The $30 Trillion Heist

The Federal Reserve
Scene Of The Crime?

The Federal Reserve Trilogy
Volume I

By: Robert L. Kelly

A JACK ASSBANKER™ PUBLICATION

The $30 Trillion Heist

The Federal Reserve

Scene Of The Crime?

By: Robert L. Kelly

Library of Congress Control Number: 2014901557

Jack Assbanker™ Publications
Attention: Robert Kelly
1732 1st Avenue #24739
New York, New York 10128

A JACK ASSBANKER™ PUBLICATION

Acknowledgements

I would like to thank every person who has continued to believe in me throughout my life. Each of you provides me with inspiration and hope to help everyone live better lives---it is what drives me forward, no matter what. I love you all, always and forever. Without your kindness, love and support this book and The Federal Reserve Trilogy would not have been possible to write.

I also want to thank God for putting Jesus in my life and giving me inspiration to write the trilogy and expose the evil which exists throughout the system. With Him, I have no fear and look forward to His powerful and triumphant return when evil shall be defeated and thrown into the gates of Hell, forever.

With best wishes and prayers for you and your loved ones, always!

Robert L. Kelly
aka:
Dad, Uncle Bob, Bob & Kel
XOXOXOXOXOXOXOXOXOXOXOXOXOXOXOXO

About The Federal Reserve Trilogy:

Mr. Kelly's warnings relating to the approaching credit crisis in 2007 and 2008 helped some people avoid devastating losses in their portfolios, because they took action *before* the crisis erupted. As everyone knows, ultimately, there was a complete stock-market meltdown and difficulty! In a "Déjà vu, all-over again" moment, Mr. Kelly is sounding the alarm bells EVEN LOUDER, yet another time.

The Federal Reserve Trilogy issues an urgent warning to all people and documents the causes, the motivations and the outcome of a devastating economic firestorm, called "D'Apocalypse™." It is swiftly approaching and set to strike nations all over the world. The trilogy unveils the secret plans of the bankers and global elite to collapse the financial system and seize control of the world's monetary policy and money supply systems. Mr. Kelly sleuths out the facts, figures, history, charts and patterns, revealing their master strategy, while compellingly providing nations, corporations and all wealth classes, specific recommendations to avoid disaster during this upcoming grab for power. The end result of D'Apocalypse™ will be social devastation and a severe economic meltdown, purposely caused by the bankers and the elite. It will rain ruin on hundreds of millions of people–with the onset of a dangerous and real global war, the likely result!

There are very few people, or organizations, with the ability to analyze and distill sets of complex information into understandable, tactical and easy-to-implement action plans. Mr. Kelly amply demonstrates these abilities, with the writing of The Federal Reserve Trilogy.

The $30 Trillion Heist–Scene Of The Crime?, and The $30 Trillion Heist–Follow The Money!, spell out how the banks, the Federal Reserve and the elite heisted nearly $30 Trillion from U.S. taxpayers–without the knowledge, or consent of Congress. Importantly, the books uncover what they are doing with this heist money. D'Apocalypse™ Now! unveils the logical conclusion and aftermath of the great heist. Reading it will help families, hedge funds, companies, and nations, avoid the worst of this purposely engineered, financial catastrophe.

Fortunes will be made and lost during the Great D'Apocalypse™ and The Federal Reserve Trilogy empowers you to assess the facts and compelling evidence, allowing you to make powerful and intelligent decisions during the course of the next several years. It is a set of books you will want to have in digital format because of their robust links, marvelous images, graphics and artwork. You may also want a hard copy for backup, just in case the lights go out and things really get bad!

A Jack Assbanker™ Publication

TABLE OF CONTENTS

© 2014 Robert L. Kelly

"FEDERAL RESERVE TOP SECRET," and other art of the author published in the Federal Reserve Trilogy, is available at http://www.jackassbanker.com. This cartoon was adapted from an Abraham Lincoln-era cartoon titled, "The 'Ins' and the 'Outs,'" created by Frank Leslie's Budget of Fun, published originally in 1861. It may be retrieved at: http://www.abrahamlincolnsclassroom.org/Cartoon_Corner/index3.asp?ID=357&TypeID=4)).

> **"And I sincerely believe, with you, that banking establishments are more dangerous than standing armies; and that the principle of spending money to be paid by posterity, under the name of funding, is but swindling futurity on a large scale. I salute you with constant friendship and respect."---THOMAS JEFFERSON**
>
> (Source: The Works of Thomas Jefferson in Twelve Volumes. Federal Edition. Collected and Edited by Paul Leicester Ford. Thomas Jefferson to John Taylor, Monticello, May 28, 1816 and retrieved from http://memory.loc.gov/cgi-bin/query/r?ammem/mtj:@field(DOCID+@lit(tj110172))).

A Personal Note from the Author

IF YOU ARE NOT INTERESTED IN READING THE AUTHOR'S BACKGROUND AND EXPERIENCE, AND/OR DO NOT WISH TO READ AN INTRODUCTION TO THE THREE BOOKS WHICH COMPRISE THE FEDERAL RESERVE TRILOGY, PLEASE SKIP TO PAGE 39 TO START THE $30 TRILLION HEIST. Thank you, rlk

In any book writing about such a sensitive topic as the Federal Reserve System, an imminent economic collapse, and a potential war, the reader deserves to know something about the author.

The subjects discussed in the three books of The Federal Reserve Trilogy (The $30 Trillion Heist---Scene Of The Crime?, The $30 Trillion Heist --- Follow The Money! and the third book, D'Apocalypse™ Now!---The Doomsday Cycle) are potentially explosive and the reader must ask him, or herself, "Is the author speaking the truth, or is he twisting facts---i.e., stirring up fear to sell books?" Readers will also inevitably ask themselves if the questions the author raises are truly important questions of our day, and if the conclusions he reached are logical----or, merely "out there" conspiracy theories?

I am a Chief Executive Officer under arrest because of inadequate disclosure of information relating to my personally owned software development company, under contract with the company I was leading. Specifically, I was charged with securities and wire fraud relating to the use of profits from my software company, derived from related-party transactions with the company I was running, as its CEO. I was never accused of rigging the books, or not disclosing the transactions.

Without protesting, or complaining, because I believe the Justice Department is just trying to do its job and I have tremendous respect for law and order, there was abundant disclosure made of all related-party transactions and the financial statements of the company were annually posted, publicly, with those disclosures in them, going as far back as 2004. There was never any question all financial statements were reported accurately because I always let the CFO, the auditors and the attorneys do their respective jobs and never interfered with their reporting process.

Unfortunately for me, as the CEO of a company in a post-Sarbanes-Oxley world, I am the man responsible for ensuring there was adequate and full disclosure. I have been informed there was not. For the last year-and-a-half, while under what amounts to house arrest, I truly believed I was

100% innocent. After spending huge amounts of time with two of the finest attorneys on earth (thanks Michael and Mark!), I can now see how securities laws may have been violated.

The bottom line is I have to make a decision to fight it out and risk losing (the statutory, meaning the legally maximum count is 20 years for each count of securities and wire fraud), or own up to the shortcomings and mistakes I have made, save the government money and graciously accept the judgment of the court.

The reader should know I never enriched myself (i.e. I didn't take money and buy Ferraris, houses, expensive clothes, etc.) and always dedicated myself, nearly 24 hours a day, to making the company I was leading a success and worked for nearly four years without a salary, right up until the day of my arrest. It represented twenty years of my life's work and I tried my hardest in, through and after the financial crisis, to make it all work, using every ounce of brain power I could muster to try and succeed.

I am also a committed Christian who hopes and prays the ordeal I am currently going through, and the mistakes I have made, will be used by God above, to help others, most of all. I hope people can learn from my mistakes and I hope others take this honesty as proof of character.

It will be an important factor when the reader assesses the sincerity and earnestness of the research effort put forth in writing The Federal Reserve Trilogy.

Securities laws are very complex in America and most CEOs probably don't realize how much risk they take when they attempt to raise capital. I sure didn't. Nevertheless, for the mistakes we make, each and every person must own up to them, freely admit those mistakes, and take responsibility---with a vow to make things better for others in the years ahead, no matter what cards we are dealt.

This is my vow.

There is no question the elite, who are targeted in this book, will try and convince anyone reading these pages, the writings are the work of a fear monger, fraud and/or nut job. The brutal truth and evidence, however, should convince anyone of the opposite. As you will soon discover, something very sinister has taken place in the United States of America by The Federal Reserve, the banks and the elite who own them.

I can also assure you---the elite, the banking establishment and many politicians will hurl protestations---with indignant finger wagging toward me. They will try and tell you these pages are filled with lies, and will try and convince you the research, its findings and its conclusions, are filled with flaws and jaded truth.

However, the evidence says something else, entirely indeed. Every reference is clearly marked and those of you reading digitally should have no problem traveling to the source of the evidence presented in any of the books of The Federal Reserve Trilogy, as the backup for nearly all the research is only a "mouse-click" away!

For the record, I am a Christian who believes in benevolent capitalism, but is dead set against the underhanded, nefarious bailouts which have taken place, and continue to take place, for the bankers and the elite by the Federal Reserve System.

In these books of exploration and detective work on the Federal Reserve System, you will discover nearly $30 Trillion in secret and unauthorized bailouts were made to the banks and the elitists, with taxpayer-backed monies, by the Federal Reserve System. You will also discover compensation of hundreds of billions of dollars to bankers, while trillions of dollars of potentially worthless securities were abominably foisted onto the American taxpayer's balance sheet.

These actions sow the seeds of disaster for our country and the entire Western financial world.

Between the three books of the trilogy, the reader has plenty of ammunition to make a definitive judgment regarding the veracity of the questions I raise, the issues I uncover and what I believe to be the undeniable conclusions these books bring to light.

There is very little overlap between the books and the primary subject matter and lessons learned are different, yet complementary, in each work. For perspective, and in case a reader hadn't read Volumes I and II of The $30 Trillion Heist (Scene Of The Crime? and Follow The Money! respectively), I incorporated some key background information and a few sections from them into D'Apocalypse™ Now!---The Doomsday Cycle, to provide a "new" reader a better understanding and better grasp of what the bankers and the elite did to us----and, particularly, what they have in store for us.

"The Heist" books (the first two books of the trilogy) describe what appears to be a massive thievery, theft and cover up which has taken place, while the last book of the trilogy, "D'Apocalypse™ Now!," describes the aftermath of these actions and what should be expected to come. This last book of the trilogy, like its two companions before it, is powerful in its implications and its far-reaching prognostications will shock you. If you take the time to read any of these works, they will prompt you to take action to protect yourself from a severe economic conflagration---an ominous collapse which is thundering our way! As most good students of history know, when economies collapse, war often happens, but this time, the danger over the next six years, will surpass anything in history. Like Pearl Harbor, like 9/11---on a perfect day, disaster will very likely strike. Woe to those who are unprepared.

The trilogy represents a substantial work and thousands and thousands of research hours I personally spent on these subjects---ultimately representing years of work in my lifetime. Because of my arrest, I thought it might be important to include a brief summary of my background in the very first volume to allow the reader to establish a sense for him, or herself, who I am as a person and the kinds of work I have undertaken during my lifetime. This summary follows.

For those who typically blow off introductions like these, feel free to do so, again. Please know the summary of my work is not meant to be braggadocios. The words are presented because my books raise explosive accusations which will demand a thorough vetting of what was written and what facts back them up. The reader will also need to rely on the character and integrity of the author, as well as his capabilities.

Because The Federal Reserve Trilogy will inevitably lead to an unrelenting, powerful effort to further blackball and discredit me, the reader will see I am a real guy who has had the good fortune to contribute to some amazing things in life. By the grace of God, I have been able to feed many people and see them live their lives through our work, together, particularly in, and through, the companies I founded. This was, and still is, the most satisfying benefit for me. This is the heart and soul of true capitalism and why it works better than any other system on earth. Creating products, creating ideas, and trying to make them successful produce value. This is what made America great.

As a Christian, I am unafraid to write against some of the most powerful people on earth, because my duty and allegiance is first and foremost, to respond to God's calling. I must and will shed light on these important and troubling subjects for our nation and people.

However, as a mere man, I must admit, it is a bit daunting! People don't take kindly to someone coming along and stirring up the sand in their sandbox, especially when the sandbox we are talking about is the sandbox of the elite, and the playground for some of the wealthiest and most powerful people on earth.

While I have written from a Christian's perspective, as I grew up Catholic and was born-again in College, the analysis, questions, answers and conclusions apply to every single person in the world who is not part of the elite's inner circle. In fact, a non-Christian will likely be interested to know someone with character wrote these pages.

I am also a red-blooded American. I always have been, and I always will be. I was born in Washington D.C. (my Dad worked for the CIA), home to the headquarters of the Federal Reserve System, and throughout my lifetime and career, I have lived and worked in several different American cities and states. I currently reside in the Big Apple, New York City, but have also lived in London, England, as well as Mexico, Venezuela and the Caribbean. I have also had the good fortune to travel extensively in the world—nearly 100% for business.

As a result, I am a well-rounded person with a global perspective on life---a perspective which is critical to understanding the ramifications of what the Federal Reserve System, the banks and their elite owners have done to us.

What I believe to be the truth will impact each and every person living in the grip of the Western financial system, particularly. Without question, the ramifications of the actions by the elite and the Federal Reserve, as described in these pages, will also cause major problems for the rest of the civilized world.

By training, I received my MBA from the University of Michigan in Ann Arbor, and my undergraduate degree from North Park College and Theological Seminary, in Chicago, graduating Magna Cum Laude, with a double major in Business and Spanish.

After I finished graduate school, I worked with and contributed to some of the world's leading technology companies, including such luminary corporations as Hewlett-Packard and Cray Research, one of the world's leading supercomputer companies. During the last two decades, most of my days and nights have been spent launching media and software companies, with unique applications which could potentially impact large sectors of the economy I felt were ripe for change. I have taken three companies public in the United States as Chief Executive Officer and/or President.

Since all three of my books are about Wall Street, the Federal Reserve and the banks, the reader will want to know my interest in financial markets not only stemmed from bringing three companies public, but also because I have actually worked for Wall Street firms and started tinkering with the building of stock market models when I worked for Cray Research. Eventually, that work and core principles of those models were integrated into a software trading platform used to trade S&P Index Futures by Morgan Stanley's professional trading group.

Ultimately, and well over a decade ago, as I read with amazement about some of the activities of the Federal Reserve and the banks (e.g., Long Term Capital Management, the "Greenspan Put," the NASDAQ bubble, and later, the Mortgage Crisis, secret bailouts, etc.), I came to understand there were some very troubling things happening on Wall Street.

I report my findings to you in these works and this book, accordingly. But first, as promised, here are some highlights from my career, followed by the concluding sections of my personal note to you, the reader.

You will find in those concluding remarks, a recounting of the author's historic ability to make some rather amazing predictions in life---all facts of the historic record and not fairy tales, each of which can be backed by a witness.

1980s Hewlett-Packard Where They Invented the Laser Printer

My technology career began with Hewlett-Packard in the division which invented the first laser printer. It was an amazing learning experience, as the engineering teams were focused and brilliant. HP's entrepreneurial spirit and drive was instilled in me at a very young age.

HP Laser Printer 2680A 1980, Price: $108,500
(Source: Hewlett-Packard, HP Computer Museum, http://www.hpmuseum.net/display_item.php?hw=442).

Hewlett-Packard "The Right Tool For The Job" 1982
(Source: Hewlett-Packard, www.yesterdaystechnology.com)

I worked at HP's Computer Peripherals Group and coordinated product launches across HP's computer divisions. The "Right Tool For The Job" campaign and a number of other product introductions were completed on my watch. With a great product line and a decision to make the next-generation printers compatible with IBM personal computers, HP stock took off like a rocket ship. I recall the company stock nearly tripling in a matter of months:

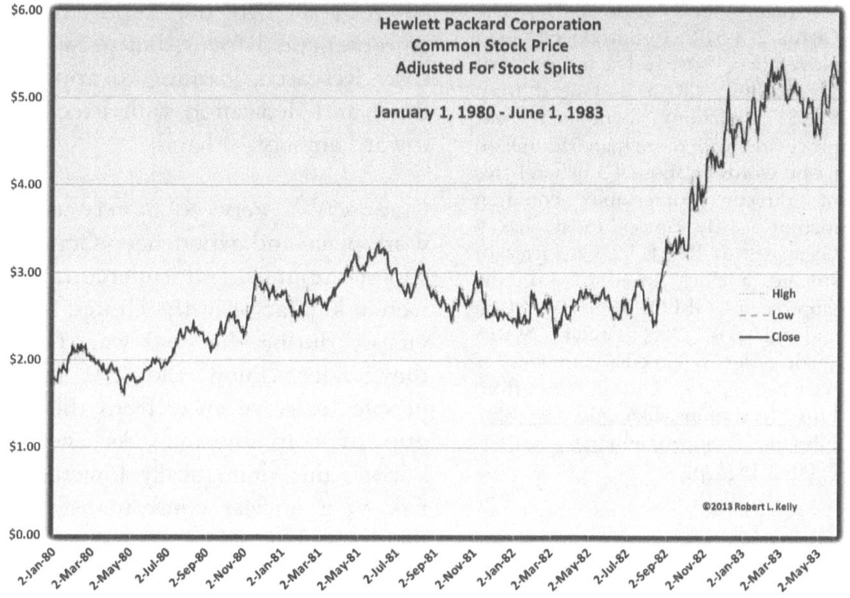

1980s-1990s the Supercomputer Years

At Cray Research, we helped defeat the Russians during the Cold War during the 80s and 90s. Of course, this wouldn't have been possible unless Ronald Reagan hadn't broken out the check book. Cray Supercomputers are legendary---and expensive---and were directly responsible for thousands of breakthroughs in commerce and defense. The company's founder and key inventor, Seymour Cray, was a national treasure and his passing should be missed by everyone. His company was filled with some of the most brilliant people I have ever met in my lifetime. You learn very quickly to listen and learn, while critically working in teams to finish a "mission."

CRAY-2 Supercomputer

The CRAY-2 performing for the Numerical Aerodynamic Simulator at NASA Ames Research Center in Mountain View, CA in 1987. The CRAY-2/4-512, introduced in November 1988, had a list price of $17 million (CRAY-2s ranged from $12-$17 Million), combined four processors with more than 512 million 64-bit words or about 4.3 billion bytes of directly addressable common memory. My laptop, today, has 4 Gigabytes of RAM, 92 Gigabytes of storage, a clock speed of 1.6 Ghz (approx. 6.4 GFLOPS), is also 64-bit and only cost $900! Credit: NASA Wade Sisler, Wikimedia commons, as retrieved from http://commons.wikimedia.org/wiki/File:Cray_2_Supercomputer_-_GPN-2000-001633.jpg

Largely because of the incredible mentor I had at Cray, my career in supercomputing would see my leadership provide successful releases for several important Cray computers, along with a special victory for the Minnesota Supercomputer Center. My mentor was, and is, a very special leader in his own right and he always demanded excellence, but was incredibly loyal. He became a great friend of mine.

In essence, I cut my teeth at HP, where I learned the importance of entrepreneurial focus, but grew up at Cray Research, learning to apply my drive and dedication with excellence, toward any task at hand.

Cray was a very cool, very unique work place and experience. Cray built supercomputers and supercomputers were a key factor in the United States' victory during the cold war, forcing the Soviet Union and 270 million people to move away from the grim grip of communism. As everyone knows, this dramatically lowered the risk of a nuclear confrontation with the Soviet Union.

Even today, Cray's are still used extensively in developing extremely advanced defense weapons and are used in thousands of commercial applications, which include advanced computational fluid dynamics (Automotive, Aerospace, Electrical, Building, Chemical Reaction, Biomedical, power generation, etc.), finite element analysis (Aerospace, Manufacturing, Bioengineering, etc.), energy science (fusion, wind energy, seismic analysis, etc.), life sciences and many, many other critical applications to the national defense and Fortune 500.

CRAY X-MP EA

Introduced 1988, price: $2.5-$14 Million (Source: © Cray Research, Inc., http://www.computerhistory.org/collections/catalog/102646184).

In 1988, NASA Cray computing power created an image from the first full-body Navier-Stokes simulation of an F-16 fighter jet showing pressure on the aircraft body and streamlines at Mach 0.90. This steady-state solution took 25 hours using a single Cray X-MP processor to solve the 500,000 grid-point problem. (Image credit to investigator Neal Chaderjian, NASA Ames Research Center).

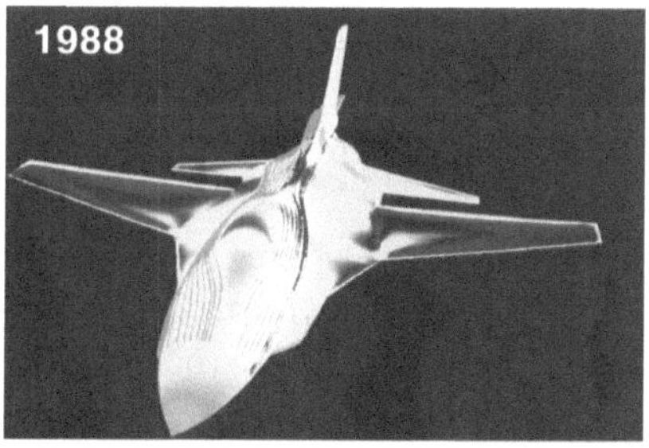

I was the Product Marketing Manager for Cray, working directly for its President, while having the responsibility for launching and coordinating the technology releases for the CRAY-2S (static memory), CRAY 2/4/512, CRAY X-MP EA (Extended Architecture) and CRAY Y-MP supercomputers. This was accomplished through "The Product Coordination Counsel," which I founded and became its Chairman, where around the room sat the key people responsible for some of our country's finest technology.

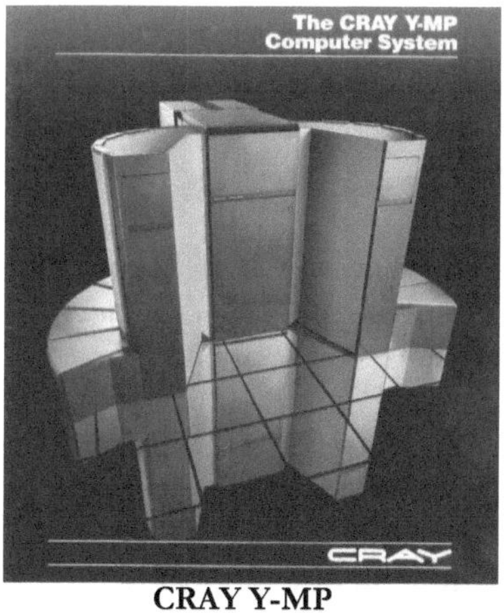

CRAY Y-MP

Introduced: 1988, Price: $5-$25 Million. (Source: © Cray Research, http://www.craywiki.com/index.php?title=Cray_YMP_Model_D).

It was indeed a humbling experience, but thrilling, at the same time.

Ultimately, I went on to work at Cray's sister company, the Minnesota Supercomputer Center, as Director of Eastern Operations, where I was responsible for business development for the Eastern United States. This included the federal government. During my tenure at this company, I directed and won a shocking and unexpected victory, overcoming all odds, in landing the U.S. Army's prestigious High Performance Computing Research Center ("AHPCRC") award.

The AHPCRC victory was amazing because we beat some of the finest minds in the country, including distinguished competitors from MIT, Georgia Tech, Carnegie Mellon, the Pittsburgh Supercomputing Center, the University of Illinois, as well as the San Diego Supercomputer Center, among many others. I was in charge of landing the program, writing the proposal (along with stellar intellects from the Supercomputer Center and University of Minnesota) and recruited Computer Sciences Corporation as a commercial partner. We buttressed our bid with academic talent from Howard University, Jackson State University, Purdue, and of course, the University of Minnesota.

With victory, the University of Minnesota and its Dean of Technology, Jim Infante, awarded me their highest honor, the Bronze Medallion. The University and State of Minnesota were the benefactors of an enormous windfall as a result of the award, landing technology, research grants and contracts worth well north of $100 Million dollars, with the initial contract worth $67 Million. They were also envied with the prestige of victory, by beating every single competitor from the National Science Foundation Centers, where the nation's national supercomputer centers (and big budgets!) were located.

> "The University of Minnesota is the lead school in the project, which also includes Jackson (Miss.) State University, Howard University in Washington, D.C., and Purdue University in West Lafayette, Ind. In addition to participating in the project with visiting faculty members, Jackson State will help to recruit minority graduate students. Howard University, which is developing a strong program in computational mathematics, will

be a "major participant" in the project and will receive about 10 percent of the grant money, Infante says, while Purdue's role will be relatively minor. Another member of the consortium is the Computer Science Corp., based in Washington, D.C."
(Source: The Scientist, by Jim Dawson, April 2, 1990, as retrieved from: http://www.the-scientist.com/?articles.view/articleNo/11043/title/Big-Award-By-Army-Sparks-Debate-On-Control-Of-Academic-Research/).

A few years into the contract with the U.S. Army, Cray bought the Minnesota Supercomputer Center, assuring Cray was in the middle of the U.S. Army's most critical, high-performance research activities, while also gaining additional inroads to supercomputer users, worldwide, which used the center's services.

CRAY RESEARCH COMPLETES $10.4 MILLION ACQUISITION OF MINNESOTA SUPERCOMPUTER CENTER

EAGAN, Minn., October 19, 1994 – "Cray Research, Inc. (NYSE:CYR) today completed the acquisition of the Minnesota Supercomputer Center, Inc. (MSCI). The company paid about $10.4 million cash to MSCI's owners, the University of Minnesota and its Foundation, to acquire MSCI and its assets. Most of the current employees at MSCI are expected to stay with Cray, the company said and also confirmed plans to continue the center's operation at its current 1200 Washington Avenue South location, in Minneapolis, under the current lease with the University.

Minnesota Supercomputer Center
Credit: (http://www.digibarn.com/collections/systems/crays/cray-q2/crayq2-minnesota-1986.html)

Following the closing, John Carlson, Cray chairman and chief executive said, 'This acquisition benefits the University, Foundation and Cray, alike. The University and Foundation are able to realize substantial value from MSCI while simultaneously retaining and expanding access to state-of-the-art supercomputing systems for students and faculty members.'"
(Source press release: as retrieved from ftp://ftp.cray.com/announcements/company/OLD/MSC_ACQUISITION.941019.txt).

My upbringing, training and natural patriotism were key factors in winning this award. It would never have been possible without the direct experience I had with working for the fine executives at Cray. My mentor taught me it wasn't enough to work hard---you had to work hard with excellence! He has continued to make major marks with some very important technology companies during his career.

From supercomputing, I went on to create a number of products and launch multiple corporations, along the way becoming a Vice President for TV Guide Networks, which occurred just after one of my companies was taken over by financiers. When building my companies, I learned the very hard lessons involved with the difficulty of raising capital--even when you have a great idea. It is a tough job, as not everyone "sees" what an inventor, or visionary, "sees" when he, or she, is creating products, or trying to solve problems.

As a result, during the course of my career, I became very curious about the financial markets and wanted to learn how they really worked. I became an avid student of Wall Street and economic history. This led me to the doorsteps of the Federal Reserve System---the key topic of the trilogy.

These are the companies (and some of their key products) I founded and took public:

1994 "Desktop TV" for Major League Baseball

1) Kelly Russell Studios created an entire line of products for Major League Baseball, the NFL, the NBA, the NHL and the U.S. Olympic Committee. It created one of the very first integrations of software and video on a CD ROM in the sports industry for Major League Baseball in the early 1990s. Images © 1994 Kelly Russell Studios.

"MINNEAPOLIS, Sept. 14 /PRNewswire/ -- Kelly Russell Studios, Inc. (Nasdaq: KRSI), a leading creator of fine art sports collectibles, today announced an agreement with PIA Merchandising

Company, Inc., a leader in the retail distribution and merchandising industry, that will propel Kelly Russell products into the most convenient and accessible consumer markets.

'We're extremely excited to join forces with one of the giants in the retail industry,' said Robert Kelly, founder and President of Kelly Russell. 'The combination of PIA's vision and expertise and the quality of our products will improve Kelly Russell's position as a supplier of sports collectibles.'

Kelly Russell specializes in creating collectible sports products featuring limited-edition prints, ceramic mugs and a new line of multi-media computer software entitled "Legends and Superstars" (referred to as DesktopTV by the Company). The CD-ROM program offers for the first time full-screen, high resolution Major League Baseball video highlights, original paintings of baseball heroes by Kelly Russell artists and the actual logos of all 28 MLB teams. The Company currently has licensing agreements with Major League Baseball, the National Football League, the National Hockey League and the U.S. Olympic Committee, as well as the Players' Associations of MLB, the NFL and the NHL."

(Source: PR Newswire, as retrieved from http://www.thefreelibrary.com/KELLY+RUSSELL+STUDIOS,+INC.+SIGNS+DISTRIBUTION+AGREEMENT+WITH+PIA-a015826258, date 9/14/94).

1998 Advanced Integration Technology for Citibank Launch of Online Banking

2) CDKnet ("K" for Kelly) created integration technology allowing a CD-ROM to interactively communicate with a target web site, with rich media content embedded onto the disk. CDK™ technology provided consumers a robust entertainment and educational platform, while overcoming the many bandwidth bottlenecks existing at the time on the Internet. It made the viewing of high-quality, full-screen video and audio possible, without the traditional "hiccups" and small, minimized screens which were standard operating procedure back then.

© 1998 Citibank

Sir Elton John was selected by Citibank to introduce their online banking services, with his songs and extensive online-banking and tutorial options integrated onto the CDK™---directly linked to Citi's web site. The technology engaged consumers and through various economic incentives built into the platform, contributed to a very successful, worldwide launch of Citibank's online banking service, which today enjoys millions of customers. Many artists and companies ultimately used the CDK™ technology.

2001-2012 WWEBNET Creates Direct Delivery of Media Directly to Computers

3) Building off the knowledge gained from CDKnet and my time as Vice President at TV Guide, I turned my focus to video and thought of an idea to create software technology capable of automatically delivering films, music and other media ***directly*** to a consumer's device (i.e., consumers wouldn't need to surf to a web site to

Artist: James Morrison, Universal Music's Streamlite Player Built by WWEBNET © Universal Music Ltd.

view a new video, film, or music release because my team had figured out a way to essentially convert a hard drive into a smart "DVR" device---allowing the direct delivery of films to a device via the seamless interaction of a web site). I reinvested my capital and profits from CDKnet and used my personally owned software development company to build the technology which powered WWEBNET and its predecessors---allowing WWEBNET to go public.

If you've heard the expression, "they rolled their eyes into the backs of their heads," it pretty much explains the years of frustration we experienced trying to convince bankers to invest in technology capable of automatically *delivering* videos over the Internet directly to a device and turning the device into a smart and interactive, portable DVR player.

As a non-bailed out "little guy," believe me when I tell you ***I understand*** the challenges associated with building businesses and trying to raise capital.

Despite the maelstrom of the credit crisis and market collapse, thereafter—particularly for small companies, we ultimately went public in 2008 and the stock traded with a market capitalization of over $150,000,000, however, the $15-$20 Million in capital we needed to purchase the film libraries and market the technology was not raised.

Several companies licensed WWEBNET's technology, including Universal Music Ltd. in the U.K., Venevision International and Comarex (Venevision and Comarex are distinguished broadcasters and distributors of Hispanic television shows, films and other media), but the vision of creating a sweeping new broadcasting network, which did not require ownership of a satellite, or cable network, to deliver films, never materialized. Theoretically, the technology could deliver a whole evening of programming to a poor family in the developing world, without the

Venevision's Broadcast Media Player
Built By WWEBNET
© Venevision International

need for a set-top box---thereby avoiding the steep cable and satellite TV charges which exist in every country on earth.

The "Light Bulb Went On"

Finally, and particularly, since D'Apocalypse™ Now! prognosticates the future, readers need to know if the writer is any good at predicting future events.

Because I am an avid reader and absorber of information from news sources all over the world, there are many times when ideas, and the gathering of intelligence, allowed me to prognosticate warnings to others, which were revealed to me. As they say, "The light bulb went on."

I have made some great predictions in my lifetime, as a result. This built-in radar gave me the ability to predict, strategically well in advance, the mortgage debacle and credit crisis, the NASDAQ bubble and the "coming" tech boom (back in the '80s). I have been both super bullish, correctly, and super bearish, correctly.

I have also been wrong, particularly if markets were being manipulated, without disclosure, in the background, as was and is the case with the Federal Reserve secretly bailing out the banks to the tune of nearly $30 Trillion, during and through the credit crisis. I have also been wrong when the entire banking system lied in their press releases and pronouncements.

I can still remember the CEO of Countrywide Financial telling the world on television all was well with his company, just before it failed. Personally, this cost me, as I was hedging against a financial collapse at the time, simply because I could read the tea leaves, when most others could not.

It is ironic all these bankers walked and only a few got fined for fraud. The SEC had this to say about the Countrywide CEO's $67.5 Million fine and no jail time, even though he outright lied in his disclosures:

> “"Mozilo's record penalty is the fitting outcome for a corporate executive who deliberately disregarded his duties to investors by concealing what he saw from inside the executive suite — a looming disaster in which Countrywide was buckling under the weight of increasing

risky mortgage underwriting, mounting defaults and delinquencies, and a deteriorating business model."

Robert Khuzami
Director
SEC Enforcement Division
(source: http://www.sec.gov/news/press/2010/2010-197.htm).

Many readers know Mr. Mozila earned nearly $460 Million from 2001-2006.

In another example of foresight, just two weeks prior to the 911 attacks on America, my spider sense went off and I warned others there was a high probability a war was coming---which wasn't on anyone's radar screen at the time. I had ***no idea*** New York would be the target of the attack, as I was living there at the time, but I definitely had a sense war was coming. There really is no magic in this particular prediction, because wars frequently happen when there is underlying economic turmoil in the world.

I also warned others of the credit and mortgage crisis, years ahead of time---and I find myself in a similar situation today, where I see an economic firestorm heading our way. As you know, or have surmised, this is an event I have christened, the "D'Apocalypse™."

Mentioning my accomplishments is not meant to be boasting, but unfortunately, it seems an author needs to present his bona fides to provide the reader confidence in the care and quality of the work and research which goes into thought-provoking books like The $30 Trillion Heist---Scene Of The Crime?, The $30 Trillion Heist---Follow The Money! and D'Apocalypse™ Now!---The Doomsday Cycle.

These books contain explosive findings and predictions.

Please accept this summary of some of my accomplishments as a humble introduction and it is not intended to impress, but is intended to provide you with a good sense of who I am. Through experience and God's direction, He inspired me to acquire the knowledge I needed to write these books and provide the warnings, predictions and uncomfortable facts contained in their pages.

Hopefully, the reader will find my honesty, experience and hardship provide credibility to my work, as the findings will undoubtedly be subject to attack by the elite, the banking establishment, The Federal Reserve---and all of their political allies.

Whether you agree with me, or not, as a Christian, or non-Christian, I pray for the sake of your families and loved ones you take heed from this carefully researched work and become just like a Boy Scout and BE PREPARED for great economic destruction…the arrival of which is imminent.

All the books present economic, political and legal facts to you—along with an astonishing story of greed and how it has driven men and women to rob the nation, and put us all in economic and social jeopardy. If, after reading any of the works you then believe I am crazy for writing them, then and only then, you will have made an informed decision.

I believe the odds are very low this will happen.

On the contrary, you may find an urgency to become prepared in order to survive and thrive in the coming great crash of D'Apocalypse™ and the aftermath of the $30 Trillion heist.

Additionally, whether, or not you are a Christian, will have little to do with the compelling facts revealed in the pages of the trilogy. While any and all proclamations and predictions were made by me (i.e. as a man who can certainly be wrong!), the motivation for writing these books was clearly inspired by God, above. The mistakes I have made, the repentance I make and the forgiveness I seek are part of my life's history---past, present and future.

Even when I failed and sinned, God has showered his steadfast love, mercy and blessings on me---even in times of great travail. As I look back, it has only been His guiding hand, working through the power of prayer, thought, insight and action, which inspired anything good I have ever accomplished.

Because of my unique experience---crossing between Wall Street, corporate life and my overriding commitment to God, writing these books just seemed like the logical course of action for me. The trilogy includes warnings and directions which have the ability to potentially help others in a time of upcoming economic crisis, chaos and war. It is with this spirit I have written these books. Hopefully, they will help all Americans seek justice against those responsible for the economic doom about to befall us all.

Of one thing I am certain, together, The Federal Reserve Trilogy not only provides a pathway of escape from a D'Apocalypse™ which is bound to strike---sooner, or later, but also provides the people with an evidence trail as to ***why it happened in the first place.***

This is perhaps the most important point because the powers who are creating the D'Apocalypse™ are masters of obfuscation and deception; they will do ***anything*** they can to point the blame away from themselves. Unfortunately, they also have control over the media to help them cover their tracks.

Keeping the Faith in God and Dad

I firmly believe God allowed my life's challenge to happen for important reasons---and three of those reasons were the writing of The $30 Trillion Heist---Scene Of The Crime?, The $30 Trillion Heist---Follow The Money! and D'Apocalypse™ Now!---The Doomsday Cycle. If I hadn't been arrested, these books would never have been written.

As blessed and inspired as my life has been, it has not been without incredible challenges and some tough times. I have worked for everything I ever had and even paid my own way through college and graduate school. At times, things have seemed insurmountable, but through it all, I have kept my faith in God and I have loved my family and cared for my loved ones and those around me, with an all-out effort.

When things have been tough, I always try and remember how hard ***others*** truly have it on earth, particular the poor, the sick and the physically persecuted---as they really have it tough. Sometimes, just a good reading of the Book of Job reminds me of the importance of one's faith and his, or her, personal walk with God.

While giving full faith and credit to God for the many gifts He has given me, I would also like to acknowledge and pay all due respect to my late Father (i.e., my Dad). His unique skills (he spoke multiple languages including Farsi, Mandarin and Japanese) and the way in which I was raised by him, provided me with a richness of experience and view of the world which looked, thought, breathed and reacted, globally.

As a personal thank you to my Dad and recognition of his role in my life, I recount, below, just one of the many principles and concepts he drove into me. My Dad loved history and wrote down the words of Theodore Roosevelt from his speech "Citizenship in a Republic," given at the Sorbonne, Paris, on April 23, 1910. He gave them to me during a moment when I was struggling to ensure success at one of my former companies. The company was at the point of near failure, but ***just before*** an enormous success when Citibank decided to use CDK™ technology to launch its electronic banking web site---worldwide. President Roosevelt's words were:

> ***"It is not the critic who counts: not the man who points out how the strong man stumbles, or where the doer of deeds could have done better. The credit belongs to the man who is actually in the arena, whose face is marred by dust and sweat and blood, who strives valiantly, who errs and comes up short again and again, because there is no effort without error or shortcoming, but who knows the great enthusiasms, the great devotions, who spends himself for a worthy cause; who, at the best, knows, in the end, the triumph of high achievement, and who, at the worst, if he fails, at least he fails while daring greatly, so that his place shall never be with those cold and timid souls who knew neither victory, nor defeat."***

My Dad KNEW there would be tough times, along with many gut-wrenching moments during one's career and life. He also knew only the men and women who strive valiantly for the great enthusiasms, the great devotions, AND WHO SPEND THEMSELVES in worthy causes—only they will experience the true character and depth of life. President Roosevelt's words hold special meaning for me and I thank my Dad and Teddy Roosevelt (and his speech writer!) for helping me make these words my own.

Being an entrepreneur carries great risks and it certainly has its ups and downs---but, my Dad knew I had been blessed with the courage, stamina and fortitude to tackle any challenge and God has always provided for me, and my loved ones---just as He has always promised.

If God's will is being done, then my work will have a special purpose for this life and it will make a difference—even at the height of a great tribulation.

Understanding an author's background, particularly when he, or she, is attempting to write about momentous events unfolding before us, is important for every reader of any book. I am convicted by the Holy Spirit to react and warn you about a whole series of events I expect to take place in the world---all of which point eventually to ARMEGEDDON and the "APOCALYPSE," with the DAY OF JUDGEMENT, coming soon.

The $30 Trillion Heist and D'Apocalypse™ Now!

The Federal Reserve Trilogy is ***NOT*** about Armageddon, or the Apocalypse, however. Volumes I and II of The $30 Trillion Heist are about understanding the root causes of a potential theft from the American people ***so*** large and ***so*** grotesque, it will be one of the leading reasons for the events described in the third book of the trilogy, D'Apocalypse™ Now!---The Doomsday Cycle.

Together, these works have the ability to help the rich and the poor, those who have faith, and those who have none, while assisting every family, every company, every pension fund AND every government prepare for, and avoid, the most devastating consequences of a banker- and elite-planned collapse of the Western financial markets.

As you read through the evidence, you can draw your own conclusions as to whether, or not, a $30 Trillion heist occurred, as a direct result of theft and sleight of hand by the Federal Reserve, the banks and the elite. They play, potentially, an important and integral part of the end-times set up for many of the warnings we have all received from the Book of Revelation---which you may also know as the Book of the Apocalypse.

Following One's Conviction

The kind of commitment required to follow one's convictions often includes great sacrifices and risks, as the willingness to speak up candidly and directly against the interests of the rich and powerful has a long history of dead bodies behind it.

Now, with God's help, courage and strength, I dare write D'Apocalypse™ Now! and The $30 Trillion Heist---in a bold trilogy. Without question, they document evidence of wrongdoing by some of the most powerful people on earth and they are written to help everyone protect themselves from the elite's egregious and diabolical plans---for all of us.

Sometimes God prepares a man a lifetime for his real work. Allowing me to experience the earthly travails and ordeals of the last four years was the last artistic touch He needed to inspire me to write these works---to His glory and not my own. Little did I realize the thousands of hours reading and assembling disparate pages of information into one coherent picture and story would lead to such complementary, compelling works---which demand a verdict!

All three books contain an "Epilogue" at the end. The Epilogue contains special words for certain readers because a soul's salvation is the most important mission in all of our lives. All other work and effort pales in comparison to this. Hopefully, either you believe in Jesus already, or perhaps you become saved and start sowing as many seeds of faith as possible, allowing the Holy Spirit to perform the great work and harvest of saving many, many souls before the Day of Judgment arrives.

Tea Leaves of History and Inspiration Help Predict the Future

Predicting the future is never easy, but doing your homework, being open to God's word and applying the lessons of the past onto a road map for the future, makes the job a lot easier.

The Vision

Unlike Constantine from ancient Rome, I did not have a "vision" which appeared in the sky, inspiring my hands to fly across the keyboard and automatically scribe the logical conclusions, predictions and action plans contained in the three books of The Federal Reserve Trilogy.

The vision for them crystallized very clearly when I was arrested.

Constantine

(Image Credit: Jean-Christophe Benoist Own Work, 3 August 2007, as retrieved from http://commons.wikimedia.org/wiki/File:Rome-Capitole-StatueConstantin.jpg).

Being arrested actually gave me the ***time*** to think---and God inspired me to write down the warnings and recommendations in these pages, in complete detail, so others might help their families during the tough times lying directly ahead of us.

Constantine, in case you don't know, is well known for being the first Roman Emperor to convert to Christianity at the height of persecution of

Christians throughout the Roman Empire. He and co-Emperor Licinius issued the Edict of Milan in 313, which first ordered the benevolent treatment of Christians by Romans throughout the land.

Before Constantine and his army attacked in a major battle, when he was heavily outnumbered, Constantine had a powerful "vision," causing him to order his soldiers to freshly engrave and paint Christ's symbol onto their shields. This is a FACT of history, as it was recorded BEFORE the battle even started and the soldiers walked into battle with the symbols on their shields!

The miraculous victory which followed, allowed Constantine to earn the title, Emperor of Rome, and he converted the entire Roman Empire to Christianity. The rest, we should say, is history.

Constantine's vision, as told by Wikipedia:

The Battle for Milvian Bridge
(Image Credit: Wikipedia, as retrieved from
http://en.wikipedia.org/wiki/Constantinian_shift).

Maxentius (the man competing with Constantine for the control of the Roman Empire) organized his forces—still twice the size of Constantine's—in long lines facing the battle plain, with their backs to the river. Constantine's army arrived at the field bearing unfamiliar symbols on either its standards or its soldiers' shields. According to Lactantius, Constantine was visited by a dream the night before the battle, wherein he was advised "to mark the heavenly sign of God on the shields of his soldiers...by means of a slanted letter X with the top of its head bent round, he marked Christ on their shields." Eusebius describes another version, where, while marching at midday, "he saw with his own eyes in the heavens a trophy of the cross arising from the light of the sun, carrying the message, *In Hoc Signo Vinces* or "with this sign, you will conquer"; in Eusebius's account, Constantine had a dream the following night, in which Christ appeared with the same heavenly sign, and told him to make a standard, the *labarum*, for his army in that form. Eusebius is vague about when and where these events took place, but it enters his narrative **before** the war against Maxentius begins. Eusebius describes the sign as Chi (X) traversed by Rho (P): ☧, a symbol representing the first two letters of the Greek spelling of the word *Christos,* or Christ. In 315 a medallion was issued at Ticinum showing Constantine wearing a helmet emblazoned with the *Chi Rho*, and coins issued at Siscia in 317/18 repeat the image. The figure was otherwise rare, however, and is uncommon in imperial iconography and propaganda before the 320s.

Constantine deployed his own forces along the whole length of Maxentius' line. He ordered his cavalry to charge, and they broke Maxentius' cavalry. He then sent his infantry against Maxentius' infantry, pushing many into the Tiber where they were slaughtered and drowned. The battle was brief: Maxentius' troops were broken before the first charge.

Maxentius' horse guards and praetorians initially held their position, but broke under the force of a Constantinian cavalry charge; they also broke ranks and fled to the river. Maxentius rode with them, and attempted to cross the bridge of boats, but he was pushed by the mass of his fleeing soldiers into the Tiber, and drowned.

The Milvian Bridge (Ponte Milvio) over the Tiber, north of Rome, where Constantine and Maxentius fought in the Battle of the Milvian Bridge. (Image Credit: October 29, 2005 by Anthony Majanlahti from Rome, Italy. Side View of Ponte Milvio, Rome, as retrieved from http://en.wikipedia.org/wiki/Battle_of_the_Milvian_Bridge).

(Source: Wikipedia, as retrieved from http://en.wikipedia.org/wiki/Constantine_the_Great).

Constantine witnessed thousands of wrongs against thousands of innocent Christian people before his conversion. He saw executions, tortures and outright murder of Christians, whose only crime was loving Jesus Christ.

Ultimately, Constantine saw so much wrong, the Holy Spirit convicted him, and Constantine changed his own life---and the lives of billions of others in the future.

I believe God will do the same thing with the bankers and the elite---many will be called, but few will be chosen. Those who respond to God's calling could make a huge difference, by potentially helping hundreds of millions of peoples' lives. This is a global and urgent need today. It will become even more pronounced when the masses fight the merciless, economic onslaught of D'Apocalypse™ and the tyrannical destruction of our way of life, at the hands of the elite, in the present and future.

For the people who read this book and support my work, please spread the word to other people and warn them of the great and troubling times approaching all of us. Tell them to prepare physically and financially as best they can, in accordance with the instructions in The Federal Reserve Trilogy, but also warn them to repair and heal themselves SPIRITUALLY. The time of the great judgment draws near. Repentance is the key to spiritual salvation and those who are shown the light of Christ, and reject Him, shall be lost forever.

And please remember---faith without works is dead. Do not be a believer sitting in a cozy suburban church, surrounded by your friends on Sunday morning drinking coffee---and eating donuts. Please get out and do something for other people.

Thanks for taking the time to read my introduction and this book.

May God's blessing be on you and yours,

Respectfully,

Robert L. Kelly

Introduction
The Federal Reserve Trilogy

Zest for Greed, Hunger for Power

Today, one of the greatest problems on earth, at odds and at issue with The Bible, The Torah, and almost any other religion, is the zest for greed and hunger for power which infects nearly every single nation on earth.

The love of money has caused wars and millions and millions of deaths. It has advanced to such a stage that a very elite group of people have figured out how to steal the wealth of nations, and thereby cause the permanent entrapment of the multitudes.

It is hoped the writings of The Federal Reserve Trilogy will enlighten the masses of the elite's despicable actions, which are lowering the standard of living for hundreds of millions of people---while enriching only a few.

As both volumes of The $30 Trillion Heist will show you in absolute detail, the international banking system has been involved in a highly complex plan to enable what appears to be a secret, direct theft of trillions of taxpayer dollars from the United States—without approval by Congress, or the people. The actions of the Federal Reserve System, along with the pure greed and avarice of bankers and the elite, shall ultimately cause a great trembling among the nations.

D'Apocalypse™ Now!---The Doomsday Cycle, if you read it carefully, will provide you, both personally and corporately, with wise suggestions for protection from this collapse and lays out a brilliant plan for governments to compete directly with the existing powers running the Western financial banking system.

Today, corruption is the byword in the West and has invaded nearly every single institution in the United States and Europe. The bold initiatives recommended in D'Apocalypse™ Now!'s pages are far more conservative and sustainable than what exists today in the bankrupt, Western banking system. Its recommendations can make governments (and their people) which institute the described initiatives in this book, billions of dollars in profits for the betterment of their nations.

Governments of any size which implement the plan and guidelines in Chapter 9 of this last book of the trilogy shall be richly rewarded, as these plans provide the foundation to create employment for potentially millions of people. The recommendations may be of particular interest to nations who are tired of being trapped by the West's web of banking-related organizations and institutions. If one, or more, bold nations adopt the plan, or elements of it, they will enjoy overwhelming profits from the endeavor and will accelerate the development of their economies.

There will be hundreds of millions more needy people in the future and providing unique and innovative ideas, like the ones suggested within the pages of D'Apocalypse™ Now!---The Doomsday Cycle, can transform entire populations. They can also turn the tables on the abhorrent behavior of the Western bankers and their elite owners.

For individuals, corporations and hedge funds, you won't want to miss the dynamic charts, entry and exit points for stocks and bullion, as well as unique recommendations to protect your capital and your businesses, during the coming economic maelstrom. As sure as there is a tomorrow, this storm will hurl destruction in all directions, if you are not prepared!

Break Up the Banks

Frankly, the author's earnest wish would be to have the United States completely change its financial system. The country should break up the banks, retake the assets which appear to be stolen from the people and adopt a plan similar to the one proposed in D'Apocalypse™ Now!---The Doomsday Cycle (see Chapter 9, "What To Do Now," subsection, "Governments").

The odds are very low such a wish will come true, as the political corruption is just too great and the intertwining relationships between bankers, bureaucrats and politicians seem insurmountable without a revolution. From a practical perspective, however, a Christian's calling is to the world and not just to the country where he, or she, lives. It is for this reason and this reason only, the ideas and forecasts in this book are written and submitted for the world's review and implementation.

Bankers and Elite Need to Change

Undoubtedly, there will be many bankers and elite who read The Federal Reserve Trilogy out of fear, or curiosity.

Rarely have pinnacle moments gone by in history when God hasn't used the conditions of the day to convict key men and women critical to those conditions, to CHANGE. Undeniable in history, He certainly did it with Constantine and the author believes He will do it, again---and this time with bankers and the elite.

Some of them can and will change.

Constantine's radical conversion and commitment to Jesus Christ is just one example of how God changes people to make things right. God's choice of Constantine allowed him to save billions of people in history through their faith in Jesus Christ, and also stopped the murdering of thousands of souls during Constantine's lifetime.

God has proven time and time again, how He will and does change lives for the good of humanity. An elite person reading this book, who becomes convicted by the Holy Spirit, will know *exactly* what he, or she, must do: feed others, clothe others, shelter others and expose the truth of the massive corruption and elite-led scheme which has invaded the West. He, or she, must also provide his, or her, testimony to Jesus Christ.

A Duty to Cast Light on Darkness

Unfortunately, we have to wait for the bankers and members of the elite to make such a conversion and expose the truth from the "inside," as *they* know it. In the meantime, we also have a duty as citizens and Christians. We must uncover the wrong doing and warn of the bankers' and elite's pre-planned takeover of the world's monetary policy and money control systems.

This is the true and predetermined goal of the bankers and elite.

Derivatives, greed and debt—all designed by the bankers, and built on a house of speculative cards and leverage, stands towering over mankind---and the common man doesn't even know it. These are the tools the elite will use to cause economic ruin and collapse, while sending a palpable and powerful fear across the land. This fear shall cause governments to shake and politicians to tremble.

Derivatives, Defaults & Interest Rates

Derivatives, defaults and interest rates are the keys to be watching in anticipation of D'Apocalypse™.

And please do not be ashamed if you do not know what a derivative is.

A derivative is simply a contract between multiple parties (typically a bank and a counter party) which involves interest rates, commodities, equities, debt, credit default swaps, futures, options, swaps, currencies, or other underlying assets, conditions, products, or items. Over 90% of the derivatives market is not even traded on an exchange, and is transacted in secret, with no transparency, leaving a small number of banks in a position of monopoly power over this enormous market.

Globally and nominally, the derivatives market is estimated at over $700 TRILLION dollars, with some insiders saying its true size approaches $1.5 QUADRILLION DOLLARS!

With the U.S. Gross Domestic Product "only" at a total of about $16 Trillion, anyone reading these few sentences can see the system is leveraged to the hilt, in a reckless and shameless manner. Disaster is inevitable.

There simply are not enough assets at the banks, or the counter-parties, to back up the massive number, and amount, of contracts the banks are underwriting. One can wonder how the market got so big, and so out-of-control, but can quickly realize why it happened---considering the banks charge enormous fees for each transaction and rake in hundreds of billions of dollars in profit, in exchange for running this mega-betting casino.

Many readers will not find it astonishing this market is nearly exclusively controlled by "The Four Horsemen of the D'Apocalypse™"--- JP Morgan Chase Bank, Goldman Sachs, Citigroup and Bank of America. They control over 90% of the U.S. Market and, along with a handful of other banks, completely control the world's market for derivatives securities.

When the bankers' preplanned collapse occurs, they will use the debt of nations and the defaults in the derivatives market to hold governments and companies hostage, worldwide. They will use this leverage and rely on their anointed governmental allies, either elected, or appointed through massive monetary contributions, to take control of the world's monetary systems (see Chapter 8 in D'Apocalypse™ Now!---The Doomsday Cycle, "The Coming Tightening…And Collapse," subsection, "Banks Reloaded With Cash, Balance Sheets Recovered…Time For Next Collapse!").

Bankers' and Elite's Allies Very Powerful

The bankers' and elite's allies in government are very powerful and are the number one reason the U.S. Justice Department and the Securities and Exchange Commission haven't been permitted to criminally prosecute, or place in jail, **ONE SINGLE SENIOR WALL STREET BANKER, TRADER, OR EXECUTIVE** who were collectively responsible for creating the credit crisis, who committed mortgage and credit fraud against millions of people, who fraudulently manipulated interest rates, and who secretly and collectively, received TRILLIONS of dollars from American taxpayer-backed funds, without approval by Congress.

Despite the preponderance of evidence documenting the bankers' fraud, their abuse of power and their incredulous heist of monies from regular Americans and regular Europeans, the entire banking industry has been basically left untouched by regulators---leaving the general public (in America) with what the evidence indicates may be a nearly $30 Trillion tax bill---enriching themselves at taxpayer expense.

In light of this, why would they, or even should they, care about window dressing, multi-billion dollar fines, when they already received nearly $30 Trillion in secret and unauthorized heist money?

The media and the Fed like to refer to this massive use of money as a "bailout." It was not a bailout, for the root of the evil runs far deeper and is far more serious than this. The author suspects the real crime lies with and around the Federal Reserve System itself.

The Federal Reserve Banks are owned and controlled by the banks and the elite---the Federal Reserve Banks are NOT owned by the U.S. Government. As The $30 Trillion Heist will show you, even the Board of Governors is controlled by the elite, as they are all on the banks' payrolls once their term of office expires---one way, or another.

The revolving door is a favorite pastime for both the Board of Governors and bureaucrats throughout the government. When board members resign from the Fed, they have to wait only two years to join the ranks of the banks, by law. In the interim period, they line their pockets with rewarding fees for speeches and consulting---provided by the grateful banks and elite they supported during their time on the Board of Governors.

In a true conspiracy with the banks and elite, the Federal Reserve allowed the banks to SECRETLY offload virtually ALL of their bad debt and worthless paper assets (e.g. toxic mortgages and derivatives assets which had little, or no, value), in exchange for nearly $30 Trillion of U.S. Treasury Securities, U.S. taxpayer-backed Fed credits and other cash-equivalents without approval, or consent, of any regulatory body. These actions were and are clearly outside the scope of the spirit, intent and law which created the Federal Reserve System.

Simultaneously, with the bank's and elite's receipt of the secret bailout money, they proceeded to pay themselves hundreds of billions of dollars in bonuses, dividends and salaries---which would not have been possible without the heist money.

All three books of The Federal Reserve Trilogy document these actions, as potentially the most shocking and sordid set of financial crimes ever committed in the history of mankind. They are crimes, if these people are ever tried and convicted, directly against the people of the United States. Their actions must be recorded to allow the people to recover everything which appears to be stolen from them, their children and their grandchildren. This will be vital when the pure torture and pain of the D'Apocalypse™ arrives on everyone's door step, leaving millions more impoverished and hungry---with everyone, once again, saying ***"How could this ever have happened?"***

The trilogy reveals the causes of this upcoming economic catastrophe---designed by the wealthy, empowered by the elite and executed by the banks to take over the world's ability to print, monitor and control the supply of money.

Hold Them Responsible

It is with great hope these tomes, and all other works of hard-working authors of the greatest heist in history, will be used as evidence in a tribunal against those who will very likely become enemies of the state.

As these facts become more well-known with the coming destruction of the debt and derivatives markets, and the population boils with anger, it is also hoped those responsible for this debacle SHALL BE HELD RESPONSIBLE, with no stone left unturned.

When the righteous anger of the people is finally unleashed against these takers, it should be with a fury and power which only comes from God above. As most of us all know, the only time The Bible ever portrays Jesus as being extremely angry is when he became furious with the bankers and merchants----i.e., the money changers.

The effort at discovery as to where all the money went, when the time comes, should include "piercing the veil" of the secret companies and thousands of shell corporations which "own" the major U.S. and international banks, Wall Street firms, the Federal Reserve System, its member banks, as well as the Bank of England. The owners behind these entities are the real culprits of society's plight, as they have taken trillions and trillions of dollars from people all over the world.

While reading any book in the trilogy, please do not forget---the Federal Reserve System has only one component federally "owned."

It is, and only is, the Board of Governors of the Federal Reserve. All twelve of the Federal Reserve Banks, who implement monetary policy and run Federal Open Market Operations for the Board of Governors, are ***privately owned*** by the commercial banks and the elites behind them!

As you will see, this system is completely rigged in a fraudulent scheme designed to heist taxpayer money away from the masses for the benefit of the bankers and their elite owners.

This is a fact, based on history---it is not conspiracy theory.

Please read the second book of the trilogy, chapter 16 of The $30 Trillion Heist---Follow The Money! Volume II, "Ownership of the Federal Reserve," if you would like to see some of the documented evidence this writer has brought to light on the subject of ownership at the Fed.

Given the recent spate of suicides among bankers around the world, some, apparently, must know their actions violate the laws of humanity. By simply growing a conscience, with perhaps some even being convicted by the Holy Spirit of the absolute evil taking place against the people, a select few may come forward and provide additional evidence of the details relating to their schemes to defraud the nations.

Those who come forward will be in the class of Constantine, for they will be very brave souls indeed, going up against Powers and Principalities which are beyond dark…and beyond evil.

These brave souls will feel elation at being delivered from deep within the bowels of a corrupt banking system. In an irony of history and in realizing the sins of their fathers, some may even come from one of the family cabals which run the banks! It could even be an individual from one of the families who have been the benefactors of money taken from the Federal Reserve for over a hundred years in the United States; and in Europe, through the Rothschild-controlled central banks, for centuries.

God will let them know who they are, and when they should come forward. In the meantime, we have an obligation to discover and disclose the activities of this evil behavior and FIGHT against it, as faith without action is dead, and a Christian's duty is to shed light on darkness.

Massive Collusion and Fraud in the Banking System

The evidence points to a massive collusion and fraud, where the bankers and elitists on the inside track ***knew*** the market would not fail because the Federal Reserve was secretly supporting the markets in a manner MORE VAST THAN AT ANY TIME BEFORE IN THE HISTORY OF MANKIND.

Because of the Fed's actions and secret, unauthorized market support, as well as the outright lies and fraud committed by the executives in the banking industry with respect to the deteriorating conditions of their balance sheets, legitimate hedgers and speculators who were reading and listening to the public information about the banking system (all very bad news), lost their money---hardly fair in a capitalistic system, where markets are supposed to make corrections and punish bankers and elitists for making poor business decisions.

Ultimately, there was no punishment for these people, of course, because the Federal Reserve ***secretly*** invested an amount of money nearly ***twice the size*** of the ***U.S. Gross Domestic Product,*** causing an outrageous, unfair distortion in financial markets. These actions were ONLY designed to help rich bankers and the elite---and nearly nobody else. This much is now obvious, especially when viewed in light of real unemployment numbers and the massive increase in food stamp recipients since the credit crisis began. It is also obvious because the United States' General Accounting Office ("GAO") confirmed the secret bailouts in its partial audit of the Federal Reserve!

There is NO conspiracy with respect to the veracity of the size of these numbers, or how the money was nefariously and secretly siphoned off to the banks and elite---without Congressional approval, as these attestations are based on documented facts.

We are schooled, taught and told by our system of government, education and regulators, the stock market is a "free" market—the "purest" form of capitalism. Everyone freely gets to "vote" on the value of a security through a purchase, or a sale of the security and it is not supposed to be a rigged event in favor of the member banks and the elite.

Capitalism, properly unleashed, is supposed to ensure weak and poorly run companies are eliminated during the bottom of a business cycle, or in a general failure of business. It also ensures the market eliminates excesses which occur during speculative bubbles. By secretly and artificially propping up the markets with U.S. taxpayer funds, the only thing the Fed has ensured is there will be a veritable implosion of markets in the coming years, with the impoverishment of millions more people because of the new bubbles it formed.

Because Ben Bernanke admitted publicly on television he used trillions of dollars to secretly support the markets and the General Accounting Office confirmed this through its partial audit, there may seem little need to write an expose on this subject and probe the extent, size, scope and nature of the actions and claims of the Federal Reserve, Mr. Bernanke, Ms. Yellen and the member banks.

However, after discovering a scathing pile of evidence pointing to potentially massive fraud and massive theft, the author determined an expose was not only needed, it was and is critical to the future of the people of the United States of America, as well as to other citizens all around the world.

Capitalism was ***not*** invented to protect rich people, or bail out bad investments, or keep politicians in office who want to use taxpayer monies to support Wall Street and the banks. As Senator Bernie Sanders from Vermont said:

> "It appears that we are very much a country in which we practice socialism for the rich and rugged capitalism for everyone else." (as documented in The $30 Trillion Heist---Follow The Money! Volume II, Chapter 1, "The $30 Trillion Heist---How the Scam Worked").

With the secret bailouts of the financial markets and insiders purchasing stocks and bonds because they were secretly and privately informed of the Fed's activities (e.g., Did Warren Buffett provide billions of dollars to Goldman Sachs, Bank of America and Wells Fargo because he is a good businessman, or was he told something we weren't and *knew* they were being secretly bailed out by the Federal Reserve???), we have a system which is now entirely corrupt.

The newly injected multi-trillion dollar, taxpayer-provided liquidity was plowed into stocks, bonds and the high-end real estate market---the favorite investments of the elite. This has driven prices in these asset classes higher and higher---an event and result this author has coined "Assflation™" (please read this book's Chapter 5 "Say Goodbye to Your Money," subsection, "Assflation™---Then Deflationary Shock & Awe," or in D'Apocalypse™ Now!---The Doomsday Cycle, Chapter 2, "Derivatives---the Ticking Time Bomb!," subsection, "When the Bubble Bursts").

If anyone else had made investments based upon the extremely material, unpublished and secret (and unauthorized by Congress) activities of the Federal Reserve, they would be in jail for insider trading and many of the conspirators would be in prison for outright theft.

Deeply Troubling Actions of the Federal Reserve

After being arrested, the revelation of the Fed's secret bailouts, the taking of nearly $30 Trillion in U.S. taxpayer-backed money and ***the fact not one banker had been put in jail***---deeply troubled the author. It awakened a thought-provoking hunch and inspiration to investigate ***exactly what happened***----asking why thousands of crooks, corrupt to the core in the banking world, were receiving a free pass, ***with no investigation and no jail time***?

Until the author started documenting, in a detailed manner, the monkey business going on behind closed doors at the Federal Reserve, the banks, and the elitists who control them, and the manner in which the system is protecting them, it just didn't make any sense.

The good news is the reader will be able to make very good sense of this conundrum after reading The Federal Reserve Trilogy.

Finally, it is clear from the research there appears to be a well-thought-out plan to ***purposely*** rob our nation and engineer, on a pre-meditated basis, the next great bubble and economic crisis, christened, "D'Apocalypse™."

Because regular people do not necessarily understand the "high-finance" of Wall Street, the author had great motivation to ensure these works were written in a manner anyone can understand, and are based upon facts, as best as the author could ascertain and document them---and they are extremely well documented.

In D'Apocalypse™ Now!---The Doomsday Cycle, the author has laid out a plan for all governments, and people, to ***fight back*** against the institutionalized corruption exposed by The Federal Reserve Trilogy---it is the only way to escape the jaws of a greedy monster called the Federal Reserve System of the United States---as controlled by the elite banks and their owners, around the world.

Whether you are a Christian, Jew, Muslim, Buddhist, or atheist (or something else!), The Federal Reserve Trilogy lays out a clear blueprint for you to see what has happened and ***what is going to happen*** during the next multi-year time period.

The prognostications contained in The Federal Reserve Trilogy are from a man, using his brains to interpret and project logical results of corrupt and despicable actions by government, the Federal Reserve, the banks and the elite. It is the author's hope those who seek protection from the coming great destruction will use collective outrage to change the system—and use any wealth they accumulate to help others, while exposing the true charlatans of our day.

One thing is a near certainty: you will become very convinced of systemic corruption in the banking and political arenas, after reading any book in The Federal Reserve Trilogy. They are destroying our country and impoverishing millions, while wrecking the "great middle class" in America.

People of all colors need to band together and fight against the real enemies---the Federal Reserve, the banks and the elitists who own them, who are taking and sucking away trillions of dollars directly from the upper middle class, the middle class, the poor and the underemployed.

The monies being taken in the form of secret bailouts and the exchange of worthless securities for valuable ones are monies which, otherwise, could have led to the creation of jobs and employment throughout the system. These culprits—the bankers and the elite---are real enemies of the people.

They include everyone who participated in the great fraud of the $30 Trillion Heist who is now sitting back, laughing, as they plan for D'Apocalypse™.

Chapter 1
Who Are The Bad Guys of this Horrid Economy, Anyway?

Everyone in America and around the world should know deep down who the real bad guys are. They start with the guys and gals in the towers of Wall Street and the world's biggest banks, including their controlling executives and the sales and trading personnel running the derivatives markets. But, importantly, it *also includes* their elite owners and benefactors of the secret and unauthorized actions of the Federal Reserve System.

As you know, collectively, these groups abominably and brazenly secretly heisted, transferred and otherwise took nearly $30 trillion dollars in taxpayer-backed monies, without any kind of approval, or oversight from Congress, or the people.

This book, the first of the trilogy, reveals what the Federal Reserve, the banks and the elite did, and how they did it. It is a detective story no American should leave unread. The second volume, Follow The Money!, reveals where the money went, what we can do about it, and provides a solution to the problem of the Federal Reserve and the people responsible for this great heist. Follow The Money! will also educate you on ***who*** the owners are of the Federal Reserve, and how the Fed and the banks hide the transactions which allowed them to take the money.

You will and should be outraged.

After reading the evidence, every reader should be screaming at their Congressman and Senator for justice and immediate action against the malevolent activities of the Fed, the banks and the elite behind them.

Our forefathers' would consider these people to be domestic and international terrorists and enemies, as the staggering amounts involved in the secret heist are twice the size of the U.S. Annual Gross Domestic Product ("GDP"). This sadly amounts to economic sabotage of the economy on a systemic basis.

Collectively, these predators will directly cause a disaster of supernatural proportions against the economy of America and the entire Western world. A virtual economic firestorm awaits us all.

When this occurs, The Federal Reserve Trilogy will be of use to those seeking to recover millions upon billions of dollars which will have vanished from the system---and have "magically" found their way into the hands of the banks and the elite.

A very brief summary of what is involved with the D'Apocalypse™ is contained within this chapter. It is included to allow the reader a better understanding to contextualize how the heist empowered the bankers to continue building the pyramid scheme of the derivatives market, which ultimately causes the great D'Apocalypse™. The author predicts this firestorm will arrive in 2015. It will pillage economies and peoples for years to come, afterward.

The details of D'Apocalypse™ Now!---The Doomsday Cycle provide the reader with extremely specific timing suggestions of ***when to buy the Dow, when to sell the Dow, when to buy Gold, when to sell Gold and what governments, pension funds and individuals should do NOW to protect themselves.*** The author presents some extraordinarily great ideas for countries, small and large, to take advantage of this looming disaster.

Did the Bad Guys Declare Economic War on America?

As time goes by, you the reader, and every other citizen in the land, will have to decide if the responsible parties for the $30 Trillion heist declared economic war on America. If Congress determines the egregious, odious and nefarious activities reported in this work amount to economic warfare against the citizens of the United States--then these parties would be guilty of high treason.

As you absorb the evidence presented in this work, you can decide this for yourself. Most people may reach a conclusion which concurs with the author, but will not be motivated to take aggressive action until the economy or nation actually implodes when the systemic collapse occurs.

This imminent collapse, caused by the greedy and heinous actions of a handful of families, companies and the Federal Reserve System is one of the key reasons which motivated the author to write The Federal Reserve Trilogy. After you read any of the books, it will probably be very difficult to come to any other conclusion, other than the fact economic sabotage was committed against our nation and people, providing a strong case for Congress to decide if, indeed, an economic war was declared against America.

These books will help you be prepared to protect your loved ones and be in a position to help millions of other people when the roof caves in, whether you are a government, a wealthy or poor individual, or successful corporation. This is the real motivation for writing them. Some of you are in a position to not only protect your family and your capital, but could also become enormously wealthy from the suggestions contained in the trilogy's pages.

For those who experience this good fortune, may God lead you to use your capital to help others, for there will be billions who are in worse trouble than ever before in history. If you even help ONE person out of your love for God, you will have a star in heaven. Hopefully, your first act of kindness will be contagious and will lead you and many others to own galaxies in the heavens! When your time is called, your largess shall be heralded by the angels above---and by God, Him very self.

As time will prove, when the economy is further destroyed in the coming years, we will witness events which are quite frankly, out of a page from the middle ages when people revolted and governments and the elite ran for cover. The brutality of the reality, however, is government has been preparing for this uprising through the purchase of billions of rounds of hollow point bullets and thousands of tanks for domestic use in the United States homeland.

While we could quite literally see kings, queens, the elite and bankers hung from light posts all over the world, it is likely governments will turn to bloodshed to quell any revolt. It will be an extraordinary time in history and we can all give thanks to the Federal Reserve, the bankers, the elite, Congress and multiple Presidential administrations. As you will learn, all of them have a hand in the blame, which will become obvious when hundreds of millions more people suffer during D'Apocalypse™.

Why does the author use colorful and strong language such as "revolt," "brutality," "hollow point bullets" and "tanks?" The reason is simple. The great heist and D'Apocalypse™, combined with our governments incredible debt load, and staggering size of the derivatives market, will cause hundreds of millions of people to be hungry---and they will not find work. The impact of the collapse will know no borders, since the $30 Trillion heist and D'Apocalypse™ are international in nature, even though the U.S. taxpayer was used to plan, architect and accomplish them.

Any time in history, when millions upon millions of people are hungry and injured, either physically, or financially, there is often a great hunt to exact justice upon those responsible for the transgressions against the people. Just as the Germans plundered the treasuries of Europe and then were hunted down mercilessly after World War II, those responsible for plundering the treasury of the United States, and burying our country economically, will also be summoned to justice---for decades to come.

Because the Federal Reserve and its co-conspirators have currently attempted to obscure their actions, with a serious effort by them to sweep the entire record of the heist under the carpet of history, millions of citizens will only awaken to its fact when our nation, and many others, lies in smoldering, economic and financial ruin. Then and only then will the fury of the people ignite and have a chance to call their actions exactly what they were and are:

A declaration of economic war on the United States of America!

If you wonder about the premise of men and women responsible for "The Heist" and D'Apocalypse™ being enemies, ask yourself, "Has there ever been one nation in the books of history which plundered another nation, when the plundered nation didn't believe it was being attacked by an enemy?"

As the Spanish Empire was thrown out of South America, so too, shall the bankers be thrown out of America and the entire Western world---after D'Apocalypse™ scorches the earth around us all.

We have enemies within our borders, inside the system, hiding as cowards behind debits, credits and intentionally complex lending, trading, accounting and leverage schemes designed to steal from a great America.

These are the enemies at the gate and the real reason our bankers and politician co-conspirators have tried to distract us from the true problems they present.

After becoming knowledgeable about the extent of their true activities, it will become obvious why they have conducted a policy of fear, using a continuing stream of boogey-man politics to intentionally frighten all Americans about terrorism, money-laundering, taxes and spying, while creating a police-state atmosphere in nearly every big city across America.

All of these policies are designed to hide the truth. The truth is the wealthy elite, the banks, and the politicians in their quest to remain in power, are walking away with the U.S. Treasury. They alone are responsible for inflation, gross unemployment and the destruction of the middle class.

The research performed in support of this book provides you with an abundance of documented evidence detailing the scheme and the shocking precipice we are about to be pushed over. It will be up to you, the reader, to decide if the evidence demands a verdict and if many of those responsible are, indeed, guilty of high treason.

If you decide to also read Volume II, Follow The Money! of The $30 Trillion Heist and/or D'Apocalypse™ Now!---The Doomsday Cycle you will not be disappointed, as the research, discoveries and recommendations are unique, and extremely powerful.

Greed is Everywhere

We know from our Bible lessons Satan will be running rampant in the end times and we are always urged to keep guard and be on the alert for "signs" from God the end days are near. With a firm belief the Apocalypse is indeed approaching, this writer knows a sign everyone should be able to see, running amuck across the entire world, is the despicable GREED, CORRUPTION and MATERIALISM which has taken the reigns of Wall Street, the banks and their elite owners.

Their love of money, through their example and model, has "trickled down" to the masses, becoming deeply entrenched in society. It is obvious something has dramatically changed in the last fifty years, as the zest and love for money seems to have infected just about everyone.

This attack on the long-standing warning against greed and the love of money by God, above, can ONLY be attributed to the work of Satan and his allies. It is quite clear from nearly every religious document on earth:

Greed is bad, it is not good---sorry about that, Gordon Gekko!

We all know the warning…"The love of money is the root of all evil" (1 Timothy 6:10—see subsection in this chapter, "The Love of Money").

The research contained in this book and its sister companion, The $30 Trillion Heist---Follow The Money!, demonstrates and documents, definitively, why this is not only the greediest time in history, but shows the imminent evil which will come of it. Make no mistake about it; the impact will affect every living soul on earth.

You will learn of the cause of the economic tragedy about to befall us and you will be able to intelligently put a warning out to those who will listen to you. D'Apocalypse™ Now!---The Doomsday Cycle even documents specifics on what you can do to protect yourself and your people from this unholy set of events furiously steaming toward us. Unfortunately, without direct intervention from God above, this book ***will NOT prevent the tragedy of systemic collapse about to firestorm across the financial system of the Western world.***

There are some people in a position of power who can also expose those who manipulated the masses and created the scheme, heist and cover up, before, during and in the aftermath of D'Apocalypse™. God will choose from among these people for His real work (despite Goldman Sachs' CEO, Lloyd Blankfein, incredulous claim he is doing "God's work"!) and they will seek redress and justice for millions of people.

Those selected will recount the millions upon millions of homes stolen from the people, the millions upon millions of jobs lost by the people, the trillions of dollars taken surreptitiously from the people and they will attest to the preplanned attack against America and the Western financial system via the explosion of the debt and derivatives time bomb---the event we call D'Apocalypse™.

Many will be led, for the betterment of mankind, to yield before God, before it is too late. These people will become part of the solution to help others BEFORE Jesus Christ returns in all power and glory to affect His Father's terrible judgment on the earth against evil doers of every kind.

Obviously, there will be nations and leaders who will read this book who do not believe Jesus is the savior. A Christian's journey is to try and help all those God puts in his, or her, way and this book is meant to help all, while also boldly heralding the coming of Christ.

As a result, this author categorically warns the men and women who rule nations they need to take action NOW to help their own people before the D'Apocalypse™ strikes and sets off the derivatives time bomb and explosion which will completely destroy the financial system and wreck their respective economies.

A leader's actions today could help save millions of people tomorrow.

The Love of Money

Our lives revolve around money and unless you barter, you must use money as a medium of exchange to live and purchase things you need and/or desire. In and of itself, money is a useful tool and has been used constantly in human history, while being discussed many times in The Bible---at length. Today, we are witnessing what we have been warned about for centuries by our ancestors, as well as by religions from all over the world:

THE LOVE OF MONEY IS THE ROOT OF ALL EVIL.

> "But godliness with contentment is great gain. For we brought nothing into *this* world, *and it is* certain we can carry nothing out. And having food and raiment let us be therewith content. But they that will be rich fall into temptation and a snare, and *into* many foolish and hurtful lusts, which drown men in destruction and perdition. For the love of money is the root of all evil: which while some coveted after, they have erred from the faith, and pierced themselves through with many sorrows." (Source: The Bible, 1 Timothy 6:10, American King James Version).

God has shown us over the ages He will use a nation's or person's pride and wickedness to bring them down and rain destruction upon those who disobey His word and laws (e.g., think Pharaoh's army being wiped out by the Red Sea).

> **"Gold is a relic of Julius Caesar and interest is an invention of Satan." Mr. Edison continued. "Gold is intrinsically of less utility than most metals. The probable reason why it is retained as the basis of money is that it is easy to control. And it is the control of money that constitutes the money question. It is the control of money that is the root of all evil."**
>
> (Source: New York Times, December 6, 1921, "Ford Sees Wealth In Muscle Shoals...Edison Backs Him Up," as retrieved from http://query.nytimes.com/mem/archivefree/pdf?res=9C04E0D7103EEE3ABC4E53DFB467838A639EDE).

Thomas Edison must have read his Bible, because he is quoted in the New York Times on December 6, 1921 and absolutely castrates the bankers in his pummeling, brief synopsis and testimony to the fact interest is the invention of Satan himself. In a direct reference and shot across the bow at the Federal Reserve System and its control over the money supply, Mr. Edison takes God's words and substitutes his own: "It is the control of money that is the root of all evil." Mr. Edison, one of the most famous inventors of all time, knew the dangers of allowing a country's central bank fall under the control of a private group of individuals and commercial banks. These are the same people who were and are up to their necks with involvement in the $30 Trillion heist and the coming great D'Apocalypse™.

The Great Heist Was Accomplished to Make D'Apocalypse™ Possible

In the case of the D'Apocalypse™, all of the elements are in place to create massive, global destruction of the electronic trading, banking, transactional and credit systems which currently support the teetering, tottering and rotting derivatives tower built by the wizards of Wall Street.

In the banks' and elites' pursuit to build a monopolized, derivatives transaction system which is not subject to regulation (or regulation is filled with many loop holes and will do nothing to protect society from the bankers' engineered collapse of the derivatives market), they unsurprisingly built an extremely profitable trading platform. Just like Las Vegas, the odds are heavily stacked in favor of the "house," but in this case, the house is the bank, or more precisely four banks.

Four primary banks control over 90% of the derivatives transactions marketplace in the United States. We call them the "4 Horsemen of the D'Apocalypse™." They include JP Morgan Chase Bank, Citigroup, Bank of America and Goldman Sachs. Why is this market important?

The derivatives market became incredibly profitable and successful for the banks, their traders and their sales people on the Street. They pyramided the transaction system, trading layer, upon layer, over transaction after transaction. Today, the world's derivatives trading platform stands ***10 TIMES LARGER THAN the size of the world's Gross Domestic Product and over 40 times the size of the GDP of the United States***! This is based on a derivatives market whose "notional amount" has been estimated at over $700 Trillion (Source: BIS Quarterly Review, December 2013 indicates total contracts of over $692 Trillion, as retrieved from http://www.bis.org/statistics/dt1920a.pdf). Many insiders believe and have reported the actual size of the derivatives market is double this size and is in excess of $1.25 QUADRILLION Dollars!

The U.S. GDP was reported at $15.6 Trillion, as of March 2013 and the world's GDP stood at approximately $71 Trillion in 2012.

Worldwide, 14 monstrous behemoths control over 80% of the derivatives market (the aforementioned American banks control approximately 40% of transactions, worldwide). These behemoths are called the Group of 14

Dealers (G14). They include JP Morgan Chase, Bank of America-Merrill Lynch, Barclays Capital, BNP Paribas, Citigroup, Credit Suisse, Deutsche Bank, Goldman Sachs, HSBC, Morgan Stanley, RBS, Societe Generale, UBS and Wells Fargo Bank. (Source: ISDA news release ISDA™, International Swaps And Derivatives Association, Inc. News Release, October 25, 2010, as retrieved from http://www2.isda.org/newsroom/press-releases/page/17).

This means only fourteen banks have leveraged the U.S. GDP 80 times and have leveraged the world's GDP by nearly 20 times, according to insiders. What is published publicly by government sources is a derivatives market which is "notionally" close to $700 Trillion. The difference between the insider's number and the published figures makes no difference---both numbers are beyond unconscionable and both numbers are destined to destroy the system they are built upon and nearly everything around it.

While the size of their casino is simply staggering, the real problem lies in the fact there are no assets to back the system up (i.e., the amount of assets underlying the transactional structure is miniscule compared to the size of the derivatives market. D'Apocalypse™ Now! provides outstanding tables where the reader can see the THOUSANDS of percent leverage the banks use in this unregulated market).

As a result, the banks, Wall Street and the G14 have endangered the entire world's economy and the livelihood of hundreds of millions of people because of their lust for power and love of money.

There is simply no other explanation.

D'Apocalypse™ - What is it?

Inevitably, we will witness the destruction of this system----literally overnight and in what will likely be a surprise to most people, it will be destroyed by the bankers themselves---AND ON PURPOSE! The demolishing crash of the derivatives system and the sound of the D'Apocalypse™ will send tremors across the world and, seemingly, greatly humble the Houses of Rockefeller, Rothschild, Morgan, as well as the minion employees in all Wall Street and banking firms around the world.

When the D'Apocalypse™ firestorm burns through balance sheets and causes utter chaos, we will witness a horrific outcry from the people and governments in all corners of the world, as thousands of companies, municipalities and ***governments*** suddenly find they have no funds, no money and no credit. Thus, the people will have no business and no way to eat.

Citizens WILL BECOME extremely upset!

For those who are prepared and can see the writing on the wall, they will be saved from the worst effects of this collapse. If governments, companies and wealthy people have made preparations, as outlined in D'Apocalypse™ Now!---The Doomsday Cycle Chapter 9, "What To Do Now," they will be in a position to help others less fortunate. Their help will be sorely needed because when the great shake and firestorm of D'Apocalypse™ sends tremors and then destruction through Wall Street and around the world, the global, primary banking system will be shut down, literally overnight.

The rain of destruction by D'Apocalypse™ will utilize every single equation, every single trading model, every single derivative and every single, really "smart" thing the wizards of Wall Street have prided themselves in building. Like the great tower of Babel before them, the derivatives tower is destined for destruction.

In Wall Street's and the bank's full-speed-ahead and all-out-dash for cash, a towering collapse of derivatives, debt and money will unleash a sea of worthless, digital account balances on the heads of bankers, elites, pension funds, governments and individuals, worldwide. Even some of the elite planners will not escape the wrath of D'Apocalypse™.

The destructive power of an infinitely leveraged capital system, devised by the wizards and sorcerers of Wall Street, will be unleashed in its full destructive potential, causing nations to lie in ruins and with its crush will also destroy many of the institutions of the elite.

This time, God will not have to use the great Red Sea to destroy those who sinned against Him. In a unique and terrible way, God will drown men in their own greed and cause great nations' to tremble, as their armies become vulnerable and their people suffer in great anguish, agonizing sorrow and tremendous trouble. Enormous change will be upon us all.

Man's own trading platforms and his "brilliant" computer programs will be turned against us and as you can imagine, the talking heads on CNN, CNBC, FOX, ABC, NBC, CBS, MSNBC, the BBC, etc. will be blabbering "Why didn't anyone see this coming?!!!"

The tremors experienced during the credit crisis of 2007-2010 and beyond were horrible, nearly destroying economic life as we knew it, but you better believe this next crisis will be much worse. The system only needs a bit more time to collapse.

The ONLY thing changed since the "credit crisis," is the fact there is even MORE DEBT in the system and the people, as a whole, have been weakened even further. The United States "official" federal government debt has more than DOUBLED to over $16 TRILLION (the real number is greater than $180 TRILLION when unfunded entitlements are factored in, as well as other debt---see Chapter 1 of D'Apocalypse™ Now!---The Doomsday Cycle "The Debt---Catalyst for D'Apocalypse™"), which is more than the U.S. GDP, while nearly 50 million people are on food stamps.

If you are listening to the pep talks from politicians and the talking heads on TV, in 2013, we are "on the road to recovery," moving full-speed ahead and unfortunately for all of us, we are just like the Titanic---with most oblivious to our fate.

Remember when these horrific things are occurring, they are part of a much bigger plan….God's plan. He has already told us before the Day of Judgment arrives there will be earthly control of every transaction on the planet by a "beast." The Federal Reserve Trilogy describes some of the integral plans to take control of monetary policy and track all economic transactions, an event, condition and precedent which must occur before the Apocalypse and return of the Messiah, Jesus Christ, as prophesied.

The critical part of the bankers', elites' and Federal Reserves' plan to accomplish this goal is to PURPOSELY bring the world into a panicked state, one more time, before they achieve their main objective of seizing control of the world's monetary policy and money supply systems. This is their end game and they will stop at nothing to achieve it, even if it means decimating billions of people's lives in the process. It is also a direct plan of Satan, as it was described thousands of years ago in the Bible.

When you witness D'Apocalypse™, brought about and made possible because of the $30 Trillion heist, you will know the squeeze is on and the plan of the elite and the banks to seize control is in play. This author expects the bankers to come out on top, setting the real stage for what we all know as Armageddon, however, Armageddon is a subject for another day and a different reading.

In conjunction with the elite, the bankers will use their leverage and control over the debt of governments by many countries to grant the bankers' and elites' ultimate wish---control of the world's transaction engine—an integrated, controlled international banking and digital currency system run by the elite. Once they achieve this objective, credit and liquidity will magically return to the markets and they will be back in business—but this time in effective control of the entire world.

This is a remarkable prediction in many people's minds, but if you are open to reading the facts of what the system is made of, you will find God has given all of us the information we need to reach the undeniable conclusion the system is going to come tumbling down---imminently and a great shakeout will empower the bankers to extend their influence and authority, in a wild and evil grasp for power.

Chapter 2
Galactic Theft

After reading the documented evidence, you will, no doubt, be angry. Ultimately, the system must be changed, but right now, this is about a warning---and presenting the pieces to the puzzle which enables people worldwide, to see how Wall Street and the bankers have heisted national assets and set us on a course of utter and total destruction.

Under the umbrella and subterfuge of clever words like "quantitative easing," "bail out," "risk management," "structured derivatives," "Federal Reserve," "fractional reserve banking," "support of non-failing institutions," etc. the bankers and Wall Street have HEISTED MORE OF YOUR MONEY, amounting to TRILLIONS and TRILLIONS of dollars, than any other singular group of people in the entire history of mankind.

They have also architected their words in such a manner to try and avoid the obvious investigation as to whether, or not, there is a possibility the Federal Reserve violated the Federal Reserve Act which, among other things, clearly states the Fed should not support failing institutions and other potential violations The $30 Trillion Heist, in both Volumes I and II, discusses in detail.

Any reasonable person would say the banks were failing and would have failed without the direct gift of capital from the Federal Reserve during the credit and mortgage crisis!

The "Piercing of the Veil" of the Federal Reserve and its Co-conspirators

This is one of the principal concerns which should be focused on with respect to understanding a great and massive fraud has occurred. In most states, Americans damaged by fraud have a legal right to go after the assets of those who defrauded them—up to six years after discovery, unless otherwise legislated by the state and/or Congress. Since the Fed has continued to hide a great many things in their books and records, only a portion of which this book reveals, it is impossible to have "discovered" the extent of the potential total fraud to date. This means the clock on the statute of limitations hasn't even started yet! The commission and the committing of fraud will also allow Americans to "pierce the corporate veil" and go after every single company and beneficial owner who participated in the fraud to begin with, should they be found guilty. Whether, or not, there was criminal intent is a matter which will be left for the reader to assess and law makers to decide.

Ben Bernanke, himself, the then Chairman of the Federal Reserve, admitted publicly the Fed had issued trillions of dollars in secret bailouts during the crisis. In a Forbes article, Mr. Bernanke claimed total credit outstanding at no more than $1.5 trillion in 2011 (it has since grown to multiple trillions of dollars, at least this is the "official version"):

> "In response to estimates that peg the Fed's emergency lending to banks anywhere from $7.7 trillion to $16 trillion or $24 trillion. 'All of these numbers are wildly inaccurate,' he says, putting the total credit outstanding at no more than $1.5 trillion at its peak." (Source: Forbes, by Steve Schaefer, December 6, 2011, "Bernanke: There Was No 'Secret' Bank Bailout, And It Was Only $1.5 Trillion," as retrieved from: http://www.forbes.com/sites/steveschaefer/2011/12/06/ bernanke-there-was-no-secret-bank-bailout-and-it-was-only-1-5-trillion/).

Mr. Bernanke also indicates the claims of secret bailouts totaling $16, or even $24 Trillion were "wildly inaccurate."

But are they, or was the Chairman of the Federal Reserve trying to fend off criticism and investigation?

As you will learn in Chapter 10, "Worthless Securities-How to Hide Them-Where They Go to Die," the Fed doesn't have to use Generally Accepted Accounting Principles ("GAAP") in its financial statements. It doesn't have to comply with GAAP because the Fed made up its own rules on its own "say so." If you can imagine such a farce and system which doesn't have to conform to the U.S. and most of the civilized world's accounting standards (even international accounting standards requires most of the normal reporting standards GAAP does), then you know there is a good possibility the Fed's system is ripe for abuse.

Because of the Fed's "special accounting rules," there seems to be particularly interesting questions to ask:

1) Did Mr. Bernanke's response to Forbes come about because there were, indeed, nearly $30 Trillion in transactions which secretly bailed out obviously bankrupt and failed institutions---BUT, somehow, the Fed covered these transactions up through its self-promulgated accounting rules? (see pages 201-204 for the General Accounting Office audit, Chapter 9, "The $30 Trillion Heist"); and

2) Did a fact like this cause a 'Ye protest too much moment' for Mr. Bernanke and deny what appears to be a glaring fact of life based on undeniable audit information available directly from the General Accounting Office?

The Fed Does Not Record Fair Market Value–Can Record Worthless Securities at Face Value

Mr. Bernanke (and Ms. Yellen, also) might be afraid to admit to the sheer magnitude of the size of the transactions and cover up if the Fed were using suspicious and non-conforming accounting standards. These highly questionable standards, as self-promulgated by the Fed, may hide the fact they may have been exchanging trillions of dollars of U.S. taxpayer monies for toxic and/or worthless debt securities of the banks---and hiding them in a variety of off-balance sheet vehicles from the public and Congress.

The Fed uses some very unique accounting tricks it has designed for itself to avoid the disclosure of the totality and true exposure of such transactions on the Fed's balance sheets. In fact, it is possible for the Fed to hide massive losses because the Fed has the ability to provide a bank, in exchange for a completely worthless debt security, the full face value (i.e. 100% of the security's original-issuance value—even if the debt security became worthless due to the credit crisis) of the security with taxpayer-backed Federal Reserve credits, cash or U.S. Treasury securities, while recording the worthless security on the Federal Reserve Bank books at 100% of its face value---despite it being really worthless!

This is the secret the Fed appears to be hiding, or hiding behind, because these special Federal Reserve accounting rules are buried in the fine print among the millions of pages of reports the Fed produces and are completely buried in their financial statement footnotes—which are definitely NOT beach-reading material!

Over Time, the U.S. Taxpayer Bears the Loss

By relying on these kinds of tactics (i.e., out of sight from just about everyone except the member Reserve Banks and the banks themselves), the Fed fully reimburses the banks' and elites' poor business decisions and investments at the expense of the U.S. taxpayer. Over time, the U.S. taxpayer will bear the loss on these investments---perhaps 30 years from now for worthless 30-year mortgage obligations which have been foreclosed upon and whose homes now sit on termite mounds in Nevada! Most of the toxic paper brought to the Fed by the banks was worth only a fraction of the value the Federal Reserve gave them in the form of taxpayer-backed cash. These totaled nearly $30 Trillion!

Additionally, some very fancy accounting tricks can be used by the Fed to simply "swap" assets—even though ½ of the swap might be worthless. In this manner, the Fed could report the "net" amount of any credits given to the banks (or other institutions) AND avoid the scrutiny and wrath of the American public and Congress, who will one day very likely discover a mountain of debt securities buried in all kinds of on- and off-balance vehicles of the Federal Reserve and its member Reserve Banks.

Fed's Secret Bailouts Would Have Given Everyone in Detroit a Check for $22 MILLION!

It is obvious to see why Mr. Bernanke might want to deflect criticism, if the above postulation is anywhere near accurate. Some quick math will tell you even a $16 Trillion secret bailout siphoned off to the domestic banks and the elite could have saved the entire city of Detroit, where a direct gift to the city would have enriched an entire population of people, with each person receiving a check for over $22 MILLION!

It doesn't take a rocket scientist to figure out scores of America's cities could have been completely transformed and obtained FULL EMPLOYMENT if the Fed didn't bail out the wealthy elite and the banks, while ignoring the rest of the country.

Looked at another way, if "only" $16 Trillion were given to ***the approximately 50 Million people on food stamps, each of them would have been given a check for $347,826!!***

Adding International Secret Bailouts, Detroiters Would Have Received $42 Million-EACH!

The numbers get EVEN WORSE when you include OVER an additional $10 TRILLION in SECRET BAILOUTS the Federal Reserve gave to FOREIGN BANKS, according to the publicly published General Accounting Office ("GAO") audit. Combining the amounts the Fed has announced could be used for "Quantitative Easing," this equates to $42,368,576 for every person in Detroit, OR $189,818,249 for each UNEMPLOYED person in this great city (see analysis and breakdown on how much has been heisted from your city, according to population estimates from the U.S. Census Bureau at the end of Chapter 6, "The Heist---Major Cause of Unemployment & Poverty," subsection, "Amount Heisted per Person per City in America").

When you hear the politicians crying out how they are helping the poor and needy with their food stamp programs and Obamacare plans, these are merely feints to hide the real theft from the system.
What the upper middle class, the middle class, the poor and people of ALL COLORS AND CREEDS need to do is stand up against the great system of architected theft which has robbed our nation blind and continues to rob and steal from it every single day.

Even after only reading a few pages from this chapter, when this knowledge is combined with the GAO audit excerpts (see Chapter 9, "The $30 Trillion Heist," subsection "The $26 Trillion as Reported by the GAO"), the reader will likely conclude ***what Mr. Bernanke stated*** in the Forbes article of December 6, 2011 is wildly inaccurate (please see previous subsection in this chapter, "The 'Piercing of the Veil' of the Federal Reserve and its Co-conspirators")!

Some might even consider the unthinkable---Mr. Bernanke's protestations are outright prevarications and lies, for the GAO boldly accounts for nearly $30 Trillion in unauthorized, secret bailout monies!

Chapter 9 (pages 201-204) in this book provides you with key portions of the General Accounting Office's partial audit of the Federal Reserve, which confirms these outrageous secret bailouts. The GAO audit also points out many other concerns for citizens of the United States with respect to the actions and activities of the Federal Reserve.

After reviewing the GAO audit and after listening to Mr. Bernanke and Ms. Yellen, what has actually transpired is today's Federal Reserve Bank has acted as an investment banker for the member banks---allowing them all to sell worthless securities back to the American Republic, with the American Republic left holding the bag.

In both the original Act, as approved by Congress in 1913, and in the amended Act as published in Congress as "U.S. Code Title 12 USC CHAPTER 3 - FEDERAL RESERVE SYSTEM § 343 - Discount of obligations arising out of actual commercial transactions," the Act only permits commercial paper to be used in collateral transactions of this nature and even in the amended Act as the law currently stands, Section 13 (which is under Section 343 of the U.S. Code available at the House of Representatives), clearly states the ONLY kind of investment paper the Fed is authorized to deal in is U.S. Government securities, or those guaranteed by the U.S. Government. Agency bonds such as the Federal

Home Loan Mortgage Corporation (Freddie Mac), the Federal National Mortgage Association (Fannie Mae), the Federal Home Loan Banks and the Federal Farm Credit Banks are Government Sponsored Entities (GSEs) and are owned by shareholders. They are not part of the federal government and these bonds are not backed by the government's "full faith and credit" guarantee and are therefore subject to credit and default risk.

The Fed had no business, or authority, under Section 13 and the original Act to work as an investment banker and while the amended Act in 1968 provided the authority to deal in agency securities as collateral for loans, the Fed is still required to apply fair market value to the transaction involving those agency securities—with a review of arms-length purchases in an open, fair market, devoid of collusion and definitely devoid of fraudulently valued toxic mortgage pools. The Fed failed to do any of this.

This goes to the core responsibility of using **reasonable risk management practices**, ***a requirement of the Act***, and ensuring the Fed is being a good custodian and guardian by exercising its fiduciary responsibility on behalf of the American public.

The banks' and elites' mortgage pools were toxic and fraudulently valued by the Federal Reserve. These worthless securities, along with many other questionable transactions, securities and collateral, are very likely hiding underneath the opaque palace of the Federal Reserve just waiting for the losses to be jammed down the throats of the American taxpayer.

This is the preamble to the original Federal Reserve Act, as you can see, it defines the purpose of the Federal Reserve in its very first paragraph:

[PUBLIC—NO. 43—63D CONGRESS.]

[H. R. 7837.]

An Act To provide for the establishment of Federal reserve banks, to furnish an elastic currency, to afford means of rediscounting commercial paper, to establish a more effective supervision of banking in the United States, and for other purposes.

Be it enacted by the Senate and House of Representatives of the United States of America in Congress assembled, **That the short title of this Act shall be the "Federal Reserve Act."**

NOTE: (see original Federal Reserve Act as retrieved from http://www.llsdc.org/assets/FRAdocs/fra-lh-pl63-43.pdf and the entirety of the amended Federal Reserve Act, or a relevant section of it for additional study, including this one, under "12 USC Sec. 343, TITLE 12 - BANKS AND BANKING, CHAPTER 3 - FEDERAL RESERVE SYSTEM,SUBCHAPTER IX - POWERS AND DUTIES OF FEDERAL RESERVE BANKS, Sec. 343, Discount of obligations arising out of actual commercial transactions" which can be retrieved from http://uscode.house.gov/view.xhtml?req=(title:12%20section:343%20edition:prelim)%20OR%20(granuleid:USC-prelim-title12-section343)&f=treesort&edition=prelim&num=0&jumpTo=true and chapter 9 of this book and its subsection "Section 13(2) Discount of commercial, agricultural and industrial paper.").

Worthless, and near worthless, collateralized debt obligations and the rest of the garbage collateral secretly taken in by the Fed ARE NOT commercial paper and they are NOT U.S. Government securities! Commercial Paper is clearly defined and has not varied over time:

> **Definition of Commercial Paper:**
> An unsecured, short-term debt instrument issued by a corporation, typically for the financing of accounts receivable, inventories and meeting short-term liabilities. Maturities on commercial paper rarely range any longer than 270 days. The debt is usually issued at a discount, reflecting prevailing market interest rates (Source: Investopedia, as retrieved from http://www.investopedia.com/terms/c/commercialpaper.asp).

What is the Galactic Theft if it isn't, Strictly Speaking, Just "The Money?"

> ***Initiated by the pillaging of nearly $30 Trillion from the America Republic and secretly bailing out the failed banking system, along with enormous and vast increases in the national debt, the galactic theft is the destruction of our way of life. It is the demeaning of our nation and people, robbing us of our freedom and well-being, two of the most important gifts U.S. citizens have enjoyed since the very foundation of our great country.***
>
> ***The Galactic Theft is placing on the head of every new born baby in America a debt which they will never be able to repay, assuring spiraling inflation, decreased wages and the creation of a 21st Century oligarchy stealing the wealth of the nation.***

Chapter 3
The Fed Shouldn't Be Used as an Investment Bank

Even in 1922, the highly prestigious, The Federal Reserve System—Its Purpose and Work, a work found in the annals of the Harvard and Yale libraries, condemned Investment Banking activity by the Fed AND the Reserve Banks:

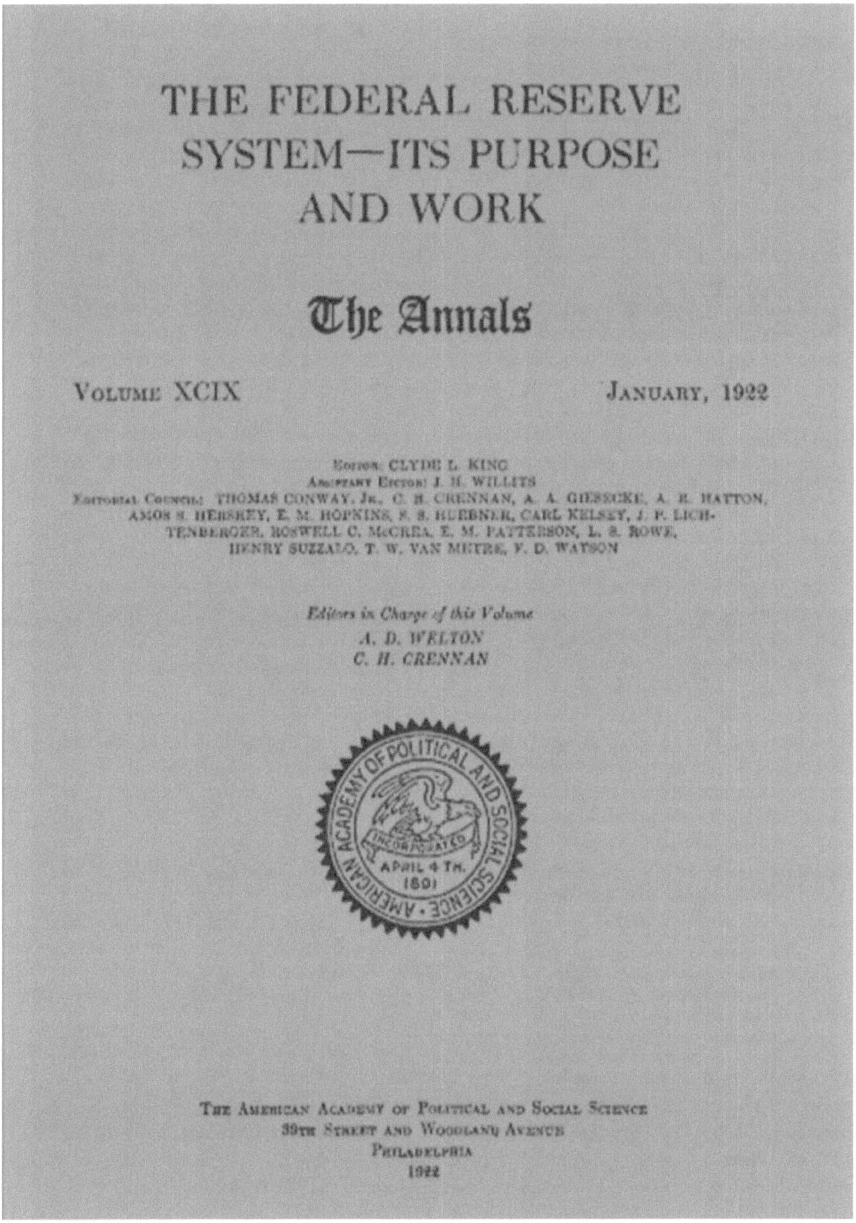

THE FEDERAL RESERVE
SYSTEM—ITS PURPOSE
AND WORK

The Annals

VOLUME XCIX — JANUARY, 1922

EDITOR: CLYDE L. KING
ASSISTANT EDITOR: J. H. WILLITS
EDITORIAL COUNCIL: THOMAS CONWAY, JR., C. H. CRENNAN, A. A. GIESECKE, A. R. HATTON, AMOS S. HERSHEY, E. M. HOPKINS, S. S. HUEBNER, CARL KELSEY, J. P. LICHTENBERGER, ROSWELL C. McCREA, E. M. PATTERSON, L. S. ROWE, HENRY SUZZALO, T. W. VAN METRE, F. D. WATSON

Editors in Charge of this Volume
A. D. WELTON
C. H. CRENNAN

THE AMERICAN ACADEMY OF POLITICAL AND SOCIAL SCIENCE
39TH STREET AND WOODLAND AVENUE
PHILADELPHIA
1922

justifiable difference. Thus will the System best perform its service in facilitating commerce. Arbitrary control, political interference and dead-level uniformity will destroy, not maintain, the integrity of the Federal Reserve System.

THE AVOIDANCE OF INVESTMENT OPERATIONS BY RESERVE BANKS

Investment banking should have no place in the operations of Federal Reserve Banks. Their reason for being is to aid commercial banking. Investment operations can be avoided by confining the paper eligible for discount at the Reserve Banks to commercial paper.[17]

Should the Federal Reserve Banks perform such agricultural credit functions as are now being developed by the War Finance Corporation and should they be "adapted" to such functions? The answer to this question will not only emphasize the distinction between commercial and investment banking—in what may be urged as a border-line case—but will also illustrate the need of confining eligible paper to that which evidences a movement of goods from producer to consumer and is self-liquidating.

The original purpose of the War Finance Corporation is of no present moment. The essential purpose of Section 24 of the War Finance Corporation Act, under which the Corporation is now operating, is to give bankers and farmers time in which to pay their obligations. Banks in various agricultural communities have made loans for "agricultural purposes" which cannot be repaid at maturity out of the proceeds of this year's crop. Some of these banks are themselves having difficulty in meeting their bills payable. This situation is too well known to need elaboration. The War Finance Corporation Act expressly permits banks with "frozen" agricultural credits to apply for advances from the Corporation for six months or a year, with a renewal privilege which may give the obligation a total life of three years. By getting time in which to retire its bills payable, the bank is in a position to give farmer borrowers time in which to make a new crop, or two if necessary, and thus clean up their obligations. The Bank's obligation must be secured by collateral which will insure ultimate payment, but time is given for payment. In short, the Corporation is functioning in the way of carrying the burden of agricultural loans that are slow but should ultimately be paid.

To the extent that the Corporation gets funds into the agricultural sections where frozen agricultural credits still prevail, the operations of the Corporation will no doubt be helpful to banks in those districts and indirectly to the farmer borrowers and the country in general. Whether Section 24 of the War Finance Corporation Act is a sound politico-economic measure need not now be debated. It is a fact. Bankers and economists have few illusions as to the probable extent or nature of its operations, but about one point there can be no doubt, namely, that this giving of time to bankers and indirectly to farmers puts the operations of the Corporation in the class of investment rather than commercial banking. If the Federal Reserve Banks were to carry loans for three years, they would be doing an investment banking business. It is the purpose of the Federal Reserve Act to deal in self-liquidating paper. The Reserve Act might conceivably be amended to

[17] The term *commercial paper*, unless in quotes in this article, means commercial paper as defined in the Federal Reserve Act and rulings of the Federal Reserve Board, and expressly includes agricultural paper. In the case of agricultural paper, however, the maturity of the paper is the essential point in giving it eligibility.

(Source: The Federal Reserve—it's Purpose and Work, The Annals, Volume XCIX January 1922, by The American Academy of Political and Social Science, Editors A.D. Welton and C.H. Crennan, Philadelphia, PA, as retrieved from fraser.stlouisfed.org/docs/publications/books/fedressys192201.pdf, page xxii).

AND SOCIAL SCIENCE

Origin and Purpose. The Academy was organized December 14, 1889, to provide a national forum for the discussion of political and social questions. The Academy does not take sides upon controverted questions, but seeks to secure and present reliable information to assist the public in forming an intelligent and accurate opinion.

Publications. The Academy publishes annually six issues of THE ANNALS dealing with the most prominent current social and political problems. Each publication contains from twenty to twenty-five papers upon the same general subject. The larger number of the papers published are solicited by the Academy; they are serious discussions, not doctrinaire expressions of opinion.

Meetings. The Academy holds scientific sessions each year during the winter months, and it also has an annual meeting extending over two full days and including six sessions. The papers of permanent value presented at the meetings are included in the Academy publications.

Membership. The subscription price of THE ANNALS of the American Academy of Political and Social Science is $5.00 per year. Single copies are sold at $2.00 each. THE ANNALS are sent to all members of the Academy, $4.00 (or more) of the annual membership fee of $5.00 being for a subscription to the publication. Membership in the Academy may be secured by applying to the Secretary, 39th Street and Woodland Avenue, Philadelphia. The annual membership fee is $5.00 and the life membership fee $100. Members not only receive the regular publications of the Academy, but are invited to all the meetings. Members also have the privilege of applying to the Editorial Council for information upon current political and social questions.

Issued bi-monthly by the American Academy of Political and Social Science at Concord, New Hampshire.
Editorial Office, 39th Street and Woodland Avenue, Philadelphia, Pa.

AGGER, E. E.—Associate Professor of Economics, Columbia University. Contributing editor to the *Standard Daily Trade Service*.

For some time Assistant to President of the National City Bank, N. Y.

Editor, American Edition of Clay's *Economics for the General Reader* and author of articles on banking subjects.

BECKHART, B. H.—Lecturer in Banking, School of Business, Columbia University, 1921; Instructor in Economics and Social Institutions, Princeton University, 1920-1921; employed at Federal Reserve Bank of New York, 1919-1920.

CASE, J. H.—Deputy Governor, Federal Reserve Bank of New York, 1917 to date.

Was Vice-President, Farmers Loan and Trust Co., New York City, also Secretary-Treasurer-Vice-President, Plainfield Trust Co., Plainfield, N. J.

CRENNAN, C. H.—Economist, Continental and Commercial National Bank, Chicago; formerly member of faculty, University of Pennsylvania, Director, Research Bureau, Pennsylvania State Chamber of Commerce, and Assistant Editor of *The Annals* of the American Academy of Political and Social Science.

Editor-in-charge of several volumes of *The Annals*.

DODGE, HOMER J.—Editor, *Federal Trade Information Service;* President, The Treasury Correspondents Association. During the War reported financial and economic news for the international News Service, covering Treasury, Federal Reserve Board and other business departments.

Author of numerous articles on economic topics. Compiled speakers' handbook for Four Minute Men which contained information about war financing.

FANCHER, E. R.—Governor, Federal Reserve Bank of Cleveland, 1914 to date.

Formerly President, Union National Bank, Cleveland.

FARWELL, J. V.—President, John V. Farwell Company, Chicago; Director, National Bank of the Republic, Chicago, and Harris Safety Deposit Co., Chicago; Director, Liverpool & London & Globe Insurance Co.; President, First State Pawners Society of Chicago.

Was President of the National Citizens League for the Promotion of a Sound Banking System.

FORGAN, J. B.—Chairman of the Board, First National Bank of Chicago.

Was with Royal Bank of Scotland for three years; later with Bank of British North America, with assignments to Montreal, New York and Halifax; Inspector of Agencies, Bank of Nova Scotia; Cashier and Manager, Northwestern National Bank, Minneapolis 1888; Vice-President, First National Bank, Chicago, 1892, President, 1900, Chairman of Board since 1916. Member Board of Directors, Federal Reserve Bank, Chicago, 1914-1919; President, Advisory Council, Federal Reserve Board, 1914-1920; Vice-Chairman, Currency Commission, American Bankers Association, 1907 to date.

GIDNEY, R. M.—Controller at Large, Federal Reserve Bank of New York.

For eight years engaged in banking at Santa Barbara and Bakersfield, California. August 1914, appointed secretary to A. C. Miller, member of the Federal Reserve Board; later, Federal Reserve examiner; 1917, Assistant Federal Reserve Agent at the Federal Reserve Bank of New York. Manager of the Buffalo Branch of the Federal Reserve Bank of New York, 1919-1921.

HARDING, W. P. G.—Governor, Federal Reserve Board, Washington, since 1916.

Vice-President, Berney National Bank, Birmingham, 1896, President 1902. Member Federal Reserve Board, Washington 1914. President, Alabama State Bankers' Association 1908 and Birmingham Chamber of Commerce, 1913.

JAY, PIERRE—Federal Reserve Agent and Chairman of Board, Federal Reserve Bank of New York since 1914.

Vice-President, Manhattan Company, New York, 1909-1914; Bank Commis-

sioner of Massachusetts, 1906-1909; Vice-President, Old Colony Trust Company, Boston, 1903-1906.

KEMMERER, E. W.—Professor of Economics and Finance, Princeton University. Professor of Economics and Finance, 1909-1912 Cornell University; Assistant Professor Political Economy, 1906-1909. Financial adviser to United States Philippine Commission, 1903; Chief, Division of Currency, P. I., 1904-06; Special Commissioner Philippine Government to Egypt, 1906; Financial adviser to Government of Mexico 1917 and to Government of Guatemala, 1919. Managing editor of the *Economic Bulletin*, 1907-1910; Associate editor, *American Economic Review* 1911-1914.

Author numerous reports on banking and currency questions; *Money and Credit Instruments in their Relation to General Prices*, 1907, *revised* 1909; *Seasonal Variations in the Relative Demands for Money and Capital in the United States* (in report of National Monetary Commission) 1910; *Modern Currency Reforms* 1916; *The United States Postal Savings System*, 1917; *Monetary System of Mexico*, 1917; *The A.B.C. of the Federal Reserve System*, 1918.

LOGAN, WALTER S.—General Counsel to the Federal Reserve Board. Practiced law in New York City in the office of Winter & Winter and also in the office of Cadwalader, Wickersham & Taft. Became Assistant Counsel to the Federal Reserve Board July 1, 1919, and General Counsel July 1, 1920.

McDOUGAL, J. B.—Governor, Federal Reserve Bank of Chicago since 1914.

National Bank examiner, 1901-1906; became official examiner of associated banks of Chicago, 1906; organized and conducted department of examination of the Chicago Clearing House and was its official head until 1914.

MILLER, A. C.—Member Federal Reserve Board of Washington, D. C. since 1914. Assistant to the Secretary of the interior, Washington, 1913-1914. Flood Professor Economics and Commerce, University of California, 1902-13; Associate Professor Political Economy and Finance, Cornell, 1891-2; Professor of Finance, University of Chicago, 1892-1902; Professor History and Politics, University of California, 1890-1; Instructor Economics, Harvard, 1889-90.

Author of papers on finance, banking, etc. in economic and financial journals.

PHILLIPS, C. A.—Dean, College of Commerce, University of Iowa. Member of the Dartmouth faculty, 1911-1920. Member, The Inter-American High Commission.

Editor, *Readings in Money and Banking* and author of *Bank Credit*.

PATTERSON, E. M.—Professor of Economics, University of Pennsylvania, 1919 to date. Formerly Assistant Professor of Economics, University of Pennsylvania, 1915-1919.

Joint author, Conway and Patterson, *The Operation of the New Bank Act*. Author, numerous articles on money and banking questions. Editor-in-charge of several issues of *The Annals*.

POWELL, CHAS. L.—Member of law firm of Mayer, Meyer, Austrian & Platt, Chicago; counsel of the Federal Reserve Bank of Chicago, 1914 to date. Practiced law for twenty years in Iowa. Student of banking, especially the legal aspects of banking questions.

REYNOLDS, ARTHUR—President, Continental and Commercial National Bank of Chicago, President, Continental and Commercial Trust and Savings Bank and President, Continental and Commercial Securities Company.

Cashier, Guthrie County National Bank, 1893; Cashier, Des Moines National Bank, 1895-97, President, 1897-1915; First Vice-President, Continental and Commercial National Bank 1915-1921. Chairman, Federal Legislative Committee, A.B.A. 1905; Member Currency Commission A.B.A., Treasurer, A.B.A. 1910; President, A.B.A. 1913.

REYNOLDS, G. M.—Chairman of the Board, Continental and Commercial National Bank of Chicago, Chairman of the Board, Continental and Commercial Trust and Savings Bank, Chairman of the Board, Continental and Commercial Securities Company. President, Continental and Commercial National Bank, 1910-1921. President, American Bankers Association, 1908; Adviser, National Monetary Commission, 1908; Director, Federal Reserve Bank of Chicago, New York Life Insurance Company, Commercial Insurance Company.

RICH, JOHN H.—Chairman of Board and Federal Reserve Agent, Federal Reserve Bank of Minneapolis, 1914 to date.

For many years president of a country bank and a manufacturer. President of the Citizens League of Minnesota, and active in the movement to secure the adoption of the Federal Reserve Act. Author of numerous monographs on Federal Reserve banking, the operations of Federal Reserve Banks and agricultural credit.

SEAY, GEORGE J.—Governor, Federal Reserve Bank of Richmond. For twenty years connected with a bank in Petersburg, Va. Later, a partner in the banking firm of Scott & Stringfellow of Richmond. In 1909 withdrew to carry on studies, following with close attention agitation for banking reform which resulted in the Reserve Act. Prepared case for selecting Richmond as Reserve Bank. Upon organization, elected Class B director. Elected Governor at first meeting of Board. Served as member of Federal Advisory Council.

Writer on banking and railroad finance.

SCOTT, WM. A.—Director of the Course in Commerce and Professor of Political Economy, University of Wisconsin. Chairman of the Board of Directors of the Commercial National Bank, Madison, Wisconsin. Professor of History and Political Science, University of South Dakota, 1887-90; Instructor in Johns Hopkins University, 1890-92.

Author, *Repudiation of State Debts*, 1893; *Money and Banking*, 1903; revised edit. 1910; *Money*, 1913; *Banking*, 1913; "Austrian School and Recent Developments," ch. VII revised edit. of Ingram's *History of Political Economy*, 1915.

SPRAGUE, O. M. W.—Professor Banking and Finance, Harvard, 1913 to date. Assistant Professor, Banking and Finance, 1908-1913; Professor Economics, Imperial University of Tokyo, 1905-08; Assistant Professor, 1904-5, Harvard.

Author *History of Crises under the National Banking System*, 1910; *Banking Reform in the United States*, 1911; *Theory and History of Banking*, 1917, and many economic articles.

WARBURG, PAUL M.—Chairman of the Board, International Acceptance Bank, Inc. Member Federal Reserve Board for term 1914-1918.

Was Director National Bank of Commerce, United States Mortgage and Trust Co., B. and O. R. R. Co., National Railways of Mexico, Wells Fargo & Co., Westinghouse Electric and Manufacturing Company. Resigned all directorships and trusteeships when appointed to Federal Reserve Board. Author many pamphlets on banking and currency, particularly in relation to the Reserve System both before and after its organization.

WELTON, A. D.—Director of Publicity, Continental and Commercial Banks, Chicago. General Secretary, National Citizens League; practiced law in Detroit; Editor, Detroit *Free Press*, 1905-1906, St. Louis *Post-Dispatch*, 1911 and *Journal of the American Bankers Association*, 1914-1918.

WESTON, N. A.—Professor of Economics, University of Illinois; Formerly Dean of the College of Commerce and Business Administration, University of Illinois.

WHEELER, H. A.—Vice-President, Union Trust Company of Chicago since 1910; Vice-President, 1899-1901, President, 1901-1910, Credit Clearing House, Chicago; General Secretary, Chicago Association of Commerce, 1906-1907, Chairman, Ways and Means Committee 1908, Vice-President, 1909, Chairman, Executive Committee, 1910, President 1911. President, Chamber of Commerce, U.S.A. 1912-1913, 1918-1919. Director and member Executive Committee, National Citizens League.

WILDMAN, MURRAY—Professor of Economics, Leland Stanford, Jr., University, 1912 to date.

Founder, Cashier and Vice-President, Henry County Bank, Spiceland, Cal. Assistant Professor Economics, Univer-

(Source: ibid, page v and vi).

The publication, as well as the eminent prestige and quality of the contributors, speaks for itself. Nearly a decade after the Fed's creation, the leading banking minds in the nation had plenty of time to absorb and digest the creation which came out of the passage of the Federal Reserve Act on December 22, 1913. THEY CLEARLY WARNED of the inappropriateness of using the Federal Reserve System as an investment bank---precisely what Ben Bernanke and Janet Yellen have been doing since the credit crisis began!

Did the Federal Reserve Bail Out Failing Institutions?

Did the Fed secretly bail out otherwise failed institutions, while taking in worthless securities which are NOT commercial paper, or other acceptable collateral according to the Federal Reserve Act? If true, then there appear to be clear violations of the law and demands should be made immediately by Congress for answers to the questions posed in this book.

If a determination is made where any of the institutions involved with transactions at the Fed window (or otherwise in dealing with the Federal Reserve) were failing institutions, the Fed is barred by law from acting to help such institutions.

The reason for this is simple. Propping up failed institutions is insidious to capitalism and creates corporations which take risks with taxpayer money. The writers of the Federal Reserve Act and every Congress since its passage in 1913, until recently, did not permit the Fed to act as an investment bank, for extremely good reasons. The reader can make up his, or her own mind on this matter, as the list of companies bailed out by the Federal Reserve (or a failed company's acquiring corporation, who in turn, was given enormous sums of money from the Fed to bail out the failed institution) is simply mind boggling.

The list includes such failures as Bear Stearns, Lehman Brothers and AIG along with many others, including permitting an obviously failing Morgan Stanley to appear at the Fed's window in more than 21,000 transactions, borrowing more than $107 Billion, more than any other entity in the Fed's history. Morgan Stanley never disclosed any of this activity to investors and it wasn't until the Fed's hand was forced to make disclosures did the information come to light (Source: Bloomberg, "Morgan Stanley Speculating to Brink of Collapse Got $107 Billion From Fed," By Bradley Keoun - Aug 22, 2011).

If some Congressmen woke up and actually read the provisions of the Federal Reserve Act, they would know Mr. Bernanke was on very thin ice. Here is what the Financial Times had to report on July 29, 2013:

> **Bernanke ordered to testify in AIG case**
> **Facing off: Ben Bernanke has never been shy about making his case for easy monetary policy**
>
> "A judge has ordered Ben Bernanke, the Federal Reserve chairman, to testify about the bailout of AIG in a case where the government is accused of illegally appropriating the insurer and using it 'to covertly funnel billions of dollars to foreign entities'." (Source: The Financial Times, by Tom Braithwaite, July 29, 2013, as retrieved from http://www.marketwatch.com/story/bernanke-ordered-to-testify-in-aig-lawsuit-report-2013-07-29).

This judge obviously saw right through the lies permeating our system and country and is asking the question---did Mr. Bernanke bail out a failed institution?! Any reasonable human being would say YES---and he bailed out a countless line of other failing companies, banks and other institutions.

Unfortunately, a Federal Appeals Court protected Mr. Bernanke from testifying and reversed the lower court's decision. Until the American public can get to the truth of the activities of the Federal Reserve System, the ability of a fiendish band of bankers to pillage wealth from the American economy will continue—to their benefit, at the expense of all Americans.

Thousands of banks and companies have failed in the world's and United States' history. There is nothing new about this. Each of them occurs because of a lack of liquidity based upon poor business decisions, huge liabilities which cannot be repaid, failed products or services and/or lending practices gone astray.

In Morgan Stanley's case, its prime brokerage operations experienced billions of dollars of demands to return client funds because the clients knew Morgan Stanley had made bad business decisions and they were fearful of losing their money! This is the epitome of a business failure when clients lose confidence in the company. The street is littered with the carcasses of corporations who went out of business because customers ceased using their services.

Without the Federal Reserve, Morgan Stanley would have failed, just as MF Global failed because of poor business decisions, along with many others. If you can't manage your balance sheet, you deserve to fail. Those are the rules and the Federal Reserve System, Mr. Bernanke and the Board of Governors did not play by them. For more discussion on AIG and this issue, please read Chapter 9, "The $30 Trillion Heist," subsection, "Have the Fed, the Federal Reserve Banks and elite Declared Economic War on America?"

Did the Federal Reserve Exchange Good U.S. Cash for Worthless Debt Securities?

If after a thorough investigation and full-blown INDEPENDENT audit, it was found, in fact, the Fed had netted out the exchange of valuable U.S. cash, U.S. securities, or Federal Reserve bank credits (potentially, up to nearly $30 Trillion) against the receipt of worthless debt securities from the banks and the elite, then there must be a day of reckoning for all those involved with the fraud.

It is of interest to perhaps some readers to note while the questioned assets may not show up on the Fed's balance sheet, as they may be parked in off-balance sheet investment vehicles, they would easily show up and be "visible" in a transaction register, like the one provided by the GAO audit.

There would be quite a stir among the people if, God forbid, this kind of activity took place. If this were found to be true, then Federal Reserve decision makers and participants would clearly be guilty of committing fraud, while also committing gross breaches of fiduciary responsibilities via the willful and wonton favor showered upon the wealthy, the banks and those who benefited from such actions---if, indeed these actions occurred. Only a full-blown audit will tell, as under the current Federal Reserve Act amendments, there are many, many carve outs for protecting the Fed and its operations from a full, no-holds-barred, audit.

The Fed and Powers That Be Shamefully Self-Promote

We often heard from "Helicopter Ben" Bernanke and from those who hail free-wheeling government spending, their policies supposedly "promote" job growth and competitiveness. Indeed, Ms. Yellen supposedly supports the same objectives, according to her public statements. They also tell us their policies are "for the good of the nation." How many times have you seen both Democrats and Republicans utter these words, while Mr. Bernanke (and Ms. Yellen) protests he didn't have any other choice but to reimburse the banks and the elite for their bad investment decisions?

Their policies caused horrendous harm and are extremely damaging to the overall economy by hurting the masses through an increase in debt and taxes on everyone, while reducing job growth (see The $30 Trillion Heist---Follow The Money! Volume II, Chapter 15 "A Word on Unemployment").

The Fed is completely disingenuous on these topics. It is disingenuous because of the nature of HOW the Fed exchanges bad paper of the banks for the good paper from the U.S. Treasury (either in the form of treasury securities directly, via cash, or through an electronic credit to a bank's Fed account). This accounting transaction provides the banking institution, or elite individual, 100% cash for the face value of a security which in reality is likely worthless, near worthless, or only worth a fraction of its face value. This sticks America with the loss equal to the difference between the cash paid out and the true fair market value of the security. As we all know, most of these mortgage pools from the credit crisis were a disaster and became worthless, or worth only a fraction of their face value.

It is also a disgustingly laughable event when the big banks merely receive multi-billion dollar fines, when collectively they pulled nearly $30 TRILLION OUT OF THE SYSTEM!! The rip off of the American taxpayer is just beyond belief.

This is something we must ponder because of the Fed's largely self-made and rubber-stamped accounting policies. Under the terms and conditions of those policies, the Fed does not have to record a worthless security at its true market value. Instead, it can be recorded at its original issuance value (its "face" value), with the asset then amortized over its entire life, or effectively written off when the security is "due." This buries the real transaction from Congress and a highly suspicious public for potentially tens of years---long after Mr. Bernanke and the co-conspirators are in the grave.

This is a particularly frightening scenario. IF there were, let's say, thousands of banks using the Fed window and they were informed the Federal Reserve would "purchase," or "loan" (at nearly 0% interest the last five years) U.S. dollars in exchange for worthless securities, you might imagine a rush to the Fed window---***far more dramatic than when the Klondike struck gold,*** with every bank in the world exchanging bad securities for good ones.

Did such a scenario take place?

It sure did! With one firm going to the Fed Window over 21,000 times and the GAO uncovering $26 Trillion in secret bailouts, only a full audit, by a group of unbiased accounting firms, will reveal the full truth. However, what little we know of the real truth is petrifying. The banks and elite flocked to the Fed's gold rush like miners to the Klondike in 1897!

This book and the trilogy believe this kind of activity indeed may have happened. If this is true, it means the Fed is potentially sitting on a MOUNTAIN of worthless securities and collateral which, when ultimately written off, will be charged to the American taxpayer—thereby further adding to our debt, while causing tremendous asset inflation along the way.

The amount of money in question is about twice the size of the United States' GDP and as discussed, the U.S. GDP stood at approximately $16 Trillion in 2012.

Fed Policies Fail to Make America More Competitive

Furthermore, the Fed's policies have failed to make America more competitive. According to the CIA Factbook for 2012, the United States was dead LAST for countries in its current account balance. The United States has a STAGGERINGLY NEGATIVE $487,200,000,000 DEFICIT—ranking 193rd---behind every nation on earth in the CIA survey of 193 nations.

193	United States	$ -487,200,000,000	2012 est

(Source: CIA Fact Book, as retrieved from https://www.cia.gov/library/publications/the-world-factbook/rankorder/2187rank.html).

This deficit amounts to approximately $690,000 per person in Detroit and amounts to about $11,000 for every person on food stamps. It is very clear the other trading nations on earth do not want American products---another eerie sign something is not working too well in the American economy.

If the policy decisions made by Mr. Bernanke, Ms. Yellen, the bankers, Congress and the current administration were on track, they would be working after six years of money pumping, exchanging cash for worthless securities and the massive debt build-up our country has experienced.

Instead, what has occurred is the United States, once the home of the greatest middle class on earth, has seen its middle class, poor and working poor devastated by the credit crisis and the Fed, with the Fed itself indicating households have only recovered 45% of what they lost during the crisis (see detailed Fed tables and discussion later in Chapter 6, "The Heist---Major Cause of Unemployment & Poverty," subsection "Massive Destruction of Wealth" and "Amount Heisted per Person per City in America").

Clearly, our system has been corrupted to serve only the bankers, the ruling elite and the powerful families behind them, as this book's analysis clearly reveals the unfairness of the actions of the Federal Reserve, but also the loss of wealth to the masses, as a result of the crisis and heist.

Historically, it is reminiscent of how old monarchies and oligarchies ruled, where the government and its preferred agents were the sole benefactors of a ruling-elite body focused solely on benefiting royalty and the top families in the empire. Similar to the Spanish, perhaps, where greedy conquistadors pillaged plunder from general populations and returned treasure, stolen from others, to the Spanish monarchy---with the loyal troops receiving their share of the spoils.

History teaches us those kinds of governments destroyed their power by taking the wealth for only a select few and leaving nothing for the masses. This, ultimately, of course, leaves the general population in utter contempt of the elite who ruled them because the elite leave the masses with nothing but a legacy of impoverishment. If you have ever traveled in, or through, Latin America, you will see the results of such a legacy in many countries. It is not a pretty sight. It is also ***centuries*** since the Spanish ruled! When the elite rob the masses, populations do not recover---UNLESS THEY TAKE THE MONEY BACK!!

There are a couple of great leaders in Latin America who are attempting to reverse the historical damage inflicted upon the general population by those monarchies and elitists. They have an enormous challenge because most of them are greatly indebted to the banks and other countries.

If you visit nearly any Spanish-speaking country on earth, you will see the legacy of the Spanish empire's monarchy and elite. About 1% of the people in most of these nations own most of the wealth, while the vast majority of people are barely surviving with millions at, or below, threshold poverty levels---living in shanty towns. To this day, people living in these nations struggle for electricity, food and water.

In a similar manner, the Federal Reserve is stripping and using assets of the Unites States people to support the wealthy elite---by creating and giving them monies ultimately backed by the U.S. Treasury. Through the direct creation of money, or electronic credits at a member bank account, the Fed allows the insiders to be reimbursed for their bad business decisions, while creating massive inflation across asset classes controlled by the rich in a series of market manipulations for the elite this author has termed "Assflation™."

The devious and nonsensical (unless you are a bank, or a member of the elite) policies of the Federal Reserve ultimately take money AWAY from the working class and poor who create products and profits for trade and commerce. The recipients and benefactors of the money---the banks and the super wealthy---simply hoard the bailout money and have invested it, primarily, in areas of liquid, asset accumulation (e.g., stocks, bonds, etc.).

The Elite---"Let Them Eat Cake"

As a group, the wealthy elite, who are the object of benevolence by the Federal Reserve, spend relatively small amounts of their wealth on riskier projects and investments which promote job growth. This is one of the key reasons America has not developed new factories, or had any real kind of industrial development in the last fifty years. As anyone can tell you, our industrial strength has all but disappeared.

The idea of a "trickle down" theory of economics, which is how the Fed and other economists attempt to characterize this kind of activity, is really a Queen Marie Antoinette "Let them eat cake" theory of economics (see <u>The $30 Trillion Heist</u>---<u>Follow The Money!</u> Volume II Chapter 21 "The Battle Between Good and Evil," subsection, "Seizing Control Through the Creation of Great Debt"), where many of the elite essentially disdain and disregard the working class and poor.

What really happens is the elite take nearly ALL the money. They then provide the poor with a subsistence-level form of survival via service industry jobs, food stamps and other entitlement programs, while slowly, but surely, destroying the middle class through inflation and cost increases via monopolies controlled by the banks and their wealthy owners—the elite.

There has been a marked decrease in the standard of living for the working class and poor because of increased taxation, increased cost of living, decreasing salaries, loss of jobs, increased healthcare costs, increased fees, increased regulations on corporations, bloated debt and bloated spending demands of government. As a result, the working class and the poor are ***worse off*** than before the credit crisis hit.

Life, however, continues to go on for the cocktail set in New York, Cannes, St. Tropez, London, L.A. and every other major city in the world.

If the elite were really smart, they would start spending their trillions on helping the masses and avoid the inevitability of a massive confrontation which will undoubtedly threaten their very lifestyle and livelihood in the not too distant future.

Chapter 4
Government Spending No Help

Government spending is replete with waste and no government in history has ever been able to innovate and create value for an economy. In conjunction with the failed Fed policies and actions, true unemployment is at record highs (as in the true unemployment—NOT the government's propaganda numbers). See The $30 Trillion Heist---Follow The Money! Volume II, Chapter 15, "A Word on Unemployment."

The only government programs which have worked have been primarily in the defense and aerospace industries, because in these sectors, money is given to the private sector AND it is constitutionally authorized. The private sector knows how to innovate, manufacture, employ and make a profit. The results of the defense industry's innovations are legendary and the program has resulted in the strongest military capability on earth.

Unfortunately, because of the increase in government expenditures across the board and the huge risk of rising interest rates which lies ahead, there will be enormous pressure to cut every budget category—including defense, over the next five to seven years, thanks to the Federal Reserve's atrocious and selfish actions, along with the profligate spending of the U.S. Congress and every single presidential administration in remembered history.

With the requirement to repay interest and principal, a significant percentage of our government's budget is apportioned to pay the bankers and the elite and this apportionment is going to increase dramatically and be far worse in the future, as the percentage of the budget dedicated to interest payments will skyrocket.

Ben Bernanke, Ms. Yellen and the Federal Reserve have artificially kept the Fed's interest rates at next to zero, for years, allowing the banks to earn billions by playing riskless arbitrage between short-term borrowing costs at the Fed (basically free) and long term rates at 3%, or thereabouts. The Fed's keeping interest rates low also kept interest expenditures as low as possible for the federal government during the last six years.

Unfortunately, this has caused the broader market to turn away from U.S. Government securities, because no one wants to purchase the U.S. Government's paper because of our government's horrendous borrowings and low rate of return on U.S. government paper.

This is also why the Federal Reserve is directly purchasing U.S. Government securities today---there is not enough demand for them!

The only thing which will help international purchases of U.S. Treasury securities is the imminent rally in the U.S. Dollar---which will be caused by a flight to "safety" (or so most will think) and rising interest rates. In 2015, interest rates should skyrocket and our government will face the prospect of paying interest and debt expenses which could ultimately approach 60% of the entire budget! This is when we will see the end of the enormously huge and unproductive social spending programs of the Western governments---with the attempt to socialize the system becoming one of the greatest disasters and experiments in human history.

Here is the math on what will happen to interest payments with an increase in rates:

Table S-1. Budget Totals

(In billions of dollars and as a percent of GDP)

	2012	2013	2014	2015	2016	2017	2018
Budget Totals in Billions of Dollars:							
Receipts	2,450	2,712	3,034	3,332	3,561	3,761	3,974
Outlays	3,537	3,685	3,778	3,908	4,090	4,247	4,449
Deficit	1,087	973	744	576	528	487	475

(Source: http://www.whitehouse.gov/sites/default/files/omb/budget/fy2014/assets/tables.pdf).

On December 7, 2013 the national debt was over $17 Trillion, but even looking at the debt *before* the 2013 budget agreement with Congress, the situation was grim. The headline debt number on March 29, 2013 was:

		% Of 2014 Budget Outlays (Above)
Interest expense on U.S. DEBT @ 3%	Interest = $502,525,770,000	13.3%
Interest expense on U.S. DEBT @ 6%	Interest = $1,005,051,540,000	26.6%
Interest expense on U.S. DEBT @ 12%	Interest = $2,010,103,080,000	53.21%
Interest expense on U.S. DEBT @ 18%	Interest = $3,015,154,620,000	79.81%

U.S Debt Clock December 7, 2013

Here is the U.S. Debt Clock for December 7, 2013 (Source: U.S. Debt Clock and U.S. National Debt figures, as retrieved from http://www.usdebtclock.org).

As you can see, with each uptick in interest rates, every budget is in danger. This ultimately, is the bankers plan. They want and need interest rates to spike higher because it will facilitate the collapse of the derivatives market, bring governments to their knees and precipitate the great D'Apocalypse™---with the bankers and elite subsequently controlling the money ***and*** governments, worldwide.

This is why President Obama attempted in 2014 to try and get Americans to buy government debt via tax-free incentives! He knows the budget is ripe for disaster and he is trying to convert the debt into a domestic problem---not an international one!

By the way, for those who question placing an 18% interest rate figure in the preceding interest table on the debt, you probably were not alive when Jimmy Carter was President. Interest rates skyrocketed during his Administration above 18%!

The pain Congress and government endured in 2012 and 2013 over inconsequential sequester cuts totaling a few hundred million dollars is nothing compared to what is coming. Increasing interest rate payments will DESTROY the budgeting process altogether, and with it, all social and spending programs.

This is what the poor, beleaguered people who are unemployed don't see. Their plight will get even worse, as food stamp money will dry up, or be inflated away into oblivion. Either way, it is very clear why Benjamin Shalom Bernanke, and now Janet Yellen, have looked frantic, at times, as they try to assure markets, globally, interest rates will remain near zero, or stable, for the foreseeable future. Ms. Janet Yellen, the new Chairman, will look even more frazzled in the years ahead.

> "The Fed said it will continue buying assets at a clip of $85 billion a month, and hold short-term interest rates at essentially 0% for the foreseeable future." (Source: FOXBusiness, "Bernanke Offers Possible Timetable for Tapering," By Dunstan Prial, June 19, 2013, as retrieved from: http://www.foxbusiness.com/economy/2013/06/19/fed-decision-on-tap/).

Unfortunately, the focus on saving the wealthy by giving away trillions of dollars, along with reckless government spending programs, has only increased the debt, while providing no investment return to the people. This is why the United States of America is DEAD LAST in its trading with the other nations and is destined to undergo the governmental version of a heart attack in the very near future.

By failing to retrain our people and invest in their future, the system is destined to fail because it is not based on God's fundamental principles of living within one's means and if you don't work---you don't eat!

"By the sweat of your brow you will eat your food until you return to the ground..."
(Source: The Bible, Genesis 3:19, New International Version).

Governments, worldwide, have spent money without regard for the budget and they will collapse, ultimately. The U.S. has gotten away with it for the moment because the dollar is the global reserve currency used for trade and the global debt is denominated primarily in dollars. But, as you shall learn and see, this too is changing.

The Pile of Debt Will Bury Us—First By Deflation, Then By Inflation

The United States' pile of debt and its inability to compete will bury us and there is no avoiding it at this point in time. God's mighty hand is coming and there will be great retribution for this country. The debt will affect everyone and all will bear witness to the great collapse and deflation, followed by a massive inflation.

This will occur regardless of which political party (Democrat, or Republican) is in power, unless there is a massive rise of a 3rd party which forces the assets of the nation to be returned by those who committed fraud against her, while balancing the budget via massive reductions in government spending---thereby lowering taxes on everyone.

If God allows the existing U.S. government (Democrat and Republican) to stay in power, the people finally will wake up, right as D'Apocalypse™ arrives. They will attempt to wrest control of the situation, but there will be tremendous hardship wrought upon the multitudes, as the poor and the middle class will be in real trouble. The poor, bought off with food stamp money, are oblivious to the real state of affairs and the real reasons behind their continued poverty and the lack of jobs on the Street.

Most people have a heart for the poor and the meek, but the entire economy has been socialized for the rich, destroying a time-tested system of a great middle class and further impoverishing the poor.

Unsustainable Government & Unsustainable Currency = Systemically Uncontrolled Risk

Unfortunately, the $30 Trillion is only a fraction of the total heist which is occurring. The greatest theft of all is a loss of freedom for the people, as politicians, deeply fearful of social unrest, continue to pass onerous laws taking away traditional freedoms in America. Out-of-control debt and out-of-control spending, along with an ongoing bleeding of the wealth from the people by the Federal Reserve System, result in an UNSUSTAINABLE currency and UNSUSTAINABLE government—and a debilitating loss of freedom for the people.

The next seven years will witness catastrophic failures in the U.S., Europe, Japan and any nation riding high on debt. Unless governments default, sparing the people the anguish of certain economic contraction, society will be punished through economic devastation, as the bankers and elite squeeze governments for debt repayment and other concessions. Treasuries will run dry and the U.S., particularly, won't be able to sell any more bonds---unless it purchases them itself! This will lead to political panic and politicians will pass even *more* laws eliminating a greater number of the most basic freedoms for Americans *and* Europeans---the result of politicians applying pressure to control, keep the peace, quell revolts and ensure the collection of every tax dollar they can from a doubting public. When the history book is written, it will show the system failed because of the short-sighted greediness of Wall Street's leaders and the wealthy elite who own the banking system, combined with an unquenchable desire to stay in power by our politicians.

Chapter 5
Say Goodbye to Your Money

When the banks ultimately collapse due to the derivatives upheaval because of systemically uncontrollable risk, many unexpected things will happen. The most serious problem immediately facing most readers will be a complete seizure of their (and everyone else's) checking and savings accounts. They will be wiped out. What most people don't realize is ***they loaned their money to the bank*** (when they made a deposit) and the bank gave them an "IOU" in return---the depositor doesn't technically "own" it, once the money is "lent" to the bank. You own the IOU from the bank!

God help us, one and all, when those IOUs become worthless…..and they surely will when the derivatives market collapses!

If monies, stocks, bonds or other assets are left in the banks, prime brokerage, hedge funds (who clear through prime brokerage), the investment banks, or the brokerage firms themselves, you can count on the fact overnight, your assets could vanish. Safety deposit boxes will not be safe if they are part of a bank which has any involvement (even if it thinks only peripherally) with the derivatives market. Those assets will be tied up in bankruptcy proceedings and people will not likely have access to their possessions for many, many months or years, while the judges, regulators and the overseers divvy up your hard earned assets for the creditors of the bank.

In a worst case scenario, you can be assured the government and bankers will promise you a brand NEW currency which will be exchanged for the OLD currency and everything will be "all right!" They will assure you the system will be stabilized and you will now be able to use the ATM, after a brief "banking holiday." For the super wealthy and those who have been able to hide their wealth offshore, they can diversify and hold assets in the private sector, which will allow them to avoid the receipt of the freshly printed and new Monopoly money. The super wealthy can purchase land, own safe deposits and vaults in private storage, hold paper certificates directly in stocks and bonds of private and/or public companies, etc. They will not be nearly as impacted as those who leave their monies and assets in the D'Apocalypse™-affected banks.

The smartest of them are investing accordingly---right now. You see them purchasing commercially viable companies, commercial real estate, farmland, gold, silver, food, stocks, corporate bonds, etc.

Warren Buffet tops this list, as you see him gobbling up companies critical to life after collapse—e.g., transportation, consumer products, etc.

SUMMARY OF WARREN BUFFETT'S HOLDINGS VIA BERKSHIRE HATHAWAY

On December 31, 2012 Berkshire Hathaway Reported:

Gross Revenues	Gross Revenues	Net Income	Cash & Cash Equivalents
$162,463,000,000	$162,463,000,000	$14,824,000,000	$46,992,000,000

Major Subsidiaries Include*:	Sector	Ownership %	Acquisition Date
GEICO	Insurance and Finance	100%	1996-08-26 (August 26, 1996)
Applied Underwriters	Insurance and Finance	100%	2004-05-22 (May 22, 2004)
General Re	Insurance and Finance	100%	1995-12-21 (December 21, 1995)
Kansas Bankers Surety Company	Insurance and Finance	100%	1998-04-10 (April 10, 1998)
National Indemnity Company	Insurance and Finance	100%	1967-03 (March, 1967) [3]
United States Liability Insurance Group	Insurance and Finance	75%	2000-08-08 [4]
Central States Indemnity Company	Insurance and Finance	100%	1982-10-20 (October 20, 1982)
Wesco Financial Corporation	Insurance and Finance	100%	1978 [5]
Dairy Queen	Food and Beverage	100%	1997-10-21 (October 21, 1997)
The Pampered Chef	Food and Beverage	100%	2002-09-23 (September 23, 2002)
See's Candies	Food and Beverage	100%	1972-01-03 (January 3, 1972)
H. J. Heinz Company	Food and Beverage	50%	2013-02-14 (February 14, 2013) [6]
Fechheimer Brothers Company	Clothing	100%	1986
Fruit of the Loom	Clothing	100%	2002-04-30 (April 30, 2002)
Garan Children's Clothing	Clothing	100%	2002-09-04 (September 4, 2002)
H.H. Brown Shoe Group	Clothing	100%	1991-07-01 (July 1, 1991)
Justin Brands	Clothing	100%	2000-08-01 (August 1, 2000)
CORT Business Services	Furniture Related	100%	2000-01-14 (January 14, 2000)
Jordan's Furniture	Furniture Related	100%	1999-10-11 (October 11, 1999)
Larson-Juhl	Furniture Related	100%	2001-12-17 (December 17, 2001)
Nebraska Furniture Mart	Furniture Related	80%	1983
RC Willey Home Furnishings	Furniture Related		1995 [7]
Star Furniture	Furniture Related	100%	1997-07-14 (July 14, 1997)
Acme Brick Company	Materials and Construction	100%	2000-08-01 (August 1, 2000)
Benjamin Moore & Co.	Materials and Construction	100%	2001-01-01 (January 1, 2001)
Clayton Homes	Materials and Construction	100%	2007-05-10 (May 10, 2007)
ISCAR Metalworking	Materials and Construction	80%	2006-05-08 (May 8, 2006)
Johns Manville	Materials and Construction	100%	2001-02-27 (February 27, 2001)
MiTek	Materials and Construction	90%	2001-06-12 [8]
Precision Steel Warehouse, Inc.	Materials and Construction		1979 [9]
Shaw Industries	Materials and Construction		2002-01-21 [10]
The Buffalo News	Media	100%	1977-04 (April, 1977)
Business Wire	Media	100%	2006-03-01 (March 1, 2006)
Omaha World-Herald	Media	100%	2011-12 (December 2011) [11]
XTRA Corporation	Logistics	100%	2001-09-20 (September 20, 2001)
McLane Company	Logistics	100%	2003-05-23 (May 23, 2003)
Ben Bridge Jewelers	Luxury Items	100%	2000-07-18 (July 18, 2000)
Borsheim's Fine Jewelry	Luxury Items	100%	1989
Helzberg Diamonds	Luxury Items	100%	1995
Scott Fetzer Companies	Other	100%	1985
MidAmerican Energy Holdings Company	Utilities	89.80%	1999-03-26 (March 26, 1999)
NetJets	Business Services	100%	1998
NetJets Europe	Business Services	100%	1998
FlightSafety	Business Services	100%	1997
CTB Inc.	Capital Goods	100%	2002
Burlington Northern Santa Fe Corp.	Railroads and Logistics	100%	2010-02-12 (February 12, 2010)
Blue Chip Stamps	Other	100%	1983-03 (March 1983)
SE Homes	Materials and Construction	100%	2007
Cavalier Homes	Materials and Construction	100%	2008
Lubrizol	Chemicals	100%	2011 (September 16, 2011)
BoatUS	Insurance		
Brooks Sports	Apparel	100%	2006 (August 2, 2006)
Forest River (company)	Materials and Construction	100%	2005 (August 31, 2005)
Marmon Group	Manufacturing & Service	100%	

* To the best knowledge at time of publication, subsidiary companies may change at any time.

(Source:
http://www.sec.gov/Archives/edgar/data/1067983/000119312513060317/d481559d13fhr.txt and http://en.wikipedia.org/wiki/List_of_assets_owned_by_Berkshire_Hathaway).

Victims of the D'Apocalypse™ will rightfully demand justice from the opportunists on Wall Street, the banking sector and the Federal Reserve. They will especially demand justice from those elitists who manipulated and took advantage of the system. They will ***try*** to go after those who bled the system dry through the burdening of debt on society, the extraction of shameful compensation and reimbursement arrangements using taxpayer money and will finally attempt to gain the cooperation of Congress in going after the guilty parties legally.

Normally, this would never be possible because Congress is in the elites' pocket, but in a collapse scenario, there will be no jobs and there will be MILLIONS of hungry and MILLIONS of very angry people in the streets. This is what will frighten Congress into ***potential*** action. It is the peoples' only hope of turning the tide against the pirates who robbed the nation and generations of children in the future.

The real battle is between the people and the banks, the people and the elite and the people and the Federal Reserve System---as the money controls Congress, the Senate and most Administrations. It remains to be seen whether the people will win during D'Apocalypse™, or not.

While this author will be with the people---we will face an uphill battle. The people are up against powers and principalities which are armed, have trillions of dollars and have control over significant portions of government. The people need to logically show those serving in government the battle ***is ONLY*** against those who were involved with the great heist. Those monies need to be returned to the American people---to the people of Detroit, Los Angeles, Dayton, Phoenix, Chicago, St. Louis, Miami, Houston, Denver, Seattle, Boston, Philadelphia, New York (to the regular people) and nearly every other city in America.

Will Our Government Open Fire on its Citizens?

When push comes to shove, will our government open fire on its citizens when the people take to the streets? You probably know the answer to this question, but at some point in time when a million people are marching in public, there will be a "moment," when a brave, courageous unarmed citizen faces down a tank---right in the middle of the street, right in front of the Capitol Building, the White House, the Supreme Court---or right in front of the Federal Reserve Bank of New York, on Maiden Lane and Liberty Streets.

This is the kind of thing which happened in Moscow when Boris Yeltsin faced down a tank and the Soviet Union fell. Their military refused to attack civilians who were just tired of the corruption and lack of freedom an oppressive, corrupt system had brought to the entire country.

Sometimes, in life, the only causes worth fighting for are the ones which appear to be lost!

New York Wakes Up

When the regular people of New York wake up and realize, they too, are victims of the actions of the Federal Reserve and the select few who were the recipients of siphoned cash from the American people, the nation will see a real change take place.

They need to vote the politicians out of office who have supported the banks in New York. This includes both Senators and every single Congressman in the five boroughs. This is a tall order, but as costs rise and the peoples' incomes continue to get squeezed, people will not be happy. The politicians and the bankers can only fool them a little while longer.

This could be an exciting revelation to every regular person in New York. It could be a magic sword and rallying cry for Jews, Christians, Buddhists, Muslims, Black Men, White Men, Yellow Men and every other person in the city and state. Hopefully, this revelation will become recognized by a few honest billionaires who did not take their money from the American treasury. It would be great to have honest wealth on the side of the people.

Remember---this trilogy supports capitalism, with benevolence, 100%. Honest rich people should be honored and protected, like every other citizen. These are the people who make life better for thousands of others through the creation of jobs, employment and capital investment in good ideas. Hopefully, they will recognize the injustice and great corruption which has taken place at, and around, the Federal Reserve System. The people will surely need their help.

A New Currency Will Be Worthless

Any new currency issued after D'Apocalypse™ begins will be worth only a FRACTION of what the old currency was worth (or, alternatively, the U.S. Dollar will be worthless because the number of dollars in circulation will skyrocket, as the government prints money to pay its bills and makes good on debt and interest payments, etc.).

Ultimately, the people will lose confidence in government, as a result. This is when bullion will soar and will be likely at the start of D'Apocalypse™ in late 2015.

Assflation™---Then Deflationary Shock & Awe

Before bullion soars, however, equity markets in the U.S. will BOOM (e.g. experience a MASSIVE RALLY). This will go into 2015, as the markets will experience a marked increase in Assflation™ across most liquid equity markets in the U.S., as the elite pivot from the overbought bond market and now put their repaired balance sheets to work in high-quality equity securities.

With up to $30 Trillion pivoting in this direction, ***equity markets should skyrocket*** in an unsustainable bubble into 2015—ultimately creating and causing a massive economic collapse which is all orchestrated with the birth of D'Apocalypse™, through rapidly rising interest rates.

Please read D'Apocalypse™ Now!---The Doomsday Cycle Chapter 9, "What to do Now" for specifics on entry and exit points and the author's thoughts on other important matters during this time of crisis.

The following chart and graphic introduces the reader, in graphical chart form, to the concept of "Assflation." There are several graph lines, the "bottom" one showing the actual Dow Jones performance, the middle graphical line showing the Dow Jones adjusted using U.S. "official" inflation figures and the "top" line, which uses the author's assumptions of true inflation.

This line actually crosses through 55,000 in 2015! Don't expect for one minute the Dow Jones will hit this number, however. Note the elliptical "Target Range" for where the author expects the Dow Jones Industrial Average to reach in late 2015.

Through the Federal Reserve's heists and manipulation of the money supply, the economy has witnessed what The $30 Trillion Heist (both Volumes I and II) and D'Apocalypse™ Now!---The Doomsday Cycle coins, for the first time ever, the word **"Assflation™."**

Assflation™ is an intentionally manipulated increase in prices across only certain asset classes or sectors, which benefit overwhelmingly and unfairly, the elite.

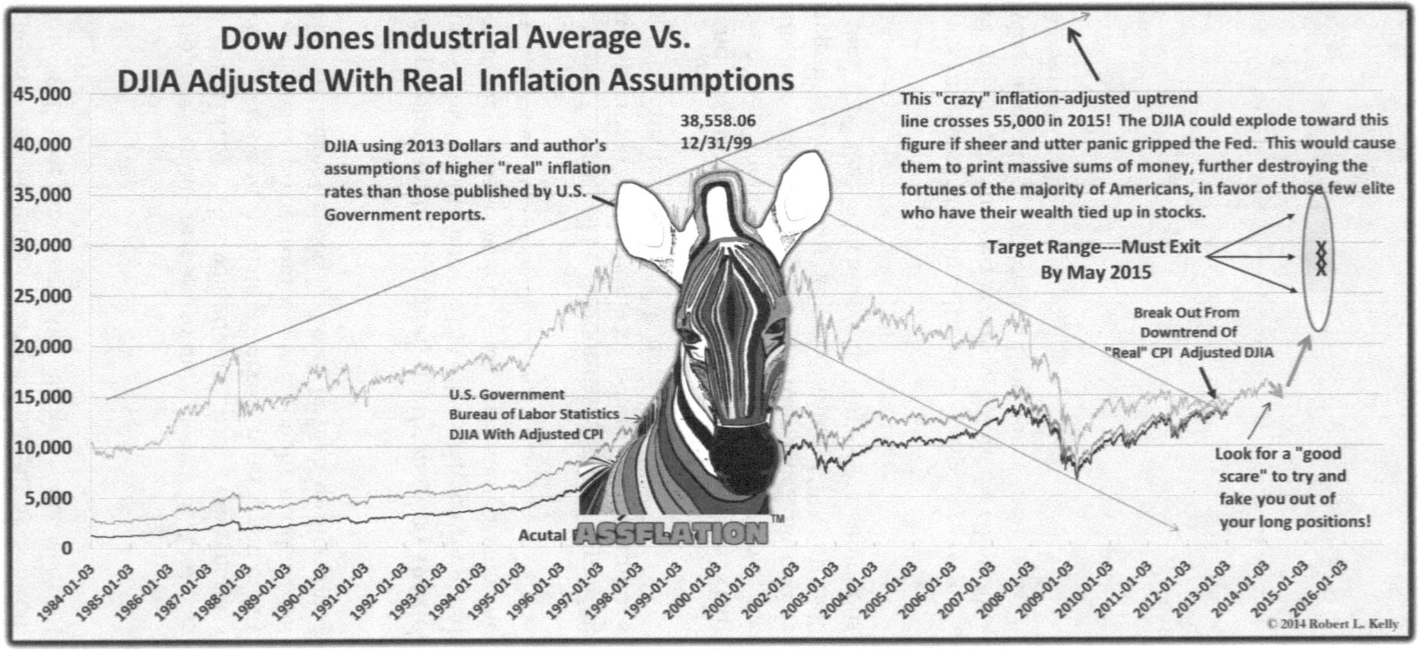

The author has created and would like to introduce to the world:

"Jack Assbanker™"

Jack commemorates and iconizes the Fed's and the banks' greedy, abominable and self-centered exercise in wealth creation for the elite.

Jack Assbanker™

They believe their actions, clever language and camouflaged financial statements can hide their egregious and nefarious activities from discovery---but exactly the opposite is true!

Jack Assbanker™

Standing out like glowing, fluorescent zebras, the elites' movements and attempts to manipulate the masses is being captured, recorded and commemorated for all time, enabling the world to see the truth of their corruption and heist of nearly $30 Trillion from the American people.

The rapacity, materialism and avarice by the bankers, elite and the Federal Reserve shall not go unrewarded---in time. Justice SHALL prevail in the end. Those who wear the colors of Jack send the signal:

WE KNOW WHO YOU ARE AND
WE KNOW WHAT YOU'RE UP TO!!

Let one picture speak a thousand words and make Jack Assbanker™ an icon to remember in this battle against powers and principalities! Visit **www.jackassbanker.com** for more information.

The bond market has nowhere to turn, as the risk of rising rates is enormous---spelling doom for anyone investing in securities locking in interest rates for any significant periods of time (i.e., stay very near term on ANY interest bearing security---no more than six months out, preferably only 90 days!).

This really just leaves the equity and currency markets for liquid capital investments, where the very big money can get in and get out, which should be its chief concern with any market during the next several years.

Massive Short Squeeze on the U.S. Dollar

Dollar and dollar-denominated liquid assets will be a great investment over the next couple of years (only until the end of May 2015, which is when the author recommends exiting from all markets, except bullion), as everyone will be seeking a safe harbor and will be scrambling to repay existing indebtedness, largely denominated in U.S. Dollars. This will create a massive short squeeze on the U.S. Dollar, creating a major bull run. Also likely to do quite well, will be the U.S. equity market. The world has very few places to put money to work and, as a result, the U.S. will benefit from this activity. The U.S., as bad as it is, is in better shape than Europe and Japan and will be a huge recipient of international capital flows, adding gasoline to the fire, blowing hot gas into the equity bubble.

Remember, ultimately be prepared to BAIL out of all equity investments and stash your cash because the markets will not only crash, but will thunder and explode with the power of an earthquake, the devastation of a hurricane and the ferociousness of a firestorm when D'Apocalypse™ strikes!

DEFLATIONARY SHOCK & AWE AWAITS ONE AND ALL!!

For more details get the book, D'Apocalypse™ Now!---The Doomsday Cycle, as it provides extremely specific recommendations and details on what to do and when to do it. You need and must confer with your financial advisor, however, before taking any action, as this author is not a registered financial advisor and the opinions expressed in the trilogy are his own.

It will be hard for most to "get out" in May because the market will be on a tear in 2015 and everyone will be making money---even the taxi driver.

How soon they all forget the "wealth effect" of equity markets can be shattered in a heartbeat, as the psychology turns and markets are no longer deemed safe, or desirable to own stock, bonds or other assets under the control of the banks, or government.

The next two years will also experience extreme volatility, shaking out the suckers, but it should march quite high---and could even double from its current levels at around 15,500. Regardless, you should have an asset plan taking your capital OUT of the system long before the U.S. Presidential elections occur in the fall of 2016. "Sell in May and go away" in 2015 would be an outstanding piece of advice to avoid the panic foreseen by this author, which will very likely begin to unfold in the fall (2015).

Just remember---don't leave anything in the banks!

Bankers Destroy Companies, Industries and Sectors, While Gobbling Up Assets

The massive inflation (note: the HUGE Assflation™ which will take place in the equity markets in the next couple of years is <u>NOT</u> the massive inflation the author expects to be awaiting consumers after D'Apocalypse™ strikes) will occur AFTER the bankers and the elite send the world into deflationary shock and awe---with the bankers destroying companies and gobbling up assets at bargain-basement prices, just as they did throughout the banker-fabricated credit crisis. After shuffling through the last five years of foreclosures, the hedge funds and banks have already repossessed, or are repurchasing for significant discounts, the best of the lovely homes stolen from the American people. We also know the bankers and elite used the credit crisis to acquire, for pennies on the dollar, many of their key competitors.

The galactic heist and actions by the banks are robbing the freedom from all Americans of the God-given rights we have enjoyed to own wonderful, yet inexpensive homes, rent nice, but inexpensive apartments, purchase cheap, but high-quality food, buy affordable, yet fashionable clothing, enjoy first-class, but low-cost education and be able to afford the finest inexpensive transportation in the world.

All of these rights we have enjoyed, historically, are now all gone because of debt, interest payments to the bankers on the debt and the continuing theft of trillions of dollars of assets from the American people, which comes back to us in the form of an inflationary tax which reduces our collective standard of living and reduces our real income.

America's historical cost advantages and historical high standard of living for nearly everyone, relative to the rest of the world, were only possible because we were born into a country without a King, Queen, Monarch, or dictator who siphoned the wealth of the nation for themselves and no one else.

Originally, until the year the Federal Reserve was created in 1913, we didn't even have to pay any income taxes, as it was (and some believe still is) outlawed by the Constitution.

The masses need to understand this is why both Mom and Dad have to work today to make a decent living. Most peoples' parents and grandparents only needed to have one person be the bread winner of the family.

This is 100% due to the actions of siphoning off the wealth of the nation into the pockets of a few abominably corrupt bankers, elitists and guardians of the Federal Reserve System.

> **American Dream Slipping as Homeownership at 18-Year Low**
> "The U.S. homeownership rate, which soared to a record high 69.2 percent in 2004, is back where it was two decades ago, before the housing bubble inflated, busted and ripped more than 7 million Americans from their homes." (Source: Bloomberg, by Prashant Gopal & Clea Benson, July 30, 2013, as retrieved from http://www.bloomberg.com/news/2013-07-30/american-dream-erased-as-homeownership-at-18-year-low.html).

A New Form of Monarchy

Today, unfortunately, a form of monarchy, or perhaps better termed oligarchy, has been placed over all of us, as the Federal Reserve has effected a hidden tax on the entire system, where the bankers and the elite have become a new form of oligarchy and along with the government, have simply taken trillions of dollars directly out of the pockets of the American people. This makes the poor, poorer, the rich, richer, and the middle class worse off through a combination of lower real wage rates and significantly higher real costs of living.

As the accumulation of assets under the control of the new oligarchs grows and grows, you can almost hear the crushing anguish of the voices of our grandchildren, decrying their loss of freedom and prosperity which were once their true inheritance.

These new 21st Century oligarchs just love to steal assets for pennies on the dollar, after calling in loans, and are happy to sell them back to the public at a profit---by reissuing a mortgage, or loan, with interest and a new 20% down payment!

Record Rents

The new oligarchs are also happy to simply rent property out to the beleaguered general public---of course rents are now at record high prices on a national level.

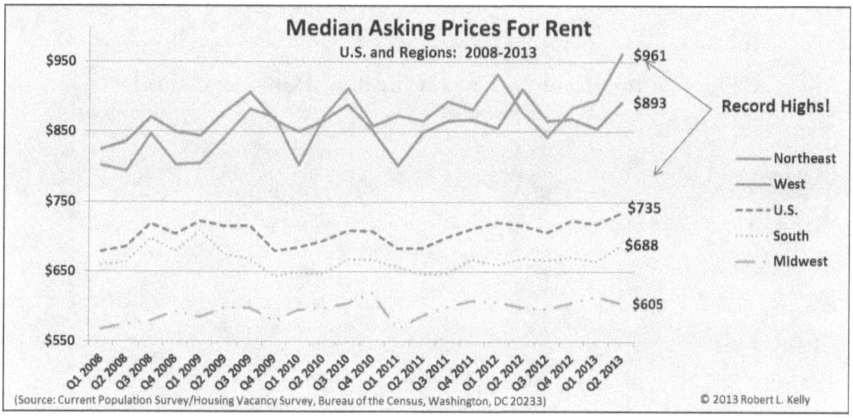

The preceding data (author's graphic) in the graph is from the U.S. Census Bureau. You can see the sharp impact on rents across the country where Assflation™ has been occurring and the $30 Trillion has been put to work. The Northeast just set a record high with the median asking price for rent at $961/month, while the U.S. national average is coming in at an all-time record high of $735!

This strategy of renting to the public has worked very well for the elite in England over the centuries, where most of the fine properties are owned by royalty, or the wealthy elite, and are rarely put up for sale. England primarily uses "lease-holds" where rent is paid to the owners, who will not allow a transfer of title to occur under any circumstances—particularly in prime areas. As a result of these actions, along with a central bank (the Bank of England) which makes a business out of indebting that nation, England has gone into the abyss as a world power, largely because of its weakened middle class, ridiculous socialistic spending policies and the shepherding of wealth to the elite.

A weakened middle class and an increase in poverty levels always mean a <u>government's tax receipts decrease</u> in inflation-adjusted dollars, pounds, etc. and the overall health of the nation declines.

For the average American, another monopoly (and/or oligopoly) is being formed in the housing sector, where prices will be manipulated, just like JP Morgan Chase has manipulated the commodities markets, the banks have fraudulently manipulated LIBOR and the banks defrauded one and all in the mortgage market and subsequently bank-engineered credit crisis. This is very bad news for Americans' traditional lifestyles.

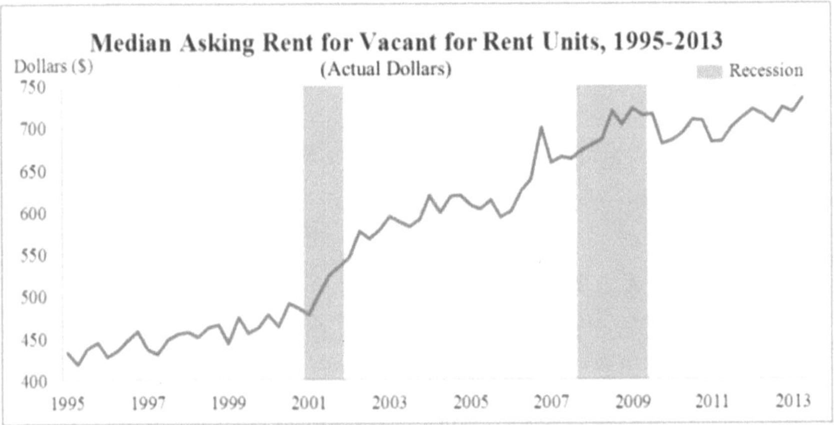

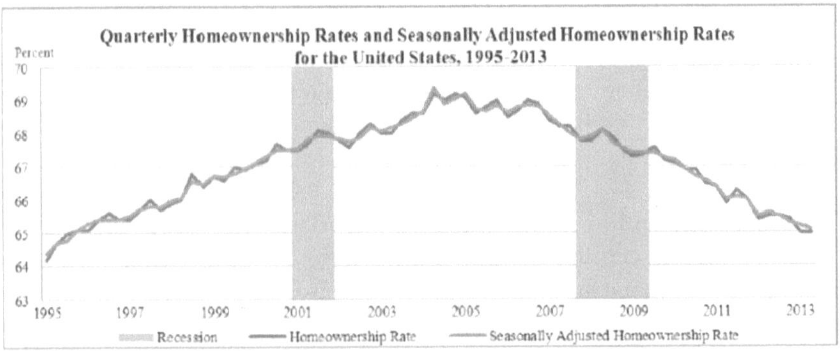

US Rents Hit Record High, Homeownership Plunges To Lowest Level Since 1995!

(Source: U.S. Census Bureau, by Robert R. Callis and Melissa Kresin, Social, Economic, and Housing Statistics Division, as retrieved from http://www.census.gov/housing/hvs/files/qtr213/q213press.pdf).

JPM facing $600M rebuke

"JPMorgan Chase was officially censured by the Federal Energy Regulatory Commission yesterday. The big bank run by CEO Dimon manipulated energy markets in California and the Midwest in 2010 and 2011 — allowing it to collect tens of millions of dollars in overpayments, according to FERC. The JPMorgan energy unit, overseen by prominent JPMorgan official Blythe Masters, is expected to get slapped with penalties of up to $600 million as soon as today, sources said." (Source: New York Post, by Mark Decambre, July 29, 2013, as retrieved from http://nypost.com/2013/07/30/jpm-facing-600m-rebuke/).

2 Billion Bullets

With oligopoly control being exercised by the big banks and the elite over many, many markets, the uncontrollable debt in the West, combined with the devastating impact the great $30 Trillion heist has had on the majority of the people, governments seem to be extremely concerned.

Between all the spying and eavesdropping on regular citizens, combined with the now well-publicized fact U.S. Homeland Security has the authorization to purchase over 2 BILLION BULLETS (most of them hollow point!), and has acquired armored tanks to police the homeland, government officials appear to be secretly panicked.

Whoever is in power in the halls of Congress at the time the derivatives debacle occurs ***will vote in favor of holding on to power mercilessly, or will simply acquiesce to the President's declaration of martial law, and the use of our military*** in an attempt to keep order among the masses.

It won't matter whether they are Republicans, or Democrats. These two parties have buried us, financially speaking, and it is highly unlikely either one of them will come to their senses any time soon. Everyone in power, in either party, is going to vote for their self-interests and if anything is true, the current set of Congressmen and Senators are interested in being re-elected and remaining in power. They will not listen to people rioting in the streets even if they are rioting because they don't have food, shelter and can't afford a new coat.

At the height of the credit crisis in 2008, when panic and fear gripped the markets around the world, our Congress and Senate, along with our President, George W. Bush, signed a bill which effectively ended Posse

Comitatus and allows Homeland Security, the military, or any other body of force, including foreign and U.N. troops to set foot on U.S. soil.

If you think this sounds farfetched and not the truth, the following is the law according to H.R. 4886:

H.R. 4986 (110th): NATIONAL DEFENSE AUTHORIZATION ACT 2008

SEC. 1068. REPEAL OF PROVISIONS IN SECTION 1076 OF PUBLIC LAW 109-364 RELATING TO USE OF ARMED FORCES IN MAJOR PUBLIC EMERGENCIES.

(a) Interference With State and Federal Laws-

(1) IN GENERAL- Section 333 of title 10, United States Code, is amended to read as follows:

`Sec. 333. Interference with State and Federal law

`The President, by using the militia or the armed forces, or both, or by any other means, shall take such measures as he considers necessary to suppress, in a State, any insurrection, domestic violence, unlawful combination, or conspiracy, if it--

`(1) so hinders the execution of the laws of that State, and of the United States within the State, that any part or class of its people is deprived of a right, privilege, immunity, or protection named in the Constitution and secured by law, and the constituted authorities of that State are unable, fail, or refuse to protect that right, privilege, or immunity, or to give that protection; or

`(2) opposes or obstructs the execution of the laws of the United States or impedes the course of justice under those laws.

(Source: http://www.govtrack.us/congress/bills/110/hr4986).

The Posse Comitatus Act's intent (in concert with the Insurrection Act of 1807), passed on June 18, 1878, was to limit the powers of Federal government in using federal military personnel to enforce the State laws (18 U.S.C. § 1385, original at 20 Stat. 152).

The United States Armed Forces, COMBINED, only used a few million rounds of ammunition A MONTH during the Afghanistan and Iraq wars combined. Why does Homeland Security need 2 BILLION BULLETS?

Why isn't there outrage in Congress as Homeland Security took it on itself to make these kinds of purchases for domestic use?

The point is some people in very powerful places are seeing something very bad happening in the future because the facts prove people in power have become very, very afraid.

Why else would one organization responsible for domestic security order 2 Billion bullets and thousands of tanks?

Get Prepared, Get Ready & Be Angry

While you may have a peace about what may happen in the future, especially if you are a Christian, God wants us to take action and use our minds. This is why He gave us a body and gave us a mind---then He connected them!

If you feel convicted to start making preparations for awful and horrific events about to unfold upon us---THEN DO SO! Make sure your family has enough basic necessities to ensure it can eat and live. You are not being a prepper; you are simply being prudent and actually following an old practice the Mormons and many other groups have relied on over centuries of time. This writer is not a Mormon, but the principle of ensuring you have enough to take care of you and yours is a sound policy at any time and should be implemented as soon as humanly possible by all readers, if they are able to do so.

God wants us to do the very best we can with what He entrusts to us, permitting us to help ourselves and the freedom to help others in the process. This is what He wants. You get to make the choice of how you live your life and He, ultimately, will be the judge of it.

Living a life at peace with God and helping others brings about great hope. Others inevitably witness the lifestyle example and discover compassion is contagious….the bad times ahead can and will be conquered through faith, hope, compassion, love and yes, charity.

Jesus had No Compassion for the Money Changers!

Jesus, however, had NO compassion for the money changers. It is the only example of pure rage and anger shown by Jesus in the entire Bible.

> ***"And Jesus went into the temple of God, and cast out all them that sold and bought in the temple, and overthrew the tables of the moneychangers, and the seats of them that sold doves, And said unto them, It is written, My house shall be called the house of prayer; but ye have made it a den of thieves. And the blind and the lame came to him in the temple; and he healed them. And when the chief priests and scribes saw the wonderful things that he did, and the children crying in the temple, and saying, Hosanna to the Son of David; they were sore displeased..."***
> (Source: The Bible, Matthew 21:12-15, King James Version).

It is beyond interesting Jesus cast His rage at probably the cleverest group of people in all the land---the money brokers, lenders and thieves who trade with and prey on the masses. Imagine---those thieves in the Temple didn't even know what a computer was and look at the rage bestowed upon them!

God have mercy on those in the banking business when the Day of Judgment arrives.

The carpet baggers of Wall Street and many of the wealthiest families on earth obtained their wealth by abusing and manipulating a corrupt banking and legal system to extract monies from the general public and they too, shall receive their just reward.

If anyone is a banker, works for a bank, or is part of the elite group who robbed America and other countries, this book and this testimony highly recommends you change your job, change your ways, make amends and get prepared to help millions of starving people during the D'Apocalypse™.

Every dollar you have placed in your pocket has the stench of greed, the squalor of avarice and the corruption of abomination all over it.

Like everyone else, you too shall be accountable for how you lived your life, who you worked for and how they earned their money.

Chapter 6
The Heist---Major Cause of Unemployment & Poverty

As you know by now, this book is not about being a bleeding-heart liberal. The author is an independent conservative, with social love in his heart and a fierce streak of liberty running through his veins. He also has exceptional disdain for the actions taken by those who have robbed the American Republic through secret bailouts, the socialization of rich people's bad investment decisions and the abusive over-spending of taxpayer monies. All of these amount to outright thefts from the people, as they cause tremendous pain for the masses.

When a person starts digging into exactly how much money was taken, one soon realizes how much good the money *could* have done to help people in real need. Today, millions upon millions of people are living under conditions of extreme stress and poverty throughout the country (and world!). One can only imagine the difference it might have made if only those trillions hadn't been siphoned off to solely aid the rich owners of the banks, the banks' employees and their managements!

Secret Heist Decided by Only 7 Unelected People!

Without boring people who don't like looking at tables, please take a look at the Population Clock.

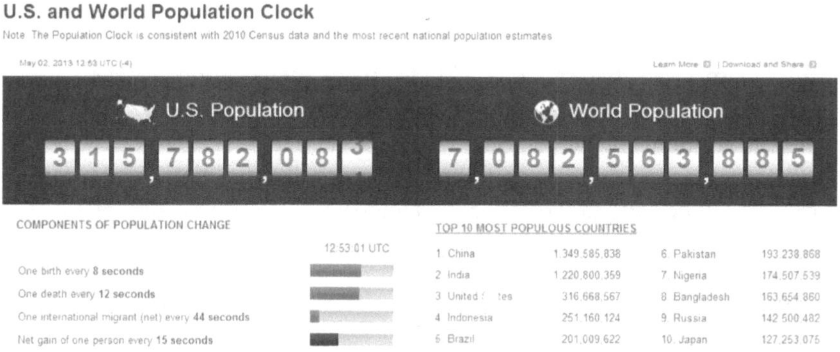

Source: U.S. Census Bureau, as retrieved from http://www.census.gov/popclock/

With over 300,000,000 people in the United States and over 7 billion people in the world, the omniscient (sarcasm intended) team of only 7 members on the Federal Reserve Board of Governors approved and delegated the authority to execute exchanges of worthless securities for U.S. taxpayer-backed monies through the Federal Open Market Committee ("FOMC") of the Federal Reserve Bank of New York, a private company. The FOMC also only consists of a very small number of unelected officials. They total only 12 people. However when one looks at many of the minutes published from FOMC meetings, only ten members appear present for voting---5 from the Federal Reserve Board of Governors and 5 members from the Reserve Banks, again, all of them unelected officials.

It is this small group who took it in their own hands to ***secretly*** decide to ***secretly*** take nearly $30 Trillion of taxpayer-backed monies and give these monies away to the banks, the elite and even, potentially, to individuals. The recent amendments to the Federal Reserve Act, pushed through Congress by the Federal Reserve and its banking allies, reverses long-standing, protective covenants in the Federal Reserve Act to NOW allow payment and exchanges with INDIVIDUALS AND CORPORATIONS at the Federal Reserve banking window. This was ***forbidden*** in the original Act, as it tried to ***prevent*** this kind of potentially treacherous behavior from occurring.

The original writers of the Act knew if these actions were not prevented by law, there would be temptation to dip into taxpayer-backed monies to reimburse banks, businesses, as well as wealthy individuals, for poor business decisions. The Federal Reserve was NOT designed with this purpose in mind. Despite the law on the books at the time of the Credit Crisis, it appears the Fed window was used in a spectacularly egregious and nefarious manner (this book describes as The $30 Trillion Heist) to secretly reimburse banks, and elitists from devastating losses. This activity, of course, was also precisely ***against, and contrary to,*** the purpose and intent of the original writers of the Act.

To this day, there appear to be gross violations of multiple sections of the Federal Reserve Act by the Federal Reserve, the banks and the elite.

The bottom line is the members of the Reserve Board and 5 representatives from the Federal Reserve Banks decided surreptitiously to secretly give away nearly $30 Trillion to banks and rich people, without approval from Congress, when billions of people on the world population clock are starving and tens of millions of Americans are out of work!

This is a travesty and shocking crime against humanity and the country, in this writer's opinion.

Collectively, these are the people responsible for making the decision to give away nearly $30 Trillion to the banks and the elite:

Members of the Federal Reserve Board During The Great Heist

Ben S. Bernanke
Chairman

Janet L. Yellen
Vice Chair

Elizabeth A. Duke

Daniel K. Tarullo

Sarah Bloom Raskin

Jeremy C. Stein

Jerome H. Powell

They, in turn, delegate the operational authority through the Federal Open Market Committee and the New York Federal Reserve Bank to conduct the open market operations to exchange the banks' bad paper for U.S. taxpayer-backed money. There are supposed to be twelve members on the FOMC, with the New York Federal Reserve Bank having a permanent seat on this Committee. 2013 Members of the FOMC are:

Federal Reserve Board Members	Federal Reserve Banks (4 Rotate)
Ben S. Bernanke, Board of Governors, Chairman	William C. Dudley, New York, Vice Chairman
Elizabeth A. Duke, Board of Governors	James Bullard, St. Louis
Jerome H. Powell, Board of Governors	Charles L. Evans, Chicago
Sarah Bloom Raskin, Board of Governors	Esther L. George, Kansas City
Jeremy C. Stein, Board of Governors	Eric S. Rosengren, Boston
Daniel K. Tarullo, Board of Governors	
Janet L. Yellen, Board of Governors	

The photographs of the Presidents of the 12 Federal Reserve Banks are online and can be easily Googled.

As you will read in Chapter 16, "Ownership of The Federal Reserve" in The $30 Trillion Heist---Follow The Money! Volume II, the Federal Reserve Banks are all owned by the commercial banks and depending on the facts of history, are also controlled by only a handful of some extremely powerful families.

Fed Board of Governors Compromised and Conflicted

As most people already realize, the Federal Reserve Board Members are taken care of by the banks when they decide to leave the Fed and are all hopelessly compromised as a result. The money for the "good" service they provide the banks and the elite is enormous and it comes in the form of speeches and appearances in the first two years after departure from the Fed and then onward and upward from there, as they can be drawn into the Chairman's office of any bank on the planet, as many Fed members have in the past.

Since the Federal Reserve Banks are owned by the commercial banks, their only interests are in serving the banks and they could care less about the economy, or people of America. MOST of the time, it is in their interests to see economic expansion occur, as the banks and the elite usually make more money in a rising economy. HOWEVER, when they decide to shut down credit and strangle the money supply, it is because they are ready to foreclose on people, businesses and industries—and take over their assets for pennies on the dollar. Just such a setup is happening presently and should be launched by them within the next two years. D'Apocalypse™ Now!---The Doomsday Cycle covers this expected event in detail.

The bankers will never look at the world population clock and use $30 Trillion to help Americans. They will only serve their masters and in this case, their masters are the rich, elite owners of the banks and the banks themselves.

On the contrary, as you will learn in these pages, the bankers and the elite used these monies to implement schemes to declare and make enormous dividend payments to the owners of the banks. They also instituted outrageous compensation schemes for their executives and employees and used trillions of dollars to run up several market sectors, creating Assflation™.

Assflation™ is unsustainable and will ultimately crash when the firestorm of D'Apocalypse™ overwhelms the markets. The Federal Reserve System under Benjamin Bernanke and Alan Greenspan temporarily manipulated markets for the favor of the elite wealthy, hurt the economy and reduced the standard of living for the people, while they appear to have simultaneously misled and withheld key facts from the general public and Congress.

Collectively, the Federal Reserve's actions allowed the bankers to walk away with multi-ten-million dollar and $100 Million+ paydays for the executives, salesmen and traders on Wall Street and many in corporate America, while also robbing the U.S. Treasury by grabbing TRILLION dollar paydays for the banks and the elite---thereby reimbursing the world's wealthiest families and corporations for their bad investment decisions.

This is the real reason unemployment is incredibly high in America and Europe. It is also why the poor are just becoming poorer around the world and the middle class is being systematically, wiped out.

True Capitalism with Faith is the Best Solution

Communism and socialism are inferior solutions to capitalism. Capitalism, combined with a profound love for God and fellow man, is the greatest system on earth, as it most efficiently uses resources and encourages ingenuity and productivity—producing JOBS---while being kind and thoughtful to everyone around it. It actually is the perfect system to HARNESS GREED (which every man and woman has in his, or her, heart), for the good of other people.

Unfortunately, as we discussed in Chapter 1's subsection, "Greed is Everywhere," contrary to the popular movie "Wall Street" and Michael Douglas' famous line, "Greed is good!," greed is NOT GOOD and is the ESSENCE OF EVIL. Greed IS the love of money, the root of all evil, and it destroys the hearts and souls of men and women.

What ***used to be*** present in nearly every single household in America (and in Europe) was a profound respect and love for God---and other people. Neighbors would help neighbors and people would gladly help the poor and the needy—regardless of their faith. Families and churches would naturally cleave together and take care of their communities and people around them. Sadly, except for very few examples today, this has gone missing in America and Europe—and by the measure of poverty, globally, is missing worldwide.

Capitalism, COMBINED with a firm belief in Jesus Christ and The Bible works because every worker is taught by God's teachings to perform their work, as if they were working for God himself. If workers are lucky enough to work for a Christian employer, then the employer knows full well his, or her, responsibility to help others and share the fruits of the company's labors. By exerting a fully-committed effort all the day long, Christians' lights are sent out powerfully and eminently to those around them and others do take notice, as they see the light of Christ shining through us. In the Christian's case, both worker and employer know this world isn't about getting rich; it is about changing one's life by asking for, and receiving automatically, the forgiveness of sins through Jesus Christ. This miracle is performed by the Holy Spirit.

As Christians, we are always forced to examine our surroundings and if obvious wrongs prevail, we must react, without fear. It is our supreme responsibility as Christians---to ACT. The Bible has one of its longest sections committed to a title of just this name—the Book of Acts!

In any event, when materialism has been obtained by ill-gotten means, at the expense of entire populations of peoples, we must and will ACT.

Greed and the love of money is the core reason the bankers took the money and have continued to manipulate the system to their advantage. It will be their own greed which will bring the entire system down on top of their heads---AND everyone else's, as well.

While they have purposely engineered D'Apocalypse™ to achieve their objective of global monetary control, there is at least a real possibility they will miscalculate (as they did in the mortgage crisis) and many of the biggest banks will fail and be forced out of business. It will be a real horse race to see which of the 4 Horsemen of the D'Apocalypse™ (i.e. JP Morgan Chase, Citigroup, Goldman Sachs and Bank of America) are left standing when the dust settles after the firestorm of D'Apocalypse™ passes through.

While the writer is an avowed capitalist, the bankers' actions are anything but capitalistic---they are supremely socialistic, as they took money from the masses for their own pockets. One could argue a new form of political party was born which combines both capitalism and communism.

When the bankers lose and make bad business decisions, they take the corrupted law of the Federal Reserve Act into their own hands and get reimbursed from the American taxpayer. As Senator Bernie Sanders states, it is **"Socialism for the rich and rugged individualized capitalism for everyone else!"** (see The $30 Trillion Heist---Follow The Money! Volume II, Chapter 1, "The $30 Trillion Heist---How the Scam Worked").

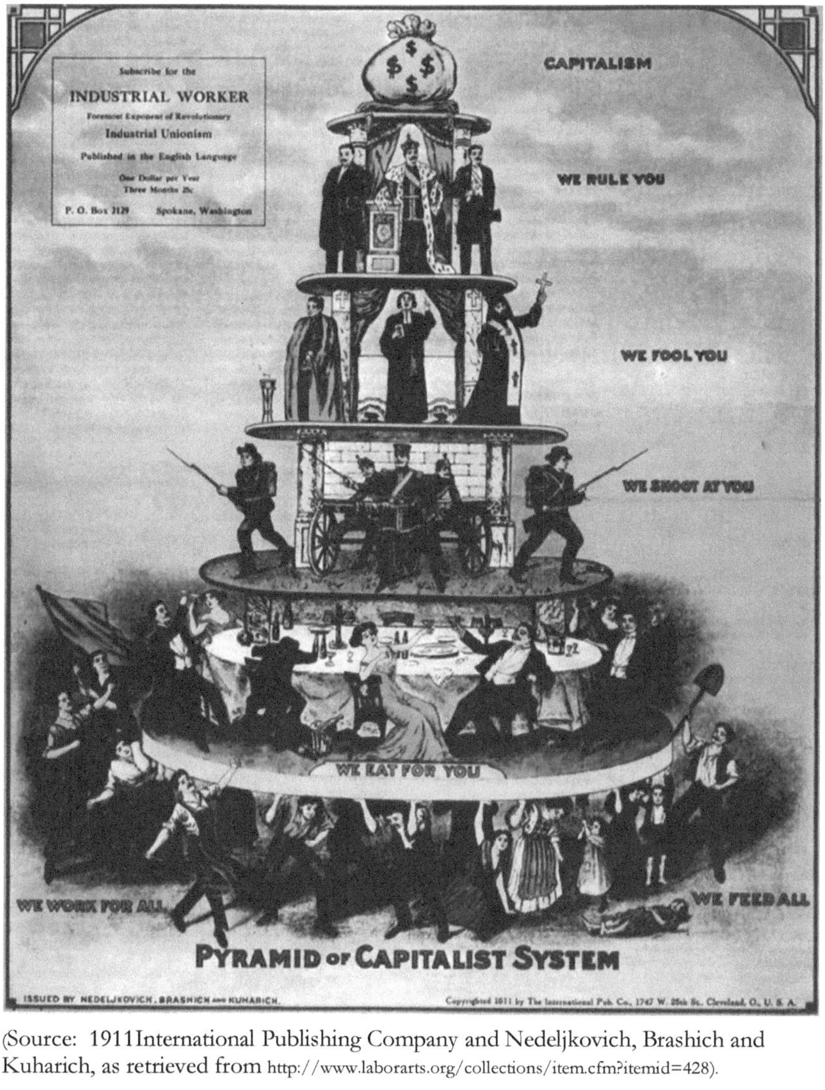

(Source: 1911International Publishing Company and Nedeljkovich, Brashich and Kuharich, as retrieved from http://www.laborarts.org/collections/item.cfm?itemid=428).

While many communists wrongfully objected to people getting rich (but didn't and don't mind enriching themselves, becoming one of the largest group of hypocrites on earth), some creative communists, intent on the destruction of capitalism, have made some fabulous illustrations over the years, where one picture is worth a thousand words.

Not much has changed since 1911, when the International Publishing Company and Nedeljkovich, Brashich and Kuharich grew frustrated with the industrialists and they published the preceding picture. The visual holds some merit today, except the bankers are now at the top of the pyramid, not even producing jobs for the industrial class! Of course, what the communists missed was the freedom for any working person to better themselves by using their freedom to create, invent, invest and otherwise use their brains to better their own lives and those around them. What this illustration does not provide the reader is a siphon which secretly takes from the industrial class and puts it into the pockets of the elite.

As our brethren in Detroit and every other crippled city can tell you, the recipients of the $30 Trillion heist have done a great job of hoarding the money for themselves and their families---and could care less about everyone else.

Capitalism No More

What is critical and important to understand is we are NOT working and living under a capitalistic system anymore. Eradicating the losses of the rich, at the expense of the upper class, the middle class and the poor is a new form of socialism---it is socialism for the elite.

While the Democrats and Republicans pound their chests and say they both help the poor (but wind up doing nothing but continuing a sad, repetitive cycle of impoverishment for those living in the inner cities and rural areas of poor parts of the country), both political parties have completely ignored the wealth guarantees secretly granted, without authorization, to the banks and the elite.

Obviously, giving the banks and elites taxpayer-backed monies coming out of the U.S. Treasury, sooner, or later, place a tax burden on all Americans.

Their ability to manipulate the entire nation is made possible because they own the Federal Reserve Banks. The commercial banks' and elites' ownership of the Federal Reserve Banks (i.e., the twelve regional Federal Reserve Banks and particularly, the New York Federal Reserve Bank) provides them with effective control, influence and power over the Federal Reserve Board of Governors and the politicians sitting on Capitol Hill. This is why inflation is ever present and the standard of living for the regular family keeps decreasing in "Amerika."

Many books and conspiracy theories exist about the ownership of the Federal Reserve. This book does NOT dwell on this subject, as it is very well documented elsewhere. However, suffice it to say, through the web of companies the elite families own they also control the Federal Reserve System—directly through the Federal Reserve Regional Banks and their effective control of the Federal Open Market Committee.

The New York Federal Reserve Bank is 100% responsible for Open Market Operations and **none of the banks has to submit, or publish, a cash flow statement due to the Fed's loose accounting policies.**

The banks have a number of ways to keep transactions (and potentially trillions of dollars in worthless assets) off of their books in the form of off-balance vehicles. They also enjoy special favor with respect to international transactions, as these are not audited and any audits conducted are filled with loopholes for the Fed to limit the audit with respect to discovery, scope and publication of findings.

The list of companies, trusts and partnerships which own the Fed will blow your mind (see Volume II in The $30 Trillion Heist---Follow The Money!, Chapter 16 "Ownership of the Federal Reserve").

The ownership diagrams and conclusions in Volume II were taken directly from a U.S. Congressional investigation and Congressional reports, as well as from amazing historical documents---see Volume II's Chapter 16, subsection, "1914 Major Shareholders of New York National Banks." It provides you a copy of the original New York Times news article which published the individual names of ownership in the major national New York banks in 1913.

This ancient article provides the names of the key people who ultimately became the major owners of the New York Federal Reserve Bank. Their legacy family members are still in control to this very day!

As stated once before in this book: **This is also not conspiracy theory. These statements are backed up by hard facts of history.**

Massive Destruction of Wealth

The result of the heist affected the United States (and the rest of the world) in several major ways.

- The first was the destruction in wealth which occurred to households across the board due to the collapse and deflation in most of the housing and building industries, with millions of homes taken away from their rightful owners;

- The second was an initial collapse in equity prices;
- The third was a dramatic increase in unemployment;
- And, finally, the fourth was the outright taking, on an unauthorized basis, of nearly $30 Trillion from the American public, without approval by Congress.

To this very day, neither the American people, nor Congress, have ANY IDEA, whether, or not, the heist money has been returned, or if the banks and the elite merely "exchanged" worthless securities for U.S. cash and U.S. cash-equivalents….leaving their toxic securities to rot at the expense of the American public.

If the toxic exchange and swap out for U.S. cash occurred, then it is HIGHLY LIKELY those worthless securities still sit on the Fed's books via "on" and "off"-balance vehicles. Additionally, they have likely been "netted out," which precludes the need to show their existence on paper, with their true worthless value "marked up" to disguise the fact the American taxpayer is stuck with nearly $30 Trillion in losses.

In this way, the Fed could cleverly hide the truth from the American public, a sound asleep Congress and two presidential administrations which allowed this activity to take place in the first place.

Only a full, independent audit will determine the truth with respect to what is really hidden in the books of the Federal Reserve and the Federal Reserve Regional Reserve Banks. Where there is no dispute, however, is the Federal Reserve secretly took nearly $30 Trillion in taxpayer monies to effect transactions with member banks, as well as non-member banks and institutions (a direct violation of the original Act's spirit and intent)--many of whom are based in other NATIONS.

Any way you cut this pie, no one has ever authorized the use of monies in this fashion to support the bad business decisions of failing international banks around the world, which all carry the bad paper of Greece, Portugal, Ireland, Italy, Spain and many, many bad bets in other countries.

Following is a chart, "% Losses Mean Net Worth 2007-2010" (created from an essay written by Ray Boshara and William Emmons of the

Federal Reserve Bank of St. Louis in May of 2013), which shows the estimated percentage losses among various demographic groups due to the credit crisis.

Messrs.' Boshara and Emmons believe the absolute destruction of the credit crisis was in the $15 Trillion range (although there are many who might dispute this figure as too low when losses in real estate, reduced incomes, GDP and monies taken from taxpayer-backed secret bailouts are included which would cause this figure to increase, dramatically), with a large chunk of this loss regained due to the goosing of the equity and bond markets by the Federal Reserve.

The hardest hit people were clearly younger, aged 0-39, but also hard hit were African-Americans, Hispanics and those who did not go on to college. As the Fed's own work demonstrates, spiking the punch bowl of equity and debt markets has done nothing to help the masses. People in the middle and lower classes do not, generally, own stocks and bonds and they make up the vast majority of the population of America.

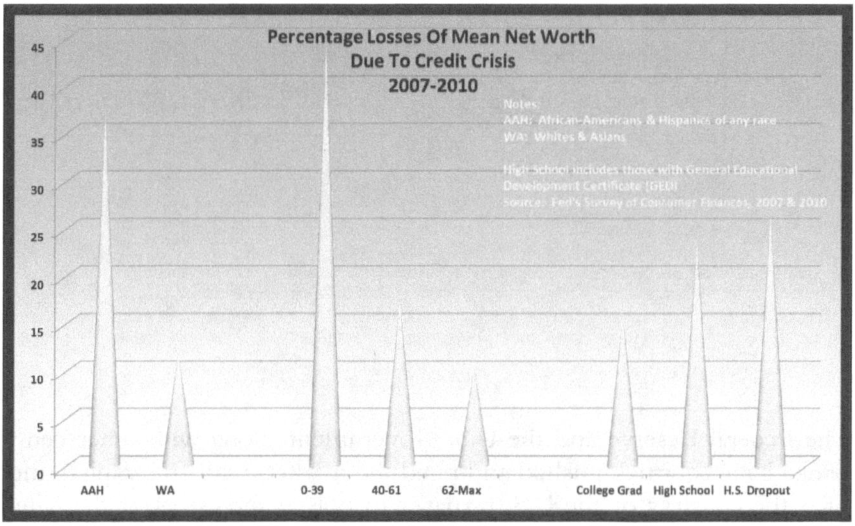

AAH: African Americans & Hispanics; WA: Whites & Asians; High School includes those with a GED Certificate

(Source: After the Fall Rebuilding Family Balance Sheets, Rebuilding the Economy, By Ray Boshara and William Emmons, published May 2013, the Federal Reserve Bank of St. Louis, retrieved from http://www.stlouisfed.org/publications/ar/2012/pages/ar12_2a.cfm).

Of the total recovery of $14.7 trillion between the first quarter of 2009 and the fourth quarter of 2012, $9.1 trillion, or 62 percent, of the gain was due to ***higher stock-market wealth.*** Since the end of 2012, the effect of Assflation™ (see The $30 Trillion Heist---Follow The Money! Volume II, Chapter 6 "Assflation™ and VaR—it's Déjà vu, All Over Again!," as well as this book's Chapter 5) has kicked into high gear, with all major equity markets up another 16-20% as of this writing in the U.S. in 2013.

Stock wealth is unevenly held, with the vast majority of stocks owned by a relatively small number of wealthy families. ***Thus, most families have recovered much less than the average amount.***

> "In the U.S., about $6.5 trillion of residential real estate value evaporated after a wave of mortgage defaults sparked the 2008 financial crisis. The median U.S. home price hit bottom in 2012 after a 33 percent drop, as measured by the National Association of Realtors." (Source: Bloomberg, "Home Value Highest Since '07 as U.S. Houses Make Cash," By Kathleen M. Howley - Mar 26, 2013 as retrieved from: http://www.bloomberg.com/news/2013-03-26/home-value-highest-since-07-as-u-s-houses-make-cash-mortgages.html).

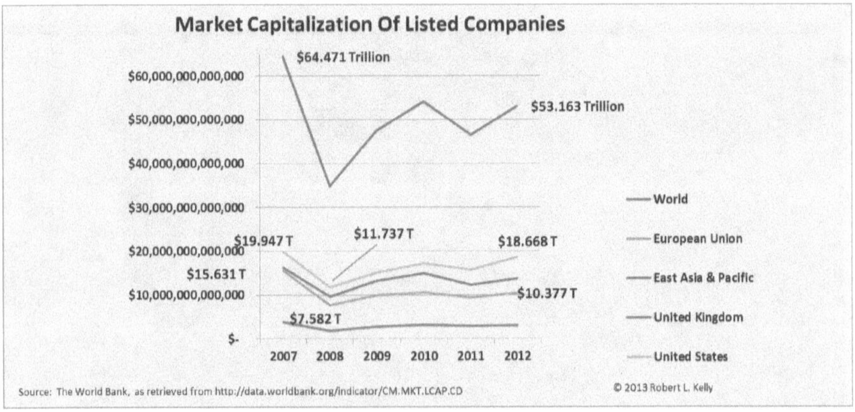

The Federal Reserve and the U.S. Government, along with other central banks have squirted, pushed and plied the markets with free capital, most of it the courtesy of the U.S. taxpayer to bolster the assets of the elite---stocks, bonds and high-end real estate!

If we review quickly how much money (using either the fully disclosed figures *or* the understated numbers which disguise the truth of the matter) the Fed has spent to support the banks and the elite, the numbers range from the $30 Trillion level, all the way down to the several trillion dollar level.

Massive Spending & Bond Issuances Have Been Used To Artificially Support Markets

Because of this massive spending, many people have feared a great hyperinflation would result from the Fed's monkey business and monetary injections into the banks' and the elites' pockets. The problem with this point of view is there has also been enormous wealth destruction in the markets, which largely cancels out the monetary infusions into the system. The result is a nominal increase in inflation on the GENERAL level, with an Assflation™ spike in certain, controlled asset markets largely controlled by the elite.

Even if we take the $30 Trillion heist money as the actual amount of "monetary infusion" from the Fed, per the GAO audit, which this book suggests is reality, then you can add up the wealth destruction (e.g., real estate, equity, unemployment, etc.), calculate the result and do at least a simple subtraction, resulting in an expected inflation number impacting the monetary base. While not exact, it will give the reader a good idea of how much "extra" fuel the Fed burned to bail out the rich and "right the ship"—at least this is what they claim they are doing.

As discussed, according to the study by the St. Louis Federal Reserve Bank, the wealth destruction totaled nearly $15 Trillion.

We also know for a fact according to the GAO partial audit, there was approximately $26 Trillion used to support the markets. This fact is published and if you also add in the announced "QE" programs (i.e. Quantitative Easing), the amount totals approximately $30 Trillion.

Most gold bugs and hyper-inflationists make the naïve assumption all the money the Fed is using to support the markets will cause a dollar for dollar "pop" in the markets, thereby forcing gold to rise to stratospheric levels (there is a whole section written on Bullion in D'Apocalypse™ Now!---The Doomsday Cycle Chapter 9, "What To Do Now," subsection, "Buy Bullion.").

The problem with this assumption is nearly HALF of the money the Fed injected goes offshore, in the form of debt purchases and support programs the Fed has launched in OTHER NATIONS (see table, as follows, "Federal Debt $16.796 Trillion-1st Quarter 2013").

Who Owns The U.S. Government Debt?

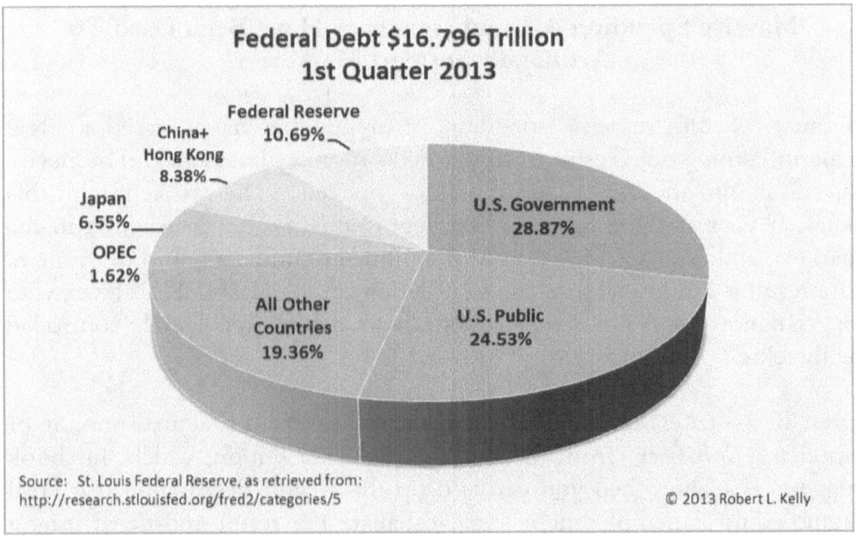

As a result, this leaves approximately $15 Trillion to cancel out the $15 Trillion of wealth destruction identified by Messrs.' Ray Boshara and William Emmons of the Federal Reserve Bank of St. Louis in May of 2013, causing no impact from an inflationary perspective on the GENERAL economy. However, because of the way in which the $30 Trillion secret give-away to the banks and the elite was siphoned off directly to the banks and elite, it has caused a massive windfall for the banks and their elite owners. This is because Assflation™ has kicked into high gear across the preferred asset classes of the rich (e.g. stocks, bonds and high-end real estate), which is making the rich, richer, and the poor, poorer.

While this analysis/illustration is simplistic and the dollar calculation is not exact, the reader should immediately begin to understand why there is no hyperinflation. The only thing which has really occurred is the people who were given the gift of heisted cash from the American taxpayer have used it to stay liquid and bid up equity, debt and high-end real estate markets, worldwide. Despite the recent rise in interest rates, the bond markets have just completed a historic bull market run.

In the post-mortem analysis of the economic devastation awaiting us all, people from all nations will demand the wrong-doers, who caused the great economic hardship and collapse to happen, be held accountable. The nation, as a whole, will very likely seek extreme accountability from nearly every working banker living today and it is also very likely the nation and peoples affected by the collapse, worldwide, will not forget the *owners* of the banks and families who were the greatest benefactors of the heist. They are the sorcerers behind the curtain and are the ones who have accumulated very great wealth at the expense of everyone else.

By secretly taking trillions of dollars, backed by our tax monies and exchanging them for worthless mortgage securities and other highly risky derivatives contracts (courtesy of Mr. Bernanke, Ms. Yellen and the Fed), these families stole our national legacy and the future from generations to come. When the Federal Reserve is finally forced into a full-blown audit and the gold reserves of the United States of America are also fully audited, there will likely be very many unpleasant surprises discovered by Americans.

Above and beyond the funny-business going on at the Fed with respect to the $30 Trillion heist, every single gold bar in storage at the Federal Reserve should be tested for tungsten cores. Counterfeit gold bars are being reported all over the world, and it would not surprise this author if many of the "gold" bars on deposit at the Fed, only have a veneer of gold on them, and are actually filled with the cheap metal, tungsten.

Sooner, or later, people will understand the real problem lies in the fact the Federal Reserve is a hopelessly flawed and conflicted institution which does not serve the American people. Its only service has been to siphon the wealth of the nation off to a bunch of greedy bankers and elite families who ultimately run and control the Fed, allowing them to corrupt the politicians in the process. This has ensured their continued monetary rule over our country.

At some point in time, the American citizens should become enraged because of the destruction rained down upon the masses by the Federal Reserve, the bankers and the elite. In this scenario, we should witness the confiscation of all of the conspirators' assets and the creation of a people's court---elected by citizens who are not corrupted by large corporate and elite-driven campaign contributions. The Federal Reserve would very likely be held as an unconstitutional institution and justice would be obtained, with the guilty parties who participated in the malevolent activities of the Fed during the last hundred years, receiving their just rewards. Their reward, or punishment in this case, would be in direct correlation with the amount of money they took and the pain, unemployment and suffering they will have caused millions of other people.

The question is if this comeuppance to these conspirators will even happen. The bankers are entrenched with the bureaucracy and, as discussed, they are extremely well capitalized and well-armed. The best chance at holding them accountable will be during the D'Apocalypse™ when the politicians are petrified.

Let it be said this book is about presenting the facts and permitting light to shine on the activities of these corrupt ones. It will be up to the people to decide their fate.

While God, alone, sits in the judgment seat, we are indeed, as Christians and peoples, REQUIRED to root out evil and DESIRE to help those in need. We are also REQUIRED TO SPEAK THE TRUTH. From this perspective, the die is already cast, as bankers, worldwide, should be hunted down and tried through a non-corrupted court system at some time in the distant future.

At least this is what the author envisions and hopes transpires if he is correct in his analysis of the activities and actions of the Federal Reserve, the banks and the elite behind the curtain.

Before any justice for these people occurs, however, the bankers will likely gain control of the global monetary system and cause <u>even more</u> hardship for people around the world.

The following is a table which puts into perspective how much taxpayer-backed cash the Federal Reserve System heisted and how much could have been given to your city (or a city near you!), if the Fed hadn't handed the money over to the banks and the elite.

We would have a much stronger economy and cities would not be bankrupt if the Fed had given the cash directly to the American people and spread the $30 Trillion out throughout the country.

We would have saved millions of homes, we would not have experienced a real estate crash and employment would not have swooned, it would have flourished, as the money would have gone directly into the economy, instead of into rich people's pockets, portfolios and cash hoards of the banks!

Amount Heisted per Person per City in America

The following tables list most of the cities in America:

EQUIVALENT AMOUNT HEISTED
BY FEDERAL RESERVE, BANKS & ELITE

*U.S. Census Burea 2011
** <u>The $30 Trillion Heist---Follow The Money!</u>
Volume II, Chapter 15
© 2014 Robert L. Kelly

-------------------$ MILLIONS-------------------

CITY	ST.	POPULATION*	TRUE UNEMPLOYED **	QE1-3 EST. $3.115 TRILLION	U.S. SECRET BAILOUT $16.115 TRILLION	FOREIGN SECRET BAILOUT $10.057 TRILLION	TOTAL HEISTED/ PERSON/ CITY	TOTAL HEISTED/ JOBLESS
New York	NY	8,244,910	1,813,880	$ 0.13	$ 1.95	$ 1.22	$ 3.31	$ 16.15
L.A.	CA	3,819,702	840,334	$ 0.29	$ 4.22	$ 2.63	$ 7.14	$ 34.85
Chicago	IL	2,707,120	595,566	$ 0.41	$ 5.95	$ 3.72	$ 10.08	$ 49.18
Houston	TX	2,145,146	471,932	$ 0.52	$ 7.51	$ 4.69	$ 12.72	$ 62.06
Phil.	PA	1,536,471	338,024	$ 0.72	$ 10.49	$ 6.55	$ 17.75	$ 86.64
Phoenix	AZ	1,469,471	323,284	$ 0.75	$ 10.97	$ 6.84	$ 18.56	$ 90.59
S. Antonio	TX	1,359,758	299,147	$ 0.81	$ 11.85	$ 7.40	$ 20.06	$ 97.90
San Diego	CA	1,326,179	291,759	$ 0.83	$ 12.15	$ 7.58	$ 20.57	$ 100.38
Dallas	TX	1,223,229	269,110	$ 0.90	$ 13.17	$ 8.22	$ 22.30	$ 108.83
San Jose	CA	967,487	212,847	$ 1.14	$ 16.66	$ 10.39	$ 28.19	$ 137.60
Jacksonvil	FL	827,908	182,140	$ 1.33	$ 19.46	$ 12.15	$ 32.95	$ 160.79
Indianapoli	IN	827,609	182,074	$ 1.34	$ 19.47	$ 12.15	$ 32.96	$ 160.85
Austin	TX	820,611	180,534	$ 1.35	$ 19.64	$ 12.26	$ 33.24	$ 162.22
S.Francisc	CA	812,826	178,822	$ 1.36	$ 19.83	$ 12.37	$ 33.56	$ 163.78
Columbus	OH	797,434	175,435	$ 1.39	$ 20.21	$ 12.61	$ 34.21	$ 166.94
Fort Worth	TX	758,738	166,922	$ 1.46	$ 21.24	$ 13.25	$ 35.95	$ 175.45
Charlotte	NC	751,087	165,239	$ 1.47	$ 21.46	$ 13.39	$ 36.32	$ 177.24
Detroit	MI	706,585	155,449	$ 1.56	$ 22.81	$ 14.23	$ 38.60	$ 188.40
El Paso	TX	665,568	146,425	$ 1.66	$ 24.21	$ 15.11	$ 40.98	$ 200.01
Memphis	TN	652,050	143,451	$ 1.69	$ 24.71	$ 15.42	$ 41.83	$ 204.16
Boston	MA	625,087	137,519	$ 1.77	$ 25.78	$ 16.09	$ 43.64	$ 212.97
Seattle	WA	620,778	136,571	$ 1.78	$ 25.96	$ 16.20	$ 43.94	$ 214.44
Denver	CO	619,968	136,393	$ 1.78	$ 25.99	$ 16.22	$ 44.00	$ 214.73
Baltimore	MD	619,493	136,288	$ 1.78	$ 26.01	$ 16.23	$ 44.03	$ 214.89
Washing'n	DC	617,996	135,959	$ 1.79	$ 26.08	$ 16.27	$ 44.14	$ 215.41
Nashvlle	TN	609,644	134,122	$ 1.81	$ 26.43	$ 16.50	$ 44.74	$ 218.36
Louisvlle	KY	602,011	132,442	$ 1.84	$ 26.77	$ 16.71	$ 45.31	$ 221.13
Milwaukee	WI	597,867	131,531	$ 1.85	$ 26.95	$ 16.82	$ 45.62	$ 222.66
Portland	OR	593,820	130,640	$ 1.86	$ 27.14	$ 16.94	$ 45.93	$ 224.18
OK City	OK	591,967	130,233	$ 1.87	$ 27.22	$ 16.99	$ 46.08	$ 224.88
Las Vegas	NV	589,317	129,650	$ 1.88	$ 27.35	$ 17.07	$ 46.29	$ 225.89

$ MILLIONS		Population	True Unemployed	QE/Per.	--Secret Bailouts/Per.--		TOTAL HEISTED/ PERSON/ CITY	TOTAL HEISTED/ JOBLESS
Albuquer.	NM	552,804	121,617	$ 5.80	$ 29.15	$ 18.19	**$ 53.14**	**$ 240.81**
Tucson	AZ	525,796	115,675	$ 6.10	$ 30.65	$ 19.13	**$ 55.87**	**$ 253.18**
Fresno	CA	501,362	110,300	$ 6.39	$ 32.14	$ 20.06	**$ 58.59**	**$ 265.52**
Sac'mento	CA	472,178	103,879	$ 6.79	$ 34.13	$ 21.30	**$ 62.22**	**$ 281.93**
Long Bch	CA	465,576	102,427	$ 6.88	$ 34.61	$ 21.60	**$ 63.10**	**$ 285.93**
Kansas C	MO	463,202	101,904	$ 6.92	$ 34.79	$ 21.71	**$ 63.42**	**$ 287.40**
Mesa	AZ	446,518	98,234	$ 7.18	$ 36.09	$ 22.52	**$ 65.79**	**$ 298.14**
Virginia B	VA	442,707	97,396	$ 7.24	$ 36.40	$ 22.72	**$ 66.36**	**$ 300.70**
Atlanta	GA	432,427	95,134	$ 7.41	$ 37.27	$ 23.26	**$ 67.94**	**$ 307.85**
C. Springs	CO	426,388	93,805	$ 7.52	$ 37.79	$ 23.59	**$ 68.90**	**$ 312.21**
Raleigh	NC	416,468	91,623	$ 7.70	$ 38.69	$ 24.15	**$ 70.54**	**$ 319.65**
Omaha	NE	415,068	91,315	$ 7.72	$ 38.82	$ 24.23	**$ 70.78**	**$ 320.73**
Miami	FL	408,750	89,925	$ 7.84	$ 39.43	$ 24.60	**$ 71.87**	**$ 325.68**
Tulsa	OK	396,466	87,223	$ 8.08	$ 40.65	$ 25.37	**$ 74.10**	**$ 335.77**
Oakland	CA	395,817	87,080	$ 8.10	$ 40.71	$ 25.41	**$ 74.22**	**$ 336.32**
Cleveland	OH	393,806	86,637	$ 8.14	$ 40.92	$ 25.54	**$ 74.60**	**$ 338.04**
Minn'polis	MN	387,753	85,306	$ 8.27	$ 41.56	$ 25.94	**$ 75.76**	**$ 343.32**
Vichita	KS	384,445	84,578	$ 8.34	$ 41.92	$ 26.16	**$ 76.41**	**$ 346.27**
Arlington	TX	373,698	82,214	$ 8.58	$ 43.12	$ 26.91	**$ 78.61**	**$ 356.23**
N. Orleans	LA	360,740	79,363	$ 8.88	$ 44.67	$ 27.88	**$ 81.44**	**$ 369.03**
Bakersf'ld	CA	352,428	77,534	$ 9.09	$ 45.73	$ 28.54	**$ 83.36**	**$ 377.73**
Tampa	FL	346,037	76,128	$ 9.26	$ 46.57	$ 29.06	**$ 84.90**	**$ 384.71**
Anaheim	CA	341,361	75,099	$ 9.39	$ 47.21	$ 29.46	**$ 86.06**	**$ 389.98**
Honolulu	HI	340,936	75,006	$ 9.40	$ 47.27	$ 29.50	**$ 86.17**	**$ 390.46**
Aurora	CO	332,354	73,118	$ 9.64	$ 48.49	$ 30.26	**$ 88.39**	**$ 400.54**
Santa Ana	CA	329,427	72,474	$ 9.73	$ 48.92	$ 30.53	**$ 89.18**	**$ 404.10**
St. Louis	MO	318,069	69,975	$ 10.08	$ 50.67	$ 31.62	**$ 92.36**	**$ 418.53**
Riverside	CA	310,651	68,343	$ 10.32	$ 51.87	$ 32.37	**$ 94.57**	**$ 428.53**
Corpus C.	TX	307,953	67,750	$ 10.41	$ 52.33	$ 32.66	**$ 95.39**	**$ 432.28**
Pittsburgh	PA	307,484	67,646	$ 10.42	$ 52.41	$ 32.71	**$ 95.54**	**$ 432.94**
Lex-Fayvl	KY	301,569	66,345	$ 10.63	$ 53.44	$ 33.35	**$ 97.41**	**$ 441.43**
Stockton	CA	296,357	65,199	$ 10.81	$ 54.38	$ 33.94	**$ 99.13**	**$ 449.20**
Cincinnati	OH	296,223	65,169	$ 10.82	$ 54.40	$ 33.95	**$ 99.17**	**$ 449.40**
Anchorage	AK	295,570	65,025	$ 10.84	$ 54.52	$ 34.03	**$ 99.39**	**$ 450.39**
St. Paul	MN	288,448	63,459	$ 11.11	$ 55.87	$ 34.87	**$ 101.85**	**$ 461.51**
Toledo	OH	286,038	62,928	$ 11.20	$ 56.34	$ 35.16	**$ 102.70**	**$ 465.40**
Nevark	NJ	277,540	61,059	$ 11.55	$ 58.06	$ 36.24	**$ 105.85**	**$ 479.65**
Gr'boro	NC	273,425	60,154	$ 11.72	$ 58.94	$ 36.78	**$ 107.44**	**$ 486.87**
Plano	TX	269,776	59,351	$ 11.88	$ 59.73	$ 37.28	**$ 108.89**	**$ 493.46**
Lincoln	NE	262,341	57,715	$ 12.22	$ 61.43	$ 38.34	**$ 111.98**	**$ 507.44**
Buffalo	NY	261,025	57,426	$ 12.28	$ 61.74	$ 38.53	**$ 112.54**	**$ 510.00**
Henderson	NV	260,068	57,215	$ 12.32	$ 61.96	$ 38.67	**$ 112.96**	**$ 511.88**
Ft Vayne	IN	255,824	56,281	$ 12.53	$ 62.99	$ 39.31	**$ 114.83**	**$ 520.37**

$ MILLIONS		Population	True Unemployed	QE/Per.	--Secret Bailouts/Per.--		TOTAL HEISTED/ PERSON/ CITY	TOTAL HEISTED/ JOBLESS
Jersey City	NJ	250,323	55,071	$ 12.80	$ 64.38	$ 40.18	**$ 117.36**	**$ 531.80**
Chula Vsta	CA	247,535	54,458	$ 12.95	$ 65.10	$ 40.63	**$ 118.68**	**$ 537.79**
S Pet'burg	FL	244,997	53,899	$ 13.08	$ 65.78	$ 41.05	**$ 119.91**	**$ 543.36**
Orlando	FL	243,195	53,503	$ 13.18	$ 66.26	$ 41.35	**$ 120.80**	**$ 547.39**
Norfolk	VA	242,628	53,378	$ 13.21	$ 66.42	$ 41.45	**$ 121.08**	**$ 548.67**
Laredo	TX	241,935	53,226	$ 13.25	$ 66.61	$ 41.57	**$ 121.43**	**$ 550.24**
Chandler	AZ	240,101	52,822	$ 13.35	$ 67.12	$ 41.89	**$ 122.35**	**$ 554.44**
Madison	WI	236,901	52,118	$ 13.53	$ 68.02	$ 42.45	**$ 124.01**	**$ 561.93**
Lubbock	TX	233,740	51,423	$ 13.71	$ 68.94	$ 43.03	**$ 125.68**	**$ 569.53**
Durham	NC	233,252	51,315	$ 13.74	$ 69.09	$ 43.12	**$ 125.95**	**$ 570.72**
W'n-Salem	NC	232,385	51,125	$ 13.79	$ 69.35	$ 43.28	**$ 126.42**	**$ 572.85**
Garland	TX	231,517	50,934	$ 13.84	$ 69.61	$ 43.44	**$ 126.89**	**$ 575.00**
Glendale	AZ	230,482	50,706	$ 13.91	$ 69.92	$ 43.63	**$ 127.46**	**$ 577.58**
Baton Rge	LA	230,139	50,631	$ 13.93	$ 70.02	$ 43.70	**$ 127.65**	**$ 578.44**
Hialeah	FL	229,969	50,593	$ 13.94	$ 70.07	$ 43.73	**$ 127.74**	**$ 578.87**
Reno	NV	227,511	50,052	$ 14.09	$ 70.83	$ 44.20	**$ 129.12**	**$ 585.13**
Chesap'ke	VA	225,050	49,511	$ 14.24	$ 71.61	$ 44.69	**$ 130.54**	**$ 591.53**
Scottsdale	AZ	221,020	48,624	$ 14.50	$ 72.91	$ 45.50	**$ 132.92**	**$ 602.31**
Irving	TX	220,702	48,554	$ 14.52	$ 73.02	$ 45.57	**$ 133.11**	**$ 603.18**
N. L. Vgas	NV	219,020	48,184	$ 14.63	$ 73.58	$ 45.92	**$ 134.13**	**$ 607.81**
Fremont	CA	216,916	47,722	$ 14.78	$ 74.29	$ 46.36	**$ 135.43**	**$ 613.71**
Irvine	CA	215,529	47,416	$ 14.87	$ 74.77	$ 46.66	**$ 136.30**	**$ 617.66**
S Bernad'o	CA	213,012	46,863	$ 15.05	$ 75.65	$ 47.21	**$ 137.91**	**$ 624.95**
Birm'ham	AL	212,413	46,731	$ 15.09	$ 75.87	$ 47.35	**$ 138.30**	**$ 626.72**
Gilbert	AZ	211,951	46,629	$ 15.12	$ 76.03	$ 47.45	**$ 138.60**	**$ 628.08**
Rochester	NY	210,855	46,388	$ 15.20	$ 76.43	$ 47.70	**$ 139.32**	**$ 631.35**
Boise City	ID	210,145	46,232	$ 15.25	$ 76.69	$ 47.86	**$ 139.79**	**$ 633.48**
Spokane	WA	210,103	46,223	$ 15.25	$ 76.70	$ 47.87	**$ 139.82**	**$ 633.61**
Monterg'y	AL	208,182	45,800	$ 15.40	$ 77.41	$ 48.31	**$ 141.11**	**$ 639.45**
Des Mne.	IA	206,599	45,452	$ 15.51	$ 78.00	$ 48.68	**$ 142.19**	**$ 644.35**
Richmond	VA	205,533	45,217	$ 15.59	$ 78.41	$ 48.93	**$ 142.93**	**$ 647.70**
Fayettv'le	NC	203,945	44,868	$ 15.72	$ 79.02	$ 49.31	**$ 144.04**	**$ 652.74**
Modesto	CA	202,751	44,605	$ 15.81	$ 79.48	$ 49.60	**$ 144.89**	**$ 656.58**
Shreveport	LA	200,975	44,215	$ 15.95	$ 80.18	$ 50.04	**$ 146.17**	**$ 662.38**
Tacoma	WA	200,678	44,149	$ 15.97	$ 80.30	$ 50.12	**$ 146.39**	**$ 663.36**
Oxnard	CA	199,943	43,987	$ 16.03	$ 80.60	$ 50.30	**$ 146.93**	**$ 665.80**
Aurora	IL	199,672	43,928	$ 16.05	$ 80.71	$ 50.37	**$ 147.13**	**$ 666.71**
Fontana	CA	199,028	43,786	$ 16.10	$ 80.97	$ 50.53	**$ 147.60**	**$ 668.86**
Akron	OH	198,402	43,648	$ 16.15	$ 81.22	$ 50.69	**$ 148.07**	**$ 670.97**
Moreno V	CA	197,838	43,524	$ 16.20	$ 81.46	$ 50.83	**$ 148.49**	**$ 672.89**
Yonkers	NY	197,399	43,428	$ 16.24	$ 81.64	$ 50.95	**$ 148.82**	**$ 674.38**
A'sta-Rich	GA	196,494	43,229	$ 16.31	$ 82.01	$ 51.18	**$ 149.51**	**$ 677.49**
Little Rock	AR	195,314	42,969	$ 16.41	$ 82.51	$ 51.49	**$ 150.41**	**$ 681.58**

$ MILLIONS		Population	True Unemployed	QE/Per.	--Secret Bailouts/Per.--		TOTAL HEISTED/ PERSON/ CITY	TOTAL HEISTED/ JOBLESS
Mobile	AL	194,914	42,881	$ 16.44	$ 82.68	$ 51.60	**$ 150.72**	**$ 682.98**
Columbus	GA	194,107	42,704	$ 16.51	$ 83.02	$ 51.81	**$ 151.34**	**$ 685.82**
AmarilLo	TX	193,675	42,609	$ 16.55	$ 83.21	$ 51.93	**$ 151.68**	**$ 687.35**
Glendale	CA	193,111	42,484	$ 16.60	$ 83.45	$ 52.08	**$ 152.12**	**$ 689.36**
Hunt. Bch.	CA	192,888	42,435	$ 16.62	$ 83.55	$ 52.14	**$ 152.30**	**$ 690.16**
Salt Lake	UT	189,899	41,778	$ 16.88	$ 84.86	$ 52.96	**$ 154.70**	**$ 701.02**
Grand Rap.	MI	189,815	41,759	$ 16.88	$ 84.90	$ 52.98	**$ 154.77**	**$ 701.33**
Tallah'ee	FL	182,965	40,252	$ 17.52	$ 88.08	$ 54.97	**$ 160.56**	**$ 727.59**
Huntsvlle	AL	182,956	40,250	$ 17.52	$ 88.08	$ 54.97	**$ 160.57**	**$ 727.62**
Vorcester	MA	181,631	39,959	$ 17.65	$ 88.72	$ 55.37	**$ 161.74**	**$ 732.93**
Knoxvlle	TN	180,761	39,767	$ 17.73	$ 89.15	$ 55.64	**$ 162.52**	**$ 736.46**
Nevport N.	VA	179,611	39,514	$ 17.84	$ 89.72	$ 55.99	**$ 163.56**	**$ 741.17**
Grand Pr.	TX	179,100	39,402	$ 17.90	$ 89.98	$ 56.15	**$ 164.03**	**$ 743.29**
Brovnsv'le	TX	178,430	39,255	$ 17.96	$ 90.32	$ 56.36	**$ 164.64**	**$ 746.08**
Prov.	RI	178,053	39,172	$ 18.00	$ 90.51	$ 56.48	**$ 164.99**	**$ 747.66**
Sta Clarita	CA	177,601	39,072	$ 18.05	$ 90.74	$ 56.63	**$ 165.41**	**$ 749.56**
Overland P	KS	176,185	38,761	$ 18.19	$ 91.47	$ 57.08	**$ 166.74**	**$ 755.58**
Jackson	MS	175,561	38,623	$ 18.26	$ 91.79	$ 57.28	**$ 167.33**	**$ 758.27**
Garden Gr'	CA	173,470	38,163	$ 18.48	$ 92.90	$ 57.98	**$ 169.35**	**$ 767.41**
Chattan'ga	TN	170,136	37,430	$ 18.84	$ 94.72	$ 59.11	**$ 172.67**	**$ 782.45**
Oceanside	CA	169,569	37,305	$ 18.90	$ 95.04	$ 59.31	**$ 173.25**	**$ 785.07**
S'ta Rosa	CA	169,292	37,244	$ 18.93	$ 95.19	$ 59.41	**$ 173.53**	**$ 786.35**
F Laud'le	FL	168,528	37,076	$ 19.02	$ 95.62	$ 59.68	**$ 174.32**	**$ 789.91**
Rcho. Cuc	CA	167,721	36,899	$ 19.11	$ 96.08	$ 59.96	**$ 175.15**	**$ 793.72**
Ontario	CA	166,390	36,606	$ 19.26	$ 96.85	$ 60.44	**$ 176.56**	**$ 800.06**
Port S Luc	FL	166,149	36,553	$ 19.29	$ 96.99	$ 60.53	**$ 176.81**	**$ 801.22**
Vancouver	VA	164,759	36,247	$ 19.45	$ 97.81	$ 61.04	**$ 178.30**	**$ 807.98**
Tempe	AZ	164,268	36,139	$ 19.51	$ 98.10	$ 61.22	**$ 178.84**	**$ 810.40**
Springfield	MO	160,660	35,345	$ 19.95	$ 100.30	$ 62.60	**$ 182.85**	**$ 828.60**
Lancaster	CA	157,693	34,692	$ 20.32	$ 102.19	$ 63.78	**$ 186.29**	**$ 844.19**
Pemb'ke P	FL	157,594	34,671	$ 20.34	$ 102.26	$ 63.82	**$ 186.41**	**$ 844.72**
Cape Cral	FL	157,476	34,645	$ 20.35	$ 102.33	$ 63.86	**$ 186.55**	**$ 845.35**
Eugene	OR	156,929	34,524	$ 20.42	$ 102.69	$ 64.09	**$ 187.20**	**$ 848.30**
Peoria	AZ	156,637	34,460	$ 20.46	$ 102.88	$ 64.21	**$ 187.55**	**$ 849.88**
Sioux Falls	SD	156,592	34,450	$ 20.47	$ 102.91	$ 64.22	**$ 187.60**	**$ 850.12**
Salem	OR	156,244	34,374	$ 20.51	$ 103.14	$ 64.37	**$ 188.02**	**$ 852.02**
Corona	CA	155,896	34,297	$ 20.56	$ 103.37	$ 64.51	**$ 188.44**	**$ 853.92**
Elk Grove	CA	154,908	34,080	$ 20.69	$ 104.03	$ 64.92	**$ 189.64**	**$ 859.37**
Palmdale	CA	153,867	33,851	$ 20.83	$ 104.73	$ 65.36	**$ 190.92**	**$ 865.18**
Springfield	MA	153,155	33,694	$ 20.93	$ 105.22	$ 65.67	**$ 191.81**	**$ 869.20**
Salinas	CA	152,994	33,659	$ 20.95	$ 105.33	$ 65.73	**$ 192.01**	**$ 870.12**
Pasadena	TX	152,281	33,502	$ 21.05	$ 105.82	$ 66.04	**$ 192.91**	**$ 874.19**
Rockford	IL	152,222	33,489	$ 21.05	$ 105.87	$ 66.07	**$ 192.99**	**$ 874.53**

$ MILLIONS		Population	True Unemployed	QE/Per.	--Secret Bailouts/Per.--		TOTAL HEISTED/ PERSON/ CITY	TOTAL HEISTED/ JOBLESS
Pomona	CA	150,119	33,026	$ 21.35	$ 107.35	$ 66.99	**$ 195.69**	**$ 886.78**
Joliet	IL	148,402	32,648	$ 21.60	$ 108.59	$ 67.77	**$ 197.96**	**$ 897.04**
F. Collins	CO	146,762	32,288	$ 21.84	$ 109.80	$ 68.53	**$ 200.17**	**$ 907.07**
Torrance	CA	146,493	32,228	$ 21.88	$ 110.01	$ 68.65	**$ 200.54**	**$ 908.73**
Kansas C	KS	146,453	32,220	$ 21.88	$ 110.04	$ 68.67	**$ 200.59**	**$ 908.98**
Paterson	NJ	146,427	32,214	$ 21.89	$ 110.05	$ 68.68	**$ 200.63**	**$ 909.14**
Hayward	CA	146,069	32,135	$ 21.94	$ 110.32	$ 68.85	**$ 201.12**	**$ 911.37**
Escondido	CA	146,032	32,127	$ 21.95	$ 110.35	$ 68.87	**$ 201.17**	**$ 911.60**
Bridgeport	CT	145,638	32,040	$ 22.01	$ 110.65	$ 69.05	**$ 201.71**	**$ 914.07**
Syracuse	NY	145,151	31,933	$ 22.08	$ 111.02	$ 69.29	**$ 202.39**	**$ 917.13**
Lakewood	CO	144,406	31,769	$ 22.19	$ 111.60	$ 69.64	**$ 203.43**	**$ 921.86**
Alexandria	VA	144,301	31,746	$ 22.21	$ 111.68	$ 69.69	**$ 203.58**	**$ 922.54**
Hollywood	FL	143,357	31,539	$ 22.36	$ 112.41	$ 70.15	**$ 204.92**	**$ 928.61**
Napervlle	IL	142,773	31,410	$ 22.45	$ 112.87	$ 70.44	**$ 205.76**	**$ 932.41**
Mesquite	TX	142,674	31,388	$ 22.46	$ 112.95	$ 70.49	**$ 205.90**	**$ 933.06**
Sunnyvale	CA	142,287	31,303	$ 22.52	$ 113.26	$ 70.68	**$ 206.46**	**$ 935.59**
Dayton	OH	142,148	31,273	$ 22.55	$ 113.37	$ 70.75	**$ 206.66**	**$ 936.51**
Cary	NC	139,633	30,719	$ 22.95	$ 115.41	$ 72.02	**$ 210.39**	**$ 953.38**
Savannah	GA	139,491	30,688	$ 22.98	$ 115.53	$ 72.10	**$ 210.60**	**$ 954.35**
Orange	CA	138,409	30,450	$ 23.16	$ 116.43	$ 72.66	**$ 212.25**	**$ 961.81**
Pasadena	CA	138,101	30,382	$ 23.21	$ 116.69	$ 72.82	**$ 212.72**	**$ 963.95**
Fullerton	CA	137,183	30,180	$ 23.36	$ 117.47	$ 73.31	**$ 214.14**	**$ 970.40**
Hampton	VA	136,401	30,008	$ 23.50	$ 118.14	$ 73.73	**$ 215.37**	**$ 975.97**
Clarksvlle	TN	136,231	29,971	$ 23.53	$ 118.29	$ 73.82	**$ 215.64**	**$ 977.18**
McKinney	TX	136,067	29,935	$ 23.55	$ 118.43	$ 73.91	**$ 215.90**	**$ 978.36**
Warren	MI	134,243	29,533	$ 23.87	$ 120.04	$ 74.92	**$ 218.83**	**$ 991.65**
McAllen	TX	133,742	29,423	$ 23.96	$ 120.49	$ 75.20	**$ 219.65**	**$ 995.37**
W Valley C	UT	131,942	29,027	$ 24.29	$ 122.14	$ 76.22	**$ 222.65**	**$ 1,008.95**
Columbia	SC	130,591	28,730	$ 24.54	$ 123.40	$ 77.01	**$ 224.95**	**$ 1,019.39**
Kileen	TX	130,018	28,604	$ 24.65	$ 123.94	$ 77.35	**$ 225.95**	**$ 1,023.88**
Sterling H	MI	129,880	28,574	$ 24.68	$ 124.08	$ 77.43	**$ 226.19**	**$ 1,024.97**
New Haven	CT	129,585	28,509	$ 24.73	$ 124.36	$ 77.61	**$ 226.70**	**$ 1,027.30**
Topeka	KS	128,188	28,201	$ 25.00	$ 125.71	$ 78.46	**$ 229.17**	**$ 1,038.50**
Thous'd O	CA	127,984	28,156	$ 25.04	$ 125.91	$ 78.58	**$ 229.54**	**$ 1,040.15**
Olathe	KS	127,907	28,140	$ 25.06	$ 125.99	$ 78.63	**$ 229.67**	**$ 1,040.78**
Cedar R	IA	127,905	28,139	$ 25.06	$ 125.99	$ 78.63	**$ 229.68**	**$ 1,040.79**
Waco	TX	126,697	27,873	$ 25.30	$ 127.19	$ 79.38	**$ 231.87**	**$ 1,050.72**
Visalia	CA	126,432	27,815	$ 25.35	$ 127.46	$ 79.54	**$ 232.35**	**$ 1,052.92**
Elizabeth	NJ	125,660	27,645	$ 25.51	$ 128.24	$ 80.03	**$ 233.78**	**$ 1,059.39**
Simi Valley	CA	125,522	27,615	$ 25.53	$ 128.38	$ 80.12	**$ 234.04**	**$ 1,060.55**
Gainesvlle	FL	125,326	27,572	$ 25.57	$ 128.58	$ 80.25	**$ 234.40**	**$ 1,062.21**
Hartford	CT	124,867	27,471	$ 25.67	$ 129.06	$ 80.54	**$ 235.27**	**$ 1,066.12**
Bellevue	WA	124,798	27,456	$ 25.68	$ 129.13	$ 80.59	**$ 235.40**	**$ 1,066.71**

$ MILLIONS		Population	True Unemployed	QE/Per.	--Secret Bailouts/Per.--		TOTAL HEISTED/ PERSON/ CITY	TOTAL HEISTED/ JOBLESS
Miramar	FL	124,302	27,346	$ 25.78	$ 129.64	$ 80.91	$ 236.34	$ 1,070.96
Concord	CA	124,055	27,292	$ 25.84	$ 129.90	$ 81.07	$ 236.81	$ 1,073.09
Stamford	CT	123,868	27,251	$ 25.87	$ 130.10	$ 81.19	$ 237.16	$ 1,074.71
Coral Spgs	FL	123,338	27,134	$ 25.99	$ 130.66	$ 81.54	$ 238.18	$ 1,079.33
Charleston	SC	122,689	26,992	$ 26.12	$ 131.35	$ 81.97	$ 239.44	$ 1,085.04
Carrollton	TX	122,640	26,981	$ 26.13	$ 131.40	$ 82.00	$ 239.54	$ 1,085.48
Lafayette	LA	122,130	26,869	$ 26.24	$ 131.95	$ 82.35	$ 240.54	$ 1,090.01
Rosevlle	CA	121,767	26,789	$ 26.32	$ 132.34	$ 82.59	$ 241.26	$ 1,093.26
Thornton	CO	121,435	26,716	$ 26.39	$ 132.70	$ 82.82	$ 241.92	$ 1,096.25
Frisco	TX	121,387	26,705	$ 26.40	$ 132.76	$ 82.85	$ 242.01	$ 1,096.68
Kent	WA	120,916	26,602	$ 26.51	$ 133.27	$ 83.17	$ 242.95	$ 1,100.95
Surprise	AZ	119,489	26,288	$ 26.82	$ 134.87	$ 84.17	$ 245.86	$ 1,114.10
Allentown	PA	119,141	26,211	$ 26.90	$ 135.26	$ 84.41	$ 246.57	$ 1,117.35
Beaumont	TX	118,548	26,081	$ 27.04	$ 135.94	$ 84.83	$ 247.81	$ 1,122.94
S. Clara	CA	118,263	26,018	$ 27.10	$ 136.26	$ 85.04	$ 248.40	$ 1,125.65
Abilene	TX	118,117	25,986	$ 27.13	$ 136.43	$ 85.14	$ 248.71	$ 1,127.04
Evansvlle	IN	117,825	25,922	$ 27.20	$ 136.77	$ 85.36	$ 249.33	$ 1,129.83
Victorvlle	CA	117,597	25,871	$ 27.25	$ 137.04	$ 85.52	$ 249.81	$ 1,132.02
Independ.	MO	117,213	25,787	$ 27.34	$ 137.48	$ 85.80	$ 250.63	$ 1,135.73
Denton	TX	117,187	25,781	$ 27.35	$ 137.52	$ 85.82	$ 250.68	$ 1,135.99
Springfield	IL	117,076	25,757	$ 27.38	$ 137.65	$ 85.90	$ 250.92	$ 1,137.06
Vallejo	CA	116,829	25,702	$ 27.43	$ 137.94	$ 86.08	$ 251.45	$ 1,139.47
Athens-C	GA	116,084	25,538	$ 27.61	$ 138.82	$ 86.64	$ 253.07	$ 1,146.78
Provo	UT	115,321	25,371	$ 27.79	$ 139.74	$ 87.21	$ 254.74	$ 1,154.37
Peoria	IL	115,234	25,351	$ 27.81	$ 139.85	$ 87.27	$ 254.93	$ 1,155.24
Ann Arbor	MI	114,925	25,284	$ 27.89	$ 140.22	$ 87.51	$ 255.62	$ 1,158.34
Lansing	MI	114,605	25,213	$ 27.97	$ 140.61	$ 87.75	$ 256.33	$ 1,161.58
El Monte	CA	114,296	25,145	$ 28.04	$ 140.99	$ 87.99	$ 257.03	$ 1,164.72
Midland	TX	113,931	25,065	$ 28.13	$ 141.45	$ 88.27	$ 257.85	$ 1,168.45
Berkeley	CA	113,905	25,059	$ 28.14	$ 141.48	$ 88.29	$ 257.91	$ 1,168.72
Norman	OK	113,273	24,920	$ 28.29	$ 142.27	$ 88.79	$ 259.35	$ 1,175.24
Downey	CA	112,584	24,768	$ 28.47	$ 143.14	$ 89.33	$ 260.93	$ 1,182.43
Costa Msa	CA	111,600	24,552	$ 28.72	$ 144.40	$ 90.12	$ 263.23	$ 1,192.86
Murfr'boro	TN	111,327	24,492	$ 28.79	$ 144.75	$ 90.34	$ 263.88	$ 1,195.78
Inglewood	CA	110,464	24,302	$ 29.01	$ 145.88	$ 91.04	$ 265.94	$ 1,205.12
Columbia	MO	110,438	24,296	$ 29.02	$ 145.92	$ 91.06	$ 266.00	$ 1,205.41
Waterbury	CT	110,189	24,242	$ 29.09	$ 146.25	$ 91.27	$ 266.61	$ 1,208.13
Manch'ter	NH	109,830	24,163	$ 29.18	$ 146.73	$ 91.57	$ 267.48	$ 1,212.08
Miami Gar.	FL	109,680	24,130	$ 29.22	$ 146.93	$ 91.69	$ 267.84	$ 1,213.74
Elgin	IL	109,104	24,003	$ 29.38	$ 147.70	$ 92.18	$ 269.26	$ 1,220.15
Wilmington	NC	108,297	23,825	$ 29.59	$ 148.80	$ 92.86	$ 271.26	$ 1,229.24
Westmin'r	CO	107,967	23,753	$ 29.68	$ 149.26	$ 93.15	$ 272.09	$ 1,232.99
Rochester	MN	107,890	23,736	$ 29.71	$ 149.37	$ 93.22	$ 272.29	$ 1,233.87

$ MILLIONS		Population	True Unemployed	QE/Per.	--Secret Bailouts/Per.--		TOTAL HEISTED/ PERSON/ CITY	TOTAL HEISTED/ JOBLESS
Clearwater	FL	107,784	23,712	$ 29.74	$ 149.51	$ 93.31	$ 272.55	$ 1,235.09
Lowell	MA	107,584	23,668	$ 29.79	$ 149.79	$ 93.48	$ 273.06	$ 1,237.38
Pueblo	CO	107,577	23,667	$ 29.79	$ 149.80	$ 93.49	$ 273.08	$ 1,237.46
Arvada	CO	107,541	23,659	$ 29.80	$ 149.85	$ 93.52	$ 273.17	$ 1,237.88
Ventura	CA	107,514	23,653	$ 29.81	$ 149.89	$ 93.54	$ 273.24	$ 1,238.19
Gresham	OR	107,439	23,637	$ 29.83	$ 149.99	$ 93.61	$ 273.43	$ 1,239.05
Fargo	ND	107,349	23,617	$ 29.86	$ 150.12	$ 93.69	$ 273.66	$ 1,240.09
Carlsbad	CA	106,888	23,515	$ 29.98	$ 150.77	$ 94.09	$ 274.84	$ 1,245.44
W Covina	CA	106,870	23,511	$ 29.99	$ 150.79	$ 94.10	$ 274.89	$ 1,245.65
Norwalk	CA	106,309	23,388	$ 30.15	$ 151.59	$ 94.60	$ 276.34	$ 1,252.22
Fairfield	CA	106,126	23,348	$ 30.20	$ 151.85	$ 94.76	$ 276.81	$ 1,254.38
Cambridge	MA	106,038	23,328	$ 30.23	$ 151.97	$ 94.84	$ 277.04	$ 1,255.42
Murrieta	CA	105,857	23,289	$ 30.28	$ 152.23	$ 95.01	$ 277.52	$ 1,257.57
Green Bay	WI	105,809	23,278	$ 30.29	$ 152.30	$ 95.05	$ 277.64	$ 1,258.14
High Point	NC	105,753	23,266	$ 30.31	$ 152.38	$ 95.10	$ 277.79	$ 1,258.81
W Jordan	UT	105,675	23,249	$ 30.33	$ 152.50	$ 95.17	$ 277.99	$ 1,259.74
BILings	MT	105,636	23,240	$ 30.34	$ 152.55	$ 95.20	$ 278.10	$ 1,260.20
Richmond	CA	105,380	23,184	$ 30.41	$ 152.92	$ 95.44	$ 278.77	$ 1,263.26
Round Rk	TX	104,664	23,026	$ 30.62	$ 153.97	$ 96.09	$ 280.68	$ 1,271.91
Everett	WA	104,295	22,945	$ 30.73	$ 154.51	$ 96.43	$ 281.67	$ 1,276.41
Burbank	CA	104,092	22,900	$ 30.79	$ 154.81	$ 96.62	$ 282.22	$ 1,278.89
Antioch	CA	104,044	22,890	$ 30.80	$ 154.89	$ 96.66	$ 282.35	$ 1,279.48
Wichita F	TX	103,931	22,865	$ 30.84	$ 155.05	$ 96.77	$ 282.66	$ 1,280.88
Palm Bay	FL	103,227	22,710	$ 31.05	$ 156.11	$ 97.43	$ 284.59	$ 1,289.61
Centennial	CO	102,603	22,573	$ 31.24	$ 157.06	$ 98.02	$ 286.32	$ 1,297.45
Temecula	CA	102,464	22,542	$ 31.28	$ 157.27	$ 98.15	$ 286.71	$ 1,299.21
Daly City	CA	102,362	22,520	$ 31.31	$ 157.43	$ 98.25	$ 286.99	$ 1,300.51
Odessa	TX	102,106	22,463	$ 31.39	$ 157.83	$ 98.50	$ 287.71	$ 1,303.77
Erie	PA	101,807	22,398	$ 31.48	$ 158.29	$ 98.78	$ 288.56	$ 1,307.60
Richrdson	TX	101,742	22,383	$ 31.50	$ 158.39	$ 98.85	$ 288.74	$ 1,308.43
Pomp'o B	FL	101,617	22,356	$ 31.54	$ 158.59	$ 98.97	$ 289.10	$ 1,310.04
Flint	MI	101,558	22,343	$ 31.56	$ 158.68	$ 99.03	$ 289.26	$ 1,310.80
S. Bend	IN	101,081	22,238	$ 31.71	$ 159.43	$ 99.49	$ 290.63	$ 1,316.99
W Palm B	FL	101,043	22,229	$ 31.72	$ 159.49	$ 99.53	$ 290.74	$ 1,317.49
El Cajon	CA	100,928	22,204	$ 31.76	$ 159.67	$ 99.65	$ 291.07	$ 1,318.99
Davenport	IA	100,802	22,176	$ 31.80	$ 159.87	$ 99.77	$ 291.43	$ 1,320.64
Rialto	CA	100,662	22,146	$ 31.84	$ 160.09	$ 99.91	$ 291.84	$ 1,322.47
Santa Mar	CA	100,277	22,061	$ 31.96	$ 160.70	$ 100.29	$ 292.96	$ 1,327.55
Br Arrow	OK	100,073	22,016	$ 32.03	$ 161.03	$ 100.50	$ 293.56	$ 1,330.26
Kenosha	WI	99,738	21,942	$ 32.13	$ 161.57	$ 100.83	$ 294.54	$ 1,334.72
N Chls'ton	SC	99,727	21,940	$ 32.14	$ 161.59	$ 100.85	$ 294.57	$ 1,334.87
Las Cruc	NM	99,665	21,926	$ 32.16	$ 161.69	$ 100.91	$ 294.76	$ 1,335.70
Boulder	CO	98,889	21,756	$ 32.41	$ 162.96	$ 101.70	$ 297.07	$ 1,346.18

$ MILLIONS		Population	True Unemployed	QE/Per.	--Secret Bailouts/Per.--		TOTAL HEISTED/ PERSON/ CITY	TOTAL HEISTED/ JOBLESS
Lewisvlle	TX	98,737	21,722	$ 32.46	$ 163.21	$ 101.86	$ 297.53	$ 1,348.26
Lakeland	FL	98,589	21,690	$ 32.51	$ 163.46	$ 102.01	$ 297.97	$ 1,350.28
Tyler	TX	98,564	21,684	$ 32.52	$ 163.50	$ 102.04	$ 298.05	$ 1,350.62
San Mateo	CA	98,391	21,646	$ 32.57	$ 163.79	$ 102.21	$ 298.57	$ 1,353.00
Lawton	OK	98,177	21,599	$ 32.65	$ 164.14	$ 102.44	$ 299.22	$ 1,355.95
Albany	NY	97,660	21,485	$ 32.82	$ 165.01	$ 102.98	$ 300.81	$ 1,363.12
Compton	CA	97,156	21,374	$ 32.99	$ 165.87	$ 103.51	$ 302.37	$ 1,370.20
Dearborn	MI	97,144	21,372	$ 32.99	$ 165.89	$ 103.53	$ 302.41	$ 1,370.36
Clovis	CA	96,929	21,324	$ 33.07	$ 166.26	$ 103.76	$ 303.08	$ 1,373.40
Sandy Spr	GA	96,856	21,308	$ 33.09	$ 166.38	$ 103.83	$ 303.31	$ 1,374.44
Roanoke	VA	96,714	21,277	$ 33.14	$ 166.63	$ 103.99	$ 303.75	$ 1,376.46
Livonia	MI	95,958	21,111	$ 33.40	$ 167.94	$ 104.81	$ 306.14	$ 1,387.30
Portsm'th	VA	95,684	21,050	$ 33.50	$ 168.42	$ 105.11	$ 307.02	$ 1,391.27
Vista	CA	95,204	20,945	$ 33.66	$ 169.27	$ 105.64	$ 308.57	$ 1,398.29
N. Bedf'd	MA	95,183	20,940	$ 33.67	$ 169.31	$ 105.66	$ 308.64	$ 1,398.60
College St	TX	95,142	20,931	$ 33.69	$ 169.38	$ 105.71	$ 308.77	$ 1,399.20
S Gat.e	CA	95,084	20,918	$ 33.71	$ 169.48	$ 105.77	$ 308.96	$ 1,400.05
Greeley	CO	94,962	20,892	$ 33.75	$ 169.70	$ 105.91	$ 309.36	$ 1,401.85
Mission V	CA	94,721	20,839	$ 33.84	$ 170.13	$ 106.17	$ 310.14	$ 1,405.42
Sn Angelo	TX	94,544	20,800	$ 33.90	$ 170.45	$ 106.37	$ 310.72	$ 1,408.05
Yuma	AZ	94,536	20,798	$ 33.90	$ 170.46	$ 106.38	$ 310.75	$ 1,408.17
Brockton	MA	94,316	20,750	$ 33.98	$ 170.86	$ 106.63	$ 311.47	$ 1,411.45
Davie	FL	93,674	20,608	$ 34.21	$ 172.03	$ 107.36	$ 313.61	$ 1,421.13
HILsboro	OR	93,455	20,560	$ 34.29	$ 172.44	$ 107.61	$ 314.34	$ 1,424.46
Pearland	TX	93,305	20,527	$ 34.35	$ 172.71	$ 107.79	$ 314.85	$ 1,426.75
Vacavlle	CA	93,088	20,479	$ 34.43	$ 173.12	$ 108.04	$ 315.58	$ 1,430.07
Quincy	MA	92,909	20,440	$ 34.50	$ 173.45	$ 108.25	$ 316.19	$ 1,432.83
Renton	WA	92,812	20,419	$ 34.53	$ 173.63	$ 108.36	$ 316.52	$ 1,434.33
Yakima	WA	92,512	20,353	$ 34.64	$ 174.19	$ 108.71	$ 317.55	$ 1,438.98
Carson	CA	92,376	20,323	$ 34.70	$ 174.45	$ 108.87	$ 318.02	$ 1,441.10
Macon	GA	91,856	20,208	$ 34.89	$ 175.44	$ 109.49	$ 319.82	$ 1,449.25
Lee's Sum	MO	91,668	20,167	$ 34.96	$ 175.80	$ 109.71	$ 320.47	$ 1,452.23
Beaverton	OR	91,625	20,158	$ 34.98	$ 175.88	$ 109.76	$ 320.62	$ 1,452.91
Tuscal'sa	AL	91,605	20,153	$ 34.99	$ 175.92	$ 109.79	$ 320.69	$ 1,453.23
Hesperia	CA	91,534	20,137	$ 35.01	$ 176.05	$ 109.87	$ 320.94	$ 1,454.35
Sparks	NV	91,195	20,063	$ 35.14	$ 176.71	$ 110.28	$ 322.13	$ 1,459.76
Roswell	GA	91,168	20,057	$ 35.15	$ 176.76	$ 110.31	$ 322.23	$ 1,460.19
Federal Wy	WA	91,085	20,039	$ 35.19	$ 176.92	$ 110.41	$ 322.52	$ 1,461.52
Westmin'r	CA	91,064	20,034	$ 35.20	$ 176.96	$ 110.44	$ 322.60	$ 1,461.86
Lynn	MA	91,040	20,029	$ 35.20	$ 177.01	$ 110.47	$ 322.68	$ 1,462.24
Orem	UT	90,727	19,960	$ 35.33	$ 177.62	$ 110.85	$ 323.80	$ 1,467.29
Santa Mon	CA	90,377	19,883	$ 35.46	$ 178.31	$ 111.28	$ 325.05	$ 1,472.97
Spokane V	WA	90,279	19,861	$ 35.50	$ 178.50	$ 111.40	$ 325.40	$ 1,474.57

$ MILLIONS		Population	True Unemployed	QE/Per.	--Secret Bailouts/Per.--		TOTAL HEISTED/ PERSON/ CITY	TOTAL HEISTED/ JOBLESS
Redding	CA	90,138	19,830	$ 35.56	$ 178.78	$ 111.57	$ 325.91	$ 1,476.88
Miami Bch	FL	89,840	19,765	$ 35.67	$ 179.37	$ 111.94	$ 326.99	$ 1,481.78
Waukegan	IL	89,426	19,674	$ 35.84	$ 180.20	$ 112.46	$ 328.51	$ 1,488.64
R Rancho	NM	89,320	19,650	$ 35.88	$ 180.42	$ 112.60	$ 328.90	$ 1,490.40
Sandy	UT	89,200	19,624	$ 35.93	$ 180.66	$ 112.75	$ 329.34	$ 1,492.41
Santa Barb	CA	89,045	19,590	$ 35.99	$ 180.98	$ 112.94	$ 329.91	$ 1,495.01
Fall River	MA	88,962	19,572	$ 36.03	$ 181.14	$ 113.05	$ 330.22	$ 1,496.40
Lawrence	KS	88,727	19,520	$ 36.12	$ 181.62	$ 113.35	$ 331.09	$ 1,500.36
Reading	PA	88,414	19,451	$ 36.25	$ 182.27	$ 113.75	$ 332.27	$ 1,505.67
Longmont	CO	87,712	19,297	$ 36.54	$ 183.73	$ 114.66	$ 334.93	$ 1,517.73
Allen	TX	87,473	19,244	$ 36.64	$ 184.23	$ 114.97	$ 335.84	$ 1,521.87
Fort Smith	AR	87,152	19,173	$ 36.77	$ 184.91	$ 115.40	$ 337.08	$ 1,527.48
Nashua	NH	86,704	19,075	$ 36.96	$ 185.86	$ 115.99	$ 338.82	$ 1,535.37
Plantation	FL	86,524	19,035	$ 37.04	$ 186.25	$ 116.23	$ 339.52	$ 1,538.56
Newport B	CA	86,484	19,026	$ 37.06	$ 186.34	$ 116.29	$ 339.68	$ 1,539.28
Norwalk	CT	86,460	19,021	$ 37.07	$ 186.39	$ 116.32	$ 339.78	$ 1,539.70
Chico	CA	86,290	18,984	$ 37.14	$ 186.75	$ 116.55	$ 340.45	$ 1,542.74
Duluth	MN	86,277	18,981	$ 37.15	$ 186.78	$ 116.57	$ 340.50	$ 1,542.97
S Leandro	CA	86,071	18,936	$ 37.24	$ 187.23	$ 116.85	$ 341.31	$ 1,546.66
Greenvlle	NC	86,017	18,924	$ 37.26	$ 187.35	$ 116.92	$ 341.53	$ 1,547.63
Sunrise	FL	85,995	18,919	$ 37.27	$ 187.39	$ 116.95	$ 341.61	$ 1,548.03
Newton	MA	85,945	18,908	$ 37.29	$ 187.50	$ 117.02	$ 341.81	$ 1,548.93
Whittier	CA	85,943	18,907	$ 37.29	$ 187.51	$ 117.02	$ 341.82	$ 1,548.97
Boca Rat	FL	85,329	18,772	$ 37.56	$ 188.86	$ 117.86	$ 344.28	$ 1,560.11
Deltona	FL	85,219	18,748	$ 37.61	$ 189.10	$ 118.01	$ 344.72	$ 1,562.12
San Marc	CA	85,022	18,705	$ 37.70	$ 189.54	$ 118.29	$ 345.52	$ 1,565.74
Suffolk	VA	84,930	18,685	$ 37.74	$ 189.74	$ 118.42	$ 345.90	$ 1,567.44
Hawthorne	CA	84,905	18,679	$ 37.75	$ 189.80	$ 118.45	$ 346.00	$ 1,567.90
Trenton	NJ	84,899	18,678	$ 37.75	$ 189.81	$ 118.46	$ 346.02	$ 1,568.01
League C	TX	84,856	18,668	$ 37.77	$ 189.91	$ 118.52	$ 346.20	$ 1,568.81
Ashevlle	NC	84,458	18,581	$ 37.95	$ 190.80	$ 119.08	$ 347.83	$ 1,576.20
Citrus Hts	CA	84,330	18,553	$ 38.01	$ 191.09	$ 119.26	$ 348.36	$ 1,578.59
Clifton	NJ	84,269	18,539	$ 38.03	$ 191.23	$ 119.34	$ 348.61	$ 1,579.74
Tracy	CA	84,266	18,539	$ 38.03	$ 191.24	$ 119.35	$ 348.62	$ 1,579.79
Cicero	IL	84,261	18,537	$ 38.04	$ 191.25	$ 119.36	$ 348.64	$ 1,579.89
Bloom'ton	MN	84,057	18,493	$ 38.13	$ 191.72	$ 119.65	$ 349.49	$ 1,583.72
Ogden	UT	83,949	18,469	$ 38.18	$ 191.96	$ 119.80	$ 349.94	$ 1,585.76
Alhambra	CA	83,693	18,412	$ 38.29	$ 192.55	$ 120.17	$ 351.01	$ 1,590.61
Westland	MI	83,239	18,313	$ 38.50	$ 193.60	$ 120.82	$ 352.92	$ 1,599.28
Sioux City	IA	82,967	18,253	$ 38.63	$ 194.23	$ 121.22	$ 354.08	$ 1,604.53
Edmond	OK	82,963	18,252	$ 38.63	$ 194.24	$ 121.22	$ 354.10	$ 1,604.60
Nampa	ID	82,755	18,206	$ 38.73	$ 194.73	$ 121.53	$ 354.99	$ 1,608.64
Warwick	RI	82,361	18,119	$ 38.91	$ 195.66	$ 122.11	$ 356.69	$ 1,616.33

$ MILLIONS		Population	True Unemployed	QE/Per.	--Secret Bailouts/Per.--		TOTAL HEISTED/ PERSON/ CITY	TOTAL HEISTED/ JOBLESS
Livermore	CA	82,039	18,049	$ 39.07	$ 196.43	$ 122.59	**$ 358.09**	**$ 1,622.68**
Hoover	AL	82,003	18,041	$ 39.08	$ 196.52	$ 122.64	**$ 358.24**	**$ 1,623.39**
Bellingham	WA	81,862	18,010	$ 39.15	$ 196.86	$ 122.85	**$ 358.86**	**$ 1,626.18**
Buena Pk	CA	81,747	17,984	$ 39.21	$ 197.13	$ 123.03	**$ 359.36**	**$ 1,628.47**
Sugar Land	TX	81,700	17,974	$ 39.23	$ 197.25	$ 123.10	**$ 359.57**	**$ 1,629.41**
Danbury	CT	81,671	17,968	$ 39.24	$ 197.32	$ 123.14	**$ 359.70**	**$ 1,629.99**
Carmel	IN	81,564	17,944	$ 39.29	$ 197.57	$ 123.30	**$ 360.17**	**$ 1,632.13**
Troy	MI	81,508	17,932	$ 39.32	$ 197.71	$ 123.39	**$ 360.42**	**$ 1,633.25**
Bloom'ton	IN	81,381	17,904	$ 39.38	$ 198.02	$ 123.58	**$ 360.98**	**$ 1,635.80**
Longview	TX	81,336	17,894	$ 39.40	$ 198.13	$ 123.65	**$ 361.18**	**$ 1,636.70**
Champaign	IL	81,291	17,884	$ 39.43	$ 198.24	$ 123.72	**$ 361.38**	**$ 1,637.61**
Parma	OH	80,968	17,813	$ 39.58	$ 199.03	$ 124.21	**$ 362.82**	**$ 1,644.14**
Hammond	IN	80,757	17,767	$ 39.69	$ 199.55	$ 124.53	**$ 363.77**	**$ 1,648.44**
Lakewood	CA	80,634	17,739	$ 39.75	$ 199.85	$ 124.72	**$ 364.33**	**$ 1,650.95**
Concord	NC	80,597	17,731	$ 39.77	$ 199.95	$ 124.78	**$ 364.49**	**$ 1,651.71**
O'Fallon	MO	80,519	17,714	$ 39.80	$ 200.14	$ 124.90	**$ 364.85**	**$ 1,653.31**
Hemet	CA	80,467	17,703	$ 39.83	$ 200.27	$ 124.98	**$ 365.08**	**$ 1,654.38**
Cranston	RI	80,392	17,686	$ 39.87	$ 200.46	$ 125.10	**$ 365.42**	**$ 1,655.92**
Farm'tn H	MI	80,258	17,657	$ 39.93	$ 200.79	$ 125.31	**$ 366.03**	**$ 1,658.68**
Merced	CA	80,232	17,651	$ 39.95	$ 200.86	$ 125.35	**$ 366.15**	**$ 1,659.22**
Gary	IN	80,221	17,649	$ 39.95	$ 200.88	$ 125.37	**$ 366.20**	**$ 1,659.45**
Mission	TX	79,368	17,461	$ 40.38	$ 203.04	$ 126.71	**$ 370.14**	**$ 1,677.28**
Menifee	CA	79,312	17,449	$ 40.41	$ 203.18	$ 126.80	**$ 370.40**	**$ 1,678.47**
Johns Crk	GA	79,192	17,422	$ 40.47	$ 203.49	$ 127.00	**$ 370.96**	**$ 1,681.01**
Edinburg	TX	79,147	17,412	$ 40.49	$ 203.61	$ 127.07	**$ 371.17**	**$ 1,681.97**
Fishers	IN	79,127	17,408	$ 40.50	$ 203.66	$ 127.10	**$ 371.26**	**$ 1,682.39**
Chino	CA	79,059	17,393	$ 40.54	$ 203.84	$ 127.21	**$ 371.58**	**$ 1,683.84**
Racine	WI	78,853	17,348	$ 40.65	$ 204.37	$ 127.54	**$ 372.55**	**$ 1,688.24**
Lk Forest	CA	78,439	17,257	$ 40.86	$ 205.45	$ 128.21	**$ 374.52**	**$ 1,697.15**
Bend	OR	77,905	17,139	$ 41.14	$ 206.85	$ 129.09	**$ 377.09**	**$ 1,708.78**
Napa	CA	77,867	17,131	$ 41.16	$ 206.96	$ 129.16	**$ 377.27**	**$ 1,709.62**
Indio	CA	77,780	17,112	$ 41.21	$ 207.19	$ 129.30	**$ 377.69**	**$ 1,711.53**
Redw'd C	CA	77,745	17,104	$ 41.22	$ 207.28	$ 129.36	**$ 377.86**	**$ 1,712.30**
Largo	FL	77,723	17,099	$ 41.24	$ 207.34	$ 129.40	**$ 377.97**	**$ 1,712.78**
Albany	GA	77,683	17,090	$ 41.26	$ 207.45	$ 129.46	**$ 378.17**	**$ 1,713.67**
N Roch'le	NY	77,606	17,073	$ 41.30	$ 207.65	$ 129.59	**$ 378.54**	**$ 1,715.37**
Avondale	AZ	77,518	17,054	$ 41.35	$ 207.89	$ 129.74	**$ 378.97**	**$ 1,717.31**
Bryan	TX	77,321	17,011	$ 41.45	$ 208.42	$ 130.07	**$ 379.94**	**$ 1,721.69**
Camden	NJ	77,283	17,002	$ 41.47	$ 208.52	$ 130.13	**$ 380.12**	**$ 1,722.54**
St. Joseph	MO	77,185	16,981	$ 41.52	$ 208.78	$ 130.30	**$ 380.61**	**$ 1,724.72**
Bellflower	CA	77,170	16,977	$ 41.53	$ 208.82	$ 130.32	**$ 380.68**	**$ 1,725.06**
Bloom'ton	IL	77,071	16,956	$ 41.59	$ 209.09	$ 130.49	**$ 381.17**	**$ 1,727.27**
Lawrence	MA	76,976	16,935	$ 41.64	$ 209.35	$ 130.65	**$ 381.64**	**$ 1,729.41**

$ MILLIONS		Population	True Unemployed	QE/Per.	--Secret Bailouts/Per.--		TOTAL HEISTED/ PERSON/ CITY	TOTAL HEISTED/ JOBLESS
Brookln Pk	MN	76,853	16,908	$ 41.70	$ 209.69	$ 130.86	$ 382.25	$ 1,732.17
Meridian	ID	76,750	16,885	$ 41.76	$ 209.97	$ 131.04	$ 382.76	$ 1,734.50
Tustin	CA	76,689	16,872	$ 41.79	$ 210.13	$ 131.14	$ 383.07	$ 1,735.88
Somervlle	MA	76,519	16,834	$ 41.89	$ 210.60	$ 131.43	$ 383.92	$ 1,739.73
Lynchburg	VA	76,504	16,831	$ 41.89	$ 210.64	$ 131.46	$ 383.99	$ 1,740.08
Palm C'st	FL	76,499	16,830	$ 41.90	$ 210.66	$ 131.47	$ 384.02	$ 1,740.19
Deerf'ld B	FL	76,389	16,806	$ 41.96	$ 210.96	$ 131.66	$ 384.57	$ 1,742.69
Kennewick	WA	76,224	16,769	$ 42.05	$ 211.42	$ 131.94	$ 385.40	$ 1,746.47
Decatur	IL	76,096	16,741	$ 42.12	$ 211.77	$ 132.16	$ 386.05	$ 1,749.41
Melbourne	FL	76,095	16,741	$ 42.12	$ 211.77	$ 132.16	$ 386.06	$ 1,749.43
Scranton	PA	75,995	16,719	$ 42.17	$ 212.05	$ 132.34	$ 386.56	$ 1,751.73
Baldwin Pk	CA	75,940	16,707	$ 42.20	$ 212.21	$ 132.43	$ 386.84	$ 1,753.00
Chino HILs	CA	75,928	16,704	$ 42.21	$ 212.24	$ 132.45	$ 386.91	$ 1,753.28
Medford	OR	75,501	16,610	$ 42.45	$ 213.44	$ 133.20	$ 389.09	$ 1,763.19
Arl'ton Hts	IL	75,428	16,594	$ 42.49	$ 213.65	$ 133.33	$ 389.47	$ 1,764.90
Bethlehem	PA	75,266	16,559	$ 42.58	$ 214.11	$ 133.62	$ 390.31	$ 1,768.70
M'tn View	CA	75,235	16,552	$ 42.60	$ 214.20	$ 133.67	$ 390.47	$ 1,769.43
Fayettev'le	AR	75,102	16,522	$ 42.68	$ 214.57	$ 133.91	$ 391.16	$ 1,772.56
Upland	CA	74,837	16,464	$ 42.83	$ 215.33	$ 134.39	$ 392.55	$ 1,778.84
Evanston	IL	74,785	16,453	$ 42.86	$ 215.48	$ 134.48	$ 392.82	$ 1,780.07
Alameda	CA	74,774	16,450	$ 42.86	$ 215.52	$ 134.50	$ 392.88	$ 1,780.33
St. George	UT	74,770	16,449	$ 42.86	$ 215.53	$ 134.51	$ 392.90	$ 1,780.43
Kalamazoo	MI	74,743	16,443	$ 42.88	$ 215.61	$ 134.55	$ 393.04	$ 1,781.07
Schaumb'g	IL	74,550	16,401	$ 42.99	$ 216.16	$ 134.90	$ 394.06	$ 1,785.68
Bolingbr'k	IL	73,802	16,236	$ 43.43	$ 218.35	$ 136.27	$ 398.05	$ 1,803.78
Sn Ramon	CA	73,333	16,133	$ 43.70	$ 219.75	$ 137.14	$ 400.60	$ 1,815.32
Baytown	TX	73,322	16,131	$ 43.71	$ 219.78	$ 137.16	$ 400.66	$ 1,815.59
N. Britain	CT	73,261	16,117	$ 43.75	$ 219.97	$ 137.28	$ 400.99	$ 1,817.10
Appleton	WI	73,243	16,113	$ 43.76	$ 220.02	$ 137.31	$ 401.09	$ 1,817.55
Folsom	CA	73,001	16,060	$ 43.90	$ 220.75	$ 137.77	$ 402.42	$ 1,823.57
Canton	OH	72,919	16,042	$ 43.95	$ 221.00	$ 137.92	$ 402.87	$ 1,825.62
Wyoming	MI	72,833	16,023	$ 44.00	$ 221.26	$ 138.08	$ 403.35	$ 1,827.78
Pharr	TX	72,513	15,953	$ 44.20	$ 222.24	$ 138.69	$ 405.13	$ 1,835.85
L. Charles	LA	72,475	15,945	$ 44.22	$ 222.35	$ 138.77	$ 405.34	$ 1,836.81
Southfield	MI	72,201	15,884	$ 44.39	$ 223.20	$ 139.29	$ 406.88	$ 1,843.78
Gastonia	NC	72,068	15,855	$ 44.47	$ 223.61	$ 139.55	$ 407.63	$ 1,847.18
Plymouth	MN	71,561	15,743	$ 44.79	$ 225.19	$ 140.54	$ 410.52	$ 1,860.27
Auburn	WA	71,517	15,734	$ 44.81	$ 225.33	$ 140.62	$ 410.77	$ 1,861.41
Rochest H	MI	71,452	15,719	$ 44.86	$ 225.54	$ 140.75	$ 411.14	$ 1,863.11
Springdale	AR	71,397	15,707	$ 44.89	$ 225.71	$ 140.86	$ 411.46	$ 1,864.54
Wilmington	DE	71,305	15,687	$ 44.95	$ 226.00	$ 141.04	$ 411.99	$ 1,866.95
Pleasantn	CA	71,215	15,667	$ 45.00	$ 226.29	$ 141.22	$ 412.51	$ 1,869.31
Pawtucket	RI	71,153	15,654	$ 45.04	$ 226.48	$ 141.34	$ 412.87	$ 1,870.94

$ MILLIONS		Population	True Unemployed	QE/Per.	--Secret Bailouts/Per.--		TOTAL HEISTED/ PERSON/ CITY	TOTAL HEISTED/ JOBLESS
Waukesha	WI	70,867	15,591	$ 45.23	$ 227.40	$ 141.91	**$ 414.54**	**$ 1,878.49**
Jackson'le	NC	70,801	15,576	$ 45.27	$ 227.61	$ 142.05	**$ 414.92**	**$ 1,880.24**
Union City	CA	70,436	15,496	$ 45.50	$ 228.79	$ 142.78	**$ 417.07**	**$ 1,889.98**
Lynwood	CA	70,257	15,457	$ 45.62	$ 229.37	$ 143.15	**$ 418.14**	**$ 1,894.80**
Apple V'ley	CA	70,172	15,438	$ 45.67	$ 229.65	$ 143.32	**$ 418.64**	**$ 1,897.09**
Muncie	IN	70,080	15,418	$ 45.73	$ 229.95	$ 143.51	**$ 419.19**	**$ 1,899.58**
Perris	CA	69,967	15,393	$ 45.81	$ 230.32	$ 143.74	**$ 419.87**	**$ 1,902.65**
Passaic	NJ	69,893	15,376	$ 45.86	$ 230.57	$ 143.89	**$ 420.31**	**$ 1,904.66**
Missouri C	TX	69,774	15,350	$ 45.93	$ 230.96	$ 144.14	**$ 421.03**	**$ 1,907.91**
Redlands	CA	69,752	15,345	$ 45.95	$ 231.03	$ 144.18	**$ 421.16**	**$ 1,908.51**
Mt Pleas't	SC	69,357	15,259	$ 46.21	$ 232.35	$ 145.00	**$ 423.56**	**$ 1,919.38**
Gulfport	MS	69,220	15,228	$ 46.30	$ 232.81	$ 145.29	**$ 424.40**	**$ 1,923.18**
Rapid City	SD	69,200	15,224	$ 46.32	$ 232.88	$ 145.33	**$ 424.52**	**$ 1,923.74**
Turlock	CA	69,089	15,200	$ 46.39	$ 233.25	$ 145.57	**$ 425.21**	**$ 1,926.83**
Boynton B	FL	68,996	15,179	$ 46.45	$ 233.56	$ 145.76	**$ 425.78**	**$ 1,929.43**
IA City	IA	68,947	15,168	$ 46.48	$ 233.73	$ 145.87	**$ 426.08**	**$ 1,930.80**
Palatine	IL	68,858	15,149	$ 46.55	$ 234.03	$ 146.05	**$ 426.63**	**$ 1,933.29**
Waterloo	IA	68,653	15,104	$ 46.68	$ 234.73	$ 146.49	**$ 427.91**	**$ 1,939.07**
Santa Fe	NM	68,642	15,101	$ 46.69	$ 234.77	$ 146.51	**$ 427.97**	**$ 1,939.38**
Jonesboro	AR	68,547	15,080	$ 46.76	$ 235.09	$ 146.72	**$ 428.57**	**$ 1,942.06**
Warner Rb	GA	68,500	15,070	$ 46.79	$ 235.26	$ 146.82	**$ 428.86**	**$ 1,943.40**
Layton	UT	68,495	15,069	$ 46.79	$ 235.27	$ 146.83	**$ 428.89**	**$ 1,943.54**
Manteca	CA	68,254	15,016	$ 46.96	$ 236.10	$ 147.35	**$ 430.41**	**$ 1,950.40**
Loveland	CO	68,203	15,005	$ 46.99	$ 236.28	$ 147.46	**$ 430.73**	**$ 1,951.86**
LauderhlL	FL	68,117	14,986	$ 47.05	$ 236.58	$ 147.64	**$ 431.27**	**$ 1,954.32**
Lafayette	IN	67,947	14,948	$ 47.17	$ 237.17	$ 148.01	**$ 432.35**	**$ 1,959.21**
Milpitas	CA	67,804	14,917	$ 47.27	$ 237.67	$ 148.32	**$ 433.26**	**$ 1,963.35**
Mt Vernon	NY	67,780	14,912	$ 47.29	$ 237.75	$ 148.38	**$ 433.42**	**$ 1,964.04**
Rock HIL	SC	67,423	14,833	$ 47.54	$ 239.01	$ 149.16	**$ 435.71**	**$ 1,974.44**
Missoula	MT	67,290	14,804	$ 47.63	$ 239.49	$ 149.46	**$ 436.57**	**$ 1,978.34**
Rdo. Bch	CA	67,233	14,791	$ 47.67	$ 239.69	$ 149.58	**$ 436.94**	**$ 1,980.02**
Temple	TX	67,188	14,781	$ 47.70	$ 239.85	$ 149.68	**$ 437.24**	**$ 1,981.35**
Union City	NJ	67,187	14,781	$ 47.70	$ 239.85	$ 149.69	**$ 437.24**	**$ 1,981.38**
Flower MD	TX	67,019	14,744	$ 47.82	$ 240.45	$ 150.06	**$ 438.34**	**$ 1,986.34**
Kenner	LA	66,715	14,677	$ 48.04	$ 241.55	$ 150.75	**$ 440.34**	**$ 1,995.39**
Eau Claire	WI	66,623	14,657	$ 48.11	$ 241.88	$ 150.95	**$ 440.94**	**$ 1,998.15**
St. Charles	MO	66,598	14,652	$ 48.12	$ 241.97	$ 151.01	**$ 441.11**	**$ 1,998.90**
Youngst'n	OH	66,571	14,646	$ 48.14	$ 242.07	$ 151.07	**$ 441.29**	**$ 1,999.71**
Weston	FL	66,544	14,640	$ 48.16	$ 242.17	$ 151.13	**$ 441.47**	**$ 2,000.52**
Portland	ME	66,363	14,600	$ 48.29	$ 242.83	$ 151.55	**$ 442.67**	**$ 2,005.98**
Oshkosh	WI	66,344	14,596	$ 48.31	$ 242.90	$ 151.59	**$ 442.80**	**$ 2,006.55**
Goodyear	AZ	66,309	14,588	$ 48.33	$ 243.03	$ 151.67	**$ 443.03**	**$ 2,007.61**
Schenec'y	NY	66,273	14,580	$ 48.36	$ 243.16	$ 151.75	**$ 443.27**	**$ 2,008.70**

$ MILLIONS		Population	True Unemployed	QE/Per.	--Secret Bailouts/Per.--		TOTAL HEISTED/ PERSON/ CITY	TOTAL HEISTED/ JOBLESS
Frederick	MD	66,169	14,557	$ 48.44	$ 243.54	$ 151.99	$ 443.97	$ 2,011.86
St. Cloud	MN	66,169	14,557	$ 48.44	$ 243.54	$ 151.99	$ 443.97	$ 2,011.86
Harlingen	TX	66,122	14,547	$ 48.47	$ 243.72	$ 152.10	$ 444.28	$ 2,013.29
Davis	CA	66,016	14,524	$ 48.55	$ 244.11	$ 152.34	$ 445.00	$ 2,016.52
Dothan	AL	66,010	14,522	$ 48.55	$ 244.13	$ 152.36	$ 445.04	$ 2,016.71
Flagstaff	AZ	65,914	14,501	$ 48.62	$ 244.49	$ 152.58	$ 445.69	$ 2,019.64
CamarlLo	CA	65,895	14,497	$ 48.64	$ 244.56	$ 152.62	$ 445.82	$ 2,020.23
R. Crdva	CA	65,606	14,433	$ 48.85	$ 245.63	$ 153.29	$ 447.78	$ 2,029.12
Palo Alto	CA	65,412	14,391	$ 49.00	$ 246.36	$ 153.75	$ 449.11	$ 2,035.14
Yorba Lin.	CA	65,215	14,347	$ 49.15	$ 247.11	$ 154.21	$ 450.46	$ 2,041.29
Valnut Cr	CA	65,211	14,346	$ 49.15	$ 247.12	$ 154.22	$ 450.49	$ 2,041.42
Jackson	TN	65,187	14,341	$ 49.17	$ 247.21	$ 154.28	$ 450.66	$ 2,042.17
Skokie	IL	65,066	14,315	$ 49.26	$ 247.67	$ 154.57	$ 451.50	$ 2,045.96
Yuba City	CA	65,050	14,311	$ 49.27	$ 247.73	$ 154.60	$ 451.61	$ 2,046.47
N Richld H	TX	64,780	14,252	$ 49.48	$ 248.77	$ 155.25	$ 453.49	$ 2,055.00
Eagan	MN	64,765	14,248	$ 49.49	$ 248.82	$ 155.28	$ 453.59	$ 2,055.47
S Clem'te	CA	64,491	14,188	$ 49.70	$ 249.88	$ 155.94	$ 455.52	$ 2,064.21
S. San Frn	CA	64,409	14,170	$ 49.76	$ 250.20	$ 156.14	$ 456.10	$ 2,066.83
E. Orange	NJ	64,365	14,160	$ 49.79	$ 250.37	$ 156.25	$ 456.41	$ 2,068.25
Franklin	TN	64,317	14,150	$ 49.83	$ 250.56	$ 156.37	$ 456.75	$ 2,069.79
Pittsburg	CA	64,294	14,145	$ 49.85	$ 250.65	$ 156.42	$ 456.92	$ 2,070.53
Lorain	OH	64,152	14,113	$ 49.96	$ 251.20	$ 156.77	$ 457.93	$ 2,075.11
Laguna N	CA	63,940	14,067	$ 50.13	$ 252.03	$ 157.29	$ 459.45	$ 2,081.99
Johnson C	TN	63,815	14,039	$ 50.22	$ 252.53	$ 157.60	$ 460.35	$ 2,086.07
Bayonne	NJ	63,722	14,019	$ 50.30	$ 252.90	$ 157.83	$ 461.02	$ 2,089.12
Fort Myers	FL	63,512	13,973	$ 50.46	$ 253.73	$ 158.35	$ 462.54	$ 2,096.02
Janesvlle	WI	63,479	13,965	$ 50.49	$ 253.86	$ 158.43	$ 462.78	$ 2,097.11
Pico Riv.	CA	63,400	13,948	$ 50.55	$ 254.18	$ 158.63	$ 463.36	$ 2,099.73
Shawnee	KS	63,219	13,908	$ 50.70	$ 254.91	$ 159.08	$ 464.69	$ 2,105.74
Pasco	VA	63,186	13,901	$ 50.72	$ 255.04	$ 159.17	$ 464.93	$ 2,106.84
Lodi	CA	63,133	13,889	$ 50.77	$ 255.25	$ 159.30	$ 465.32	$ 2,108.61
Victoria	TX	63,131	13,889	$ 50.77	$ 255.26	$ 159.30	$ 465.33	$ 2,108.67
Monteb'lo	CA	62,954	13,850	$ 50.91	$ 255.98	$ 159.75	$ 466.64	$ 2,114.60
N Little R.	AR	62,886	13,835	$ 50.97	$ 256.26	$ 159.92	$ 467.15	$ 2,116.89
Hamilton	OH	62,795	13,815	$ 51.04	$ 256.63	$ 160.16	$ 467.82	$ 2,119.96
Woodbury	MN	62,787	13,813	$ 51.05	$ 256.66	$ 160.18	$ 467.88	$ 2,120.23
Bossier C.	LA	62,745	13,804	$ 51.08	$ 256.83	$ 160.28	$ 468.20	$ 2,121.65
Bismarck	ND	62,665	13,786	$ 51.14	$ 257.16	$ 160.49	$ 468.79	$ 2,124.36
Taylor	MI	62,489	13,748	$ 51.29	$ 257.89	$ 160.94	$ 470.11	$ 2,130.34
Council Bl	IA	62,466	13,743	$ 51.31	$ 257.98	$ 161.00	$ 470.29	$ 2,131.12
Maple Gr.	MN	62,440	13,737	$ 51.33	$ 258.09	$ 161.07	$ 470.48	$ 2,132.01
Rockvlle	MD	62,334	13,713	$ 51.42	$ 258.53	$ 161.34	$ 471.28	$ 2,135.64
Madera	CA	62,219	13,688	$ 51.51	$ 259.00	$ 161.64	$ 472.15	$ 2,139.58

$ MILLIONS		Population	True Unemployed	QE/Per.	--Secret Bailouts/Per.--		TOTAL HEISTED/ PERSON/ CITY	TOTAL HEISTED/ JOBLESS
Utica	NY	62,110	13,664	$ 51.60	$ 259.46	$ 161.92	**$ 472.98**	**$ 2,143.34**
Homest'd	FL	61,940	13,627	$ 51.74	$ 260.17	$ 162.37	**$ 474.28**	**$ 2,149.22**
Coon Rap.	MN	61,904	13,619	$ 51.77	$ 260.32	$ 162.46	**$ 474.56**	**$ 2,150.47**
Eden Pr.	MN	61,657	13,565	$ 51.98	$ 261.37	$ 163.11	**$ 476.46**	**$ 2,159.09**
Tamarac	FL	61,542	13,539	$ 52.08	$ 261.85	$ 163.42	**$ 477.35**	**$ 2,163.12**
HaverhiL	MA	61,351	13,497	$ 52.24	$ 262.67	$ 163.93	**$ 478.83**	**$ 2,169.85**
Kissimmee	FL	61,346	13,496	$ 52.24	$ 262.69	$ 163.94	**$ 478.87**	**$ 2,170.03**
Delray B.	FL	61,209	13,466	$ 52.36	$ 263.28	$ 164.31	**$ 479.95**	**$ 2,174.89**
Valtham	MA	61,181	13,460	$ 52.39	$ 263.40	$ 164.38	**$ 480.17**	**$ 2,175.88**
La Habra	CA	61,164	13,456	$ 52.40	$ 263.47	$ 164.43	**$ 480.30**	**$ 2,176.49**
Gatherb'rg	MD	61,045	13,430	$ 52.50	$ 263.99	$ 164.75	**$ 481.24**	**$ 2,180.73**
Daytona B	FL	61,028	13,426	$ 52.52	$ 264.06	$ 164.79	**$ 481.37**	**$ 2,181.34**
Terre Hte	IN	60,961	13,411	$ 52.57	$ 264.35	$ 164.97	**$ 481.90**	**$ 2,183.74**
Vineland	NJ	60,952	13,409	$ 52.58	$ 264.39	$ 165.00	**$ 481.97**	**$ 2,184.06**
Burnsvlle	MN	60,828	13,382	$ 52.69	$ 264.93	$ 165.34	**$ 482.95**	**$ 2,188.51**
Marysvlle	VA	60,785	13,373	$ 52.73	$ 265.11	$ 165.45	**$ 483.29**	**$ 2,190.06**
Meriden	CT	60,770	13,369	$ 52.74	$ 265.18	$ 165.49	**$ 483.41**	**$ 2,190.60**
Vest Allis	VI	60,714	13,357	$ 52.79	$ 265.42	$ 165.65	**$ 483.86**	**$ 2,192.62**
Mont'y Pk.	CA	60,707	13,356	$ 52.79	$ 265.46	$ 165.66	**$ 483.91**	**$ 2,192.87**
Bristol	CT	60,525	13,316	$ 52.95	$ 266.25	$ 166.16	**$ 485.37**	**$ 2,199.47**
Conway	AR	60,470	13,303	$ 53.00	$ 266.50	$ 166.31	**$ 485.81**	**$ 2,201.47**
Encinitas	CA	60,400	13,288	$ 53.06	$ 266.80	$ 166.51	**$ 486.37**	**$ 2,204.02**
Greenvlle	SC	60,379	13,283	$ 53.08	$ 266.90	$ 166.56	**$ 486.54**	**$ 2,204.79**
Santa Cruz	CA	60,342	13,275	$ 53.11	$ 267.06	$ 166.67	**$ 486.84**	**$ 2,206.14**
Springfield	OH	60,333	13,273	$ 53.12	$ 267.10	$ 166.69	**$ 486.91**	**$ 2,206.47**
Tulare	CA	60,289	13,264	$ 53.16	$ 267.30	$ 166.81	**$ 487.27**	**$ 2,208.08**
N. Miami	FL	60,143	13,231	$ 53.29	$ 267.94	$ 167.22	**$ 488.45**	**$ 2,213.44**
Cheyenne	VY	60,096	13,221	$ 53.33	$ 268.15	$ 167.35	**$ 488.83**	**$ 2,215.17**
Malden	MA	60,071	13,216	$ 53.35	$ 268.27	$ 167.42	**$ 489.04**	**$ 2,216.09**
Lancaster	PA	60,058	13,213	$ 53.37	$ 268.32	$ 167.45	**$ 489.14**	**$ 2,216.57**
Pontiac	MI	59,887	13,175	$ 53.52	$ 269.09	$ 167.93	**$ 490.54**	**$ 2,222.90**
St. Clair S	MI	59,798	13,156	$ 53.60	$ 269.49	$ 168.18	**$ 491.27**	**$ 2,226.21**
Taylorsv'le	UT	59,767	13,149	$ 53.62	$ 269.63	$ 168.27	**$ 491.53**	**$ 2,227.36**
Springfield	OR	59,695	13,133	$ 53.69	$ 269.96	$ 168.47	**$ 492.12**	**$ 2,230.05**
N Braunf.	TX	59,590	13,110	$ 53.78	$ 270.43	$ 168.77	**$ 492.99**	**$ 2,233.98**
Alpharetta	GA	59,397	13,067	$ 53.96	$ 271.31	$ 169.32	**$ 494.59**	**$ 2,241.24**
Nat'l City	CA	59,369	13,061	$ 53.98	$ 271.44	$ 169.40	**$ 494.82**	**$ 2,242.29**
Gardena	CA	59,253	13,036	$ 54.09	$ 271.97	$ 169.73	**$ 495.79**	**$ 2,246.68**
Cupertino	CA	59,220	13,028	$ 54.12	$ 272.12	$ 169.82	**$ 496.07**	**$ 2,247.94**
Ames	IA	59,042	12,989	$ 54.28	$ 272.94	$ 170.34	**$ 497.56**	**$ 2,254.71**
Conroe	TX	58,973	12,974	$ 54.35	$ 273.26	$ 170.54	**$ 498.14**	**$ 2,257.35**
Great Falls	MT	58,950	12,969	$ 54.37	$ 273.37	$ 170.60	**$ 498.34**	**$ 2,258.23**
Bovling G.	KY	58,894	12,957	$ 54.42	$ 273.63	$ 170.76	**$ 498.81**	**$ 2,260.38**

$ MILLIONS

		Population	True Unemployed	QE/Per.	Secret Bailouts/Per.		TOTAL HEISTED/ PERSON/ CITY	TOTAL HEISTED/ JOBLESS
Lakewood	VA	58,839	12,945	$ 54.47	$ 273.88	$ 170.92	$ 499.28	$ 2,262.49
Grand Jct.	CO	58,704	12,915	$ 54.60	$ 274.51	$ 171.32	$ 500.43	$ 2,267.69
D' Plaines	IL	58,617	12,896	$ 54.68	$ 274.92	$ 171.57	$ 501.17	$ 2,271.06
Hunt'gtn P	CA	58,536	12,878	$ 54.75	$ 275.30	$ 171.81	$ 501.86	$ 2,274.20
Petaluma	CA	58,453	12,860	$ 54.83	$ 275.69	$ 172.05	$ 502.57	$ 2,277.43
Rocklin	CA	58,324	12,831	$ 54.95	$ 276.30	$ 172.43	$ 503.69	$ 2,282.47
San Rafael	CA	58,313	12,829	$ 54.96	$ 276.35	$ 172.47	$ 503.78	$ 2,282.90
Dubuque	IA	58,234	12,811	$ 55.04	$ 276.73	$ 172.70	$ 504.46	$ 2,286.00
Chapel HIL	NC	58,011	12,762	$ 55.25	$ 277.79	$ 173.36	$ 506.40	$ 2,294.78
W.Des Mn	IA	57,909	12,740	$ 55.35	$ 278.28	$ 173.67	$ 507.30	$ 2,298.83
La Mesa	CA	57,907	12,740	$ 55.35	$ 278.29	$ 173.68	$ 507.31	$ 2,298.91
North Port	FL	57,780	12,712	$ 55.47	$ 278.90	$ 174.06	$ 508.43	$ 2,303.96
ID Falls	ID	57,646	12,682	$ 55.60	$ 279.55	$ 174.46	$ 509.61	$ 2,309.31
Mansfield	TX	57,627	12,678	$ 55.62	$ 279.64	$ 174.52	$ 509.78	$ 2,310.08
Royal Oak	MI	57,607	12,674	$ 55.64	$ 279.74	$ 174.58	$ 509.96	$ 2,310.88
Owensb'o	KY	57,605	12,673	$ 55.64	$ 279.75	$ 174.59	$ 509.97	$ 2,310.96
Blaine	MN	57,584	12,668	$ 55.66	$ 279.85	$ 174.65	$ 510.16	$ 2,311.80
Rogers	AR	57,539	12,659	$ 55.70	$ 280.07	$ 174.79	$ 510.56	$ 2,313.61
Rowlett	TX	57,463	12,642	$ 55.78	$ 280.44	$ 175.02	$ 511.23	$ 2,316.67
Rocky Mt.	NC	57,433	12,635	$ 55.80	$ 280.59	$ 175.11	$ 511.50	$ 2,317.88
Marietta	GA	57,357	12,619	$ 55.88	$ 280.96	$ 175.34	$ 512.18	$ 2,320.95
Broomf'ld	CO	57,352	12,617	$ 55.88	$ 280.98	$ 175.36	$ 512.22	$ 2,321.15
White Pl.	NY	57,258	12,597	$ 55.97	$ 281.45	$ 175.64	$ 513.06	$ 2,324.96
Dearbn Ht	MI	57,186	12,581	$ 56.05	$ 281.80	$ 175.86	$ 513.71	$ 2,327.89
Wellington	FL	57,163	12,576	$ 56.07	$ 281.91	$ 175.94	$ 513.92	$ 2,328.83
Orland P.	IL	57,016	12,544	$ 56.21	$ 282.64	$ 176.39	$ 515.24	$ 2,334.83
Tinley Pk	IL	56,965	12,532	$ 56.26	$ 282.89	$ 176.55	$ 515.70	$ 2,336.92
Oak Lawn	IL	56,937	12,526	$ 56.29	$ 283.03	$ 176.63	$ 515.96	$ 2,338.07
Berwyn	IL	56,906	12,519	$ 56.32	$ 283.19	$ 176.73	$ 516.24	$ 2,339.34
Arcadia	CA	56,769	12,489	$ 56.46	$ 283.87	$ 177.16	$ 517.48	$ 2,344.99
Medford	MA	56,738	12,482	$ 56.49	$ 284.02	$ 177.25	$ 517.77	$ 2,346.27
Prt Orange	FL	56,529	12,436	$ 56.70	$ 285.07	$ 177.91	$ 519.68	$ 2,354.95
Ocala	FL	56,517	12,434	$ 56.71	$ 285.14	$ 177.95	$ 519.79	$ 2,355.45
Lakevlle	MN	56,443	12,417	$ 56.78	$ 285.51	$ 178.18	$ 520.47	$ 2,358.53
Kettering	OH	56,427	12,414	$ 56.80	$ 285.59	$ 178.23	$ 520.62	$ 2,359.20
Moore	OK	56,315	12,389	$ 56.91	$ 286.16	$ 178.58	$ 521.65	$ 2,363.89
Fountain V	CA	56,153	12,354	$ 57.08	$ 286.98	$ 179.10	$ 523.16	$ 2,370.71
Valdosta	GA	56,019	12,324	$ 57.21	$ 287.67	$ 179.53	$ 524.41	$ 2,376.39
Casper	WY	55,988	12,317	$ 57.24	$ 287.83	$ 179.63	$ 524.70	$ 2,377.70
Anderson	IN	55,957	12,311	$ 57.28	$ 287.99	$ 179.73	$ 524.99	$ 2,379.02
Diamond B	CA	55,951	12,309	$ 57.28	$ 288.02	$ 179.75	$ 525.05	$ 2,379.27
Taunton	MA	55,940	12,307	$ 57.29	$ 288.08	$ 179.78	$ 525.15	$ 2,379.74
Jupiter	FL	55,911	12,300	$ 57.32	$ 288.23	$ 179.88	$ 525.42	$ 2,380.98

		$ MILLIONS Population	True Unemployed	QE/Per.		Secret Bailouts/Per.	TOTAL HEISTED/ PERSON/ CITY	TOTAL HEISTED/ JOBLESS
Decatur	AL	55,902	12,298	$ 57.33	$ 288.27	$ 179.90	$ **525.51**	**$ 2,381.36**
Woodland	CA	55,806	12,277	$ 57.43	$ 288.77	$ 180.21	$ **526.41**	**$ 2,385.46**
Novi	MI	55,583	12,228	$ 57.66	$ 289.93	$ 180.94	$ **528.52**	**$ 2,395.03**
W. Haven	CT	55,477	12,205	$ 57.77	$ 290.48	$ 181.28	$ **529.53**	**$ 2,399.60**
N. B'nswk	NJ	55,444	12,198	$ 57.81	$ 290.65	$ 181.39	$ **529.85**	**$ 2,401.03**
Carson	NV	55,439	12,197	$ 57.81	$ 290.68	$ 181.41	$ **529.90**	**$ 2,401.25**
Midwest C.	OK	55,427	12,194	$ 57.82	$ 290.74	$ 181.45	$ **530.01**	**$ 2,401.77**
Chicopee	MA	55,333	12,173	$ 57.92	$ 291.24	$ 181.75	$ **530.91**	**$ 2,405.85**
Bowie	MD	55,232	12,151	$ 58.03	$ 291.77	$ 182.09	$ **531.88**	**$ 2,410.25**
Redmond	WA	55,228	12,150	$ 58.03	$ 291.79	$ 182.10	$ **531.92**	**$ 2,410.42**
Bartlett	TN	55,055	12,112	$ 58.21	$ 292.71	$ 182.67	$ **533.59**	**$ 2,418.00**
Portervlle	CA	55,023	12,105	$ 58.25	$ 292.88	$ 182.78	$ **533.90**	**$ 2,419.40**
Eastvale	CA	54,930	12,085	$ 58.35	$ 293.37	$ 183.09	$ **534.81**	**$ 2,423.50**
Pocatello	ID	54,810	12,058	$ 58.47	$ 294.02	$ 183.49	$ **535.98**	**$ 2,428.80**
Corvallis	OR	54,674	12,028	$ 58.62	$ 294.75	$ 183.94	$ **537.31**	**$ 2,434.85**
Elyria	OH	54,581	12,008	$ 58.72	$ 295.25	$ 184.26	$ **538.23**	**$ 2,438.99**
Auburn	AL	54,566	12,005	$ 58.74	$ 295.33	$ 184.31	$ **538.38**	**$ 2,439.66**
Paramount	CA	54,492	11,988	$ 58.82	$ 295.73	$ 184.56	$ **539.11**	**$ 2,442.98**
M. Pr'pect	IL	54,403	11,969	$ 58.91	$ 296.22	$ 184.86	$ **539.99**	**$ 2,446.97**
Hanford	CA	54,284	11,942	$ 59.04	$ 296.86	$ 185.27	$ **541.17**	**$ 2,452.34**
Margate	FL	54,270	11,939	$ 59.06	$ 296.94	$ 185.31	$ **541.31**	**$ 2,452.97**
Santee	CA	54,197	11,923	$ 59.14	$ 297.34	$ 185.56	$ **542.04**	**$ 2,456.27**
Rosemead	CA	54,154	11,914	$ 59.18	$ 297.58	$ 185.71	$ **542.47**	**$ 2,458.23**
Weymouth	MA	54,116	11,906	$ 59.22	$ 297.79	$ 185.84	$ **542.85**	**$ 2,459.95**
Hempst'd	NY	54,088	11,899	$ 59.26	$ 297.94	$ 185.94	$ **543.13**	**$ 2,461.22**
Shoreline	WA	54,044	11,890	$ 59.30	$ 298.18	$ 186.09	$ **543.58**	**$ 2,463.23**
Port Art'r	TX	53,937	11,866	$ 59.42	$ 298.77	$ 186.46	$ **544.65**	**$ 2,468.12**
Sanford	FL	53,926	11,864	$ 59.43	$ 298.84	$ 186.50	$ **544.77**	**$ 2,468.62**
Coconut C	FL	53,915	11,861	$ 59.45	$ 298.90	$ 186.53	$ **544.88**	**$ 2,469.12**
Highland	CA	53,903	11,859	$ 59.46	$ 298.96	$ 186.58	$ **545.00**	**$ 2,469.67**
Delano	CA	53,819	11,840	$ 59.55	$ 299.43	$ 186.87	$ **545.85**	**$ 2,473.53**
Manhattan	KS	53,678	11,809	$ 59.71	$ 300.22	$ 187.36	$ **547.28**	**$ 2,480.02**
Noblesv'le	IN	53,515	11,773	$ 59.89	$ 301.13	$ 187.93	$ **548.95**	**$ 2,487.58**
L. Elsinore	CA	53,417	11,752	$ 60.00	$ 301.68	$ 188.27	$ **549.96**	**$ 2,492.14**
St. Peters	MO	53,264	11,718	$ 60.17	$ 302.55	$ 188.81	$ **551.54**	**$ 2,499.30**
Wheaton	IL	53,238	11,712	$ 60.20	$ 302.70	$ 188.91	$ **551.81**	**$ 2,500.52**
Colton	CA	52,940	11,647	$ 60.54	$ 304.40	$ 189.97	$ **554.91**	**$ 2,514.60**
L. Havasu	AZ	52,935	11,646	$ 60.55	$ 304.43	$ 189.99	$ **554.96**	**$ 2,514.83**
Normal	IL	52,772	11,610	$ 60.73	$ 305.37	$ 190.57	$ **556.68**	**$ 2,522.60**
Bl Springs	MO	52,749	11,605	$ 60.76	$ 305.50	$ 190.66	$ **556.92**	**$ 2,523.70**
Grand Fks	ND	52,631	11,579	$ 60.90	$ 306.19	$ 191.09	$ **558.17**	**$ 2,529.36**
Revere	MA	52,459	11,541	$ 61.10	$ 307.19	$ 191.71	$ **560.00**	**$ 2,537.65**
Novato	CA	52,456	11,540	$ 61.10	$ 307.21	$ 191.72	$ **560.03**	**$ 2,537.80**

		$ MILLIONS					TOTAL HEISTED/ PERSON/ CITY	TOTAL HEISTED/ JOBLESS
		Population	True Unemployed	QE/Per.	Secret Bailouts/Per.			
Euless	TX	52,443	11,537	$ 61.11	$ 307.29	$ 191.77	$ 560.17	$ 2,538.43
Cath.City	CA	52,381	11,524	$ 61.19	$ 307.65	$ 192.00	$ 560.83	$ 2,541.43
H'sonvlle	TN	52,349	11,517	$ 61.22	$ 307.84	$ 192.11	$ 561.18	$ 2,542.99
Sarasota	FL	52,341	11,515	$ 61.23	$ 307.88	$ 192.14	$ 561.26	$ 2,543.37
Brentwood	CA	52,326	11,512	$ 61.25	$ 307.97	$ 192.20	$ 561.42	$ 2,544.10
Pensacola	FL	52,197	11,483	$ 61.40	$ 308.73	$ 192.67	$ 562.81	$ 2,550.39
Florissant	MO	52,145	11,472	$ 61.46	$ 309.04	$ 192.87	$ 563.37	$ 2,552.93
Yucaipa	CA	52,139	11,471	$ 61.47	$ 309.08	$ 192.89	$ 563.44	$ 2,553.23
Hof. Est.	IL	52,124	11,467	$ 61.49	$ 309.17	$ 192.94	$ 563.60	$ 2,553.96
Oak Park	IL	52,104	11,463	$ 61.51	$ 309.29	$ 193.02	$ 563.81	$ 2,554.94
Battle Crk.	MI	52,093	11,460	$ 61.52	$ 309.35	$ 193.06	$ 563.93	$ 2,555.48
Smyrna	GA	51,982	11,436	$ 61.66	$ 310.01	$ 193.47	$ 565.14	$ 2,560.94
Lakewood	OH	51,724	11,379	$ 61.96	$ 311.56	$ 194.44	$ 567.96	$ 2,573.71
La Crosse	WI	51,719	11,378	$ 61.97	$ 311.59	$ 194.45	$ 568.01	$ 2,573.96
Peabody	MA	51,653	11,364	$ 62.05	$ 311.99	$ 194.70	$ 568.74	$ 2,577.25
Buckeye	AZ	51,649	11,363	$ 62.05	$ 312.01	$ 194.72	$ 568.78	$ 2,577.45
Watsonv'le	CA	51,586	11,349	$ 62.13	$ 312.39	$ 194.96	$ 569.48	$ 2,580.60
Greenw'd	IN	51,584	11,348	$ 62.13	$ 312.40	$ 194.96	$ 569.50	$ 2,580.70
S. Jordan	UT	51,377	11,303	$ 62.38	$ 313.66	$ 195.75	$ 571.79	$ 2,591.10
Elkhart	IN	51,320	11,290	$ 62.45	$ 314.01	$ 195.97	$ 572.43	$ 2,593.97
Bellevue	NE	51,319	11,290	$ 62.45	$ 314.02	$ 195.97	$ 572.44	$ 2,594.02
Placentia	CA	51,302	11,286	$ 62.47	$ 314.12	$ 196.04	$ 572.63	$ 2,594.88
Cedar Pk	TX	51,283	11,282	$ 62.50	$ 314.24	$ 196.11	$ 572.84	$ 2,595.85
Saginaw	MI	51,230	11,271	$ 62.56	$ 314.56	$ 196.31	$ 573.43	$ 2,598.53
Milford	CT	51,189	11,262	$ 62.61	$ 314.81	$ 196.47	$ 573.89	$ 2,600.61
Charleston	WV	51,177	11,259	$ 62.63	$ 314.89	$ 196.51	$ 574.03	$ 2,601.22
Per Amboy	NJ	51,093	11,240	$ 62.73	$ 315.41	$ 196.84	$ 574.97	$ 2,605.50
Burlington	NC	50,925	11,204	$ 62.94	$ 316.45	$ 197.49	$ 576.87	$ 2,614.09
Albany	OR	50,724	11,159	$ 63.19	$ 317.70	$ 198.27	$ 579.15	$ 2,624.45
Joplin	MO	50,559	11,123	$ 63.39	$ 318.74	$ 198.92	$ 581.04	$ 2,633.02
Hoboken	NJ	50,545	11,120	$ 63.41	$ 318.82	$ 198.97	$ 581.20	$ 2,633.75
Glendora	CA	50,435	11,096	$ 63.55	$ 319.52	$ 199.41	$ 582.47	$ 2,639.49
Minnetonk	MN	50,435	11,096	$ 63.55	$ 319.52	$ 199.41	$ 582.47	$ 2,639.49
W. N. York	NJ	50,260	11,057	$ 63.77	$ 320.63	$ 200.10	$ 584.50	$ 2,648.68
Bradenton	FL	50,193	11,042	$ 63.85	$ 321.06	$ 200.37	$ 585.28	$ 2,652.22
Troy	NY	50,120	11,026	$ 63.95	$ 321.53	$ 200.66	$ 586.13	$ 2,656.08
Niagara F.	NY	50,086	11,019	$ 63.99	$ 321.75	$ 200.79	$ 586.53	$ 2,657.88
Plainfield	NJ	50,085	11,019	$ 63.99	$ 321.75	$ 200.80	$ 586.54	$ 2,657.94
DeSoto	TX	50,045	11,010	$ 64.04	$ 322.01	$ 200.96	$ 587.01	$ 2,660.06

Chapter 7
Our Constitution—Just a Quick Word---You Won't Be Bored!

As clearly stated in the U.S. Constitution:

We the People

Article. I

ARTICLE I, SECTION 8:

The Congress shall have power to lay and collect taxes, duties, imposts and excises, to pay the debts and provide for the common defense and general welfare of the United States; but all duties, imposts and excises shall be uniform throughout the United States;

To borrow money on the credit of the United States;

To regulate commerce with foreign nations, and among the several states, and with the Indian tribes;

To establish a uniform rule of naturalization, and uniform laws on the subject of bankruptcies throughout the United States;

To coin money, regulate the value thereof, and of foreign coin, and fix the standard of weights and measures;

(Source: U.S. Archives, as retrieved from http://www.archives.gov/exhibits/charters/charters_downloads.html)

As you can read, Congress is supposed to be directly in charge of our money supply. Men like George Washington, Thomas Jefferson, Benjamin Franklin, John Adams and many other Founding Fathers **knew** what the banking system did to the European nations, where the bankers indebted the nations and manipulated the money supply, causing economic havoc when it was in the bankers' interests to do so. By systematically contracting and expanding the economy, through the manipulation of the money supply and interest rates, over time, the bankers and the elite have been able to acquire most, if not all of the prime property in Europe. The same thing is happening today in America.

To this day in Europe and particularly in England, most people are just modern-day versions of serfs in the middle ages---a time when the common man never owned his home. Today, the elite in England and the elite in most parts of Europe only will rent their properties via "leasehold" agreements, allowing them to own their properties for generation after generation.

> "More than a third of Britain's land is still in the hands of a tiny group of aristocrats, according to the most extensive ownership survey in nearly 140 years.
>
> In a shock to those who believed the landed gentry were a dying breed, blue-blooded owners still control vast swathes of the country within their inherited estates.
>
> A group of 36,000 individuals – only 0.6 per cent of the population – own 50 per cent of rural land." (Source: "Look who owns Britain: A third of the country STILL belongs to the aristocracy "Mail Online, By Tamara Cohen, November 10, 2010, as retrieved from http://www.dailymail.co.uk/news/article-1328270/A-Britain-STILL-belongs-aristocracy.html#ixzz2ZEMjRdqB).
>
> "The wealthiest property owner in the country, Gerald Grosvenor, the 6th Duke of Westminster regularly tops rich lists and appears in Forbes' world rankings of billionaires. The Duke is head of the Grosvenor family, which through various trusts established for current and future family members, owns more than 100 acres in Mayfair and Belgravia, including Grosvenor Square on which the American Embassy is built. He has refused to sell the freehold to the American government, and resigned from the Conservative Party after the leasehold reform of 1993 which gave flat tenants the rights to extend their leases or unite with other tenants to buy their freehold. Grosvenor also has extensive other property interests and has built 23 shopping centres in the UK and Ireland since 1965."

(Source: The Telegraph, "British business people: The top 1,000: Property 20 to 1,"By Andrew Cave, 19 Feb 2008, as retrieved from http://www.telegraph.co.uk/finance/newsbysector/constructionandproperty/2954853/British-business-people-The-top-1000-Property-20-to-1.html)

America Going Down the Same Path As England

Any living person who reads the papers, or who has watched television the last five years, has seen the lengths the bankers and elite have taken to repossess millions of homes across America and the world. Our Forefathers had tremendous foresight and witnessed, first hand, how the European and English bankers financed wars (and incited wars, knowing wars are good for business) and lent money <u>at interest</u> to the great nations and their people, thereby indebting the governments and peoples to the banking families. Once this was accomplished, the bankers could expand and contract the supply of money, thereby creating recessions and depressions at will. This capability served and serves a very important purpose for the elite, as it created (and creates) vulture-like opportunities to snatch away assets for pennies on the dollar from unsuspecting consumers, businesses and governments.

Because they can engineer recessions and depressions, they not only cause populations of people to go hungry, but they force monarchies and governments, alike, to INCREASE taxes at exactly the wrong time. When the economy downturns and with the debt in place, government spending does not stop and the government must increase taxes to pay its bills. This exacerbates the plight of the poor and middle class the most and makes the bankers and elite rich---while keeping the masses hanging on by the string of a thread.

After centuries of this activity, most real estate and major businesses are controlled by the banking families and their affiliated institutions in Europe. This cancer has quickly moved across the Atlantic Ocean to the relatively new territory of the United States.

Our Forefathers Tried To Make Sure Our Government Would Not Pay Interest

Our Forefathers tried to make sure this didn't happen to us and truly attempted to make OUR government DIFFERENT, with the ability to print money and pay its bills—WITHOUT INTEREST! With this capability assured by the Constitution, there is only one question to ask:

Why in the world are we currently, or should we EVER be paying debt and interest to a group of elite families and bankers when Congress is empowered to print money without interest and without debt?

The short answer is Congress should have NEVER delegated this authority to the Federal Reserve, an entity whose key operating components are owned by the commercial banks and the banking families. They control the Federal Reserve Board of Governors, directly or indirectly and exercise virtually absolute control over their own Regional Federal Reserve Banks.

The U.S. Congress also answers this question in a terrific summary on our monetary system in 1964:

> **69. If the Government can issue bonds, why can't it issue money and save the interest?**
>
> "A few clear-headed and firm individuals, such as Abraham Lincoln, have insisted that the Government should. The late Thomas A. Edison stated the matter this way: If our nation can issue a dollar bond it can issue a dollar bill. The element that makes the bond good makes the bill good also * * *. It is absurd to say that our country can issue $30 million in bonds and not $30 million in currency. Both are promises to pay: but one promise fattens the usurer and the other helps the people. However, it has long been one of the political facts of life that private banks must be allowed to create the lion's share of the money, even if not all of the money. Thus there is little opposition to the Goverment's [*sic*] printing bonds and then permitting the banks to create the money with which to buy those bonds; but proposals that the Government itself create the money instead of the bond have always set off tremendous political upheavals. For example, Abraham Lincoln set off a political furor when he insisted upon having the Government issue $346 million in money (the so-called "greenbacks") instead of issuing interest-bearing bonds and paying interest on the money."
>
> (Source: COMMITTEE ON BANKING AND CURRENCY, HOUSE OF REPRESENTATIVES, SUBCOMITTEE ON DOMESTIC FINANCE, 88th Congress, 2nd Session, SEPTEMBER 21, 1964, by Wright Patman, Chairman, Chapter I, PREFACE, Chapter III, point 69, as retrieved from http://www.baldwinlivingtrust.com/pdfs/AllAboutMoney.pdf).

Ultimately, President Lincoln was assassinated, as were other Presidents and politicians who dared to wrest control of monetary policy away from the bankers.

The perfect relationship between the Federal Reserve and Congress allows Congress to spend indiscriminately, while keeping the bankers in business, all at the expense of the taxpayer. Each and EVERY time the politicians have threatened and/or succeeded in wresting banking control away from the elite, the banks immediately tighten credit lines and shrink the money supply, forcing horrific economic consequences on the general public. This results in political upheaval for elected officials and very little real change has occurred to this system because of the deep, underlying, corruption involved. As long as the politicians play ball, the bankers generally behave---until the temptation to foreclose on trillions of dollars of assets gets too high.

If there ever is a permanent change to the system, control of monetary policy must be taken by a government for the people, by the people and with the people, 100%. The system unfortunately, has gotten too incestuous and is filled with too many conflicts of interest. As a result, until it collapses, there is very little chance of real change, short of a miracle from God above.

Federal Reserve Act Passage 1913

The research completed by many others on this subject points to huge amounts of bribe money paid to Senators and Congressman to assure the Federal Reserve Act's passage in 1913. This was purportedly the courtesy of the Rothschild's in England and their principal agents and co-conspirators who included the houses of JP Morgan, Paul Warburg, the Mellons, the Rockefellers, other founders of the Fed, a host of politicians, major media owners at the time, as well as many others.

These are the people and families who, in the early 1900s, hijacked and took control from Congress the power to coin and print money by creating the Federal Reserve System, an entity comprised of 12 private banking companies and an agency whose board of governors include seven people, appointed by the President and ultimately, controlled by the banks and the elite.

Federal Reserve Operates With Impunity

Such authority and power granted to a small group of men and women has allowed the elite to manipulate and corrupt the system. Today, the Federal Reserve is operating with little or no accountability to Congress, or the people, despite supposed reforms enacted after the credit crisis broke open.

The problem is Congress is dealing with people who are among the most brilliant and educated in the world. They have also spent hundreds of BILLIONS of dollars to ensure the system of the Federal Reserve and its policies are protected for the benefit of the elites' ***future*** family generations who control the shares of the Federal Reserve and commercial banks.

Their successful long-term self-entitlement strategy is aided and abetted by portraying monetary policy and the Federal Reserve System as complex and as confusing as possible--so the common man never has a real clue as to what is really transpiring.

Unfortunately, this includes an ignorant, willing or conspiring Congress, ensuring very few people ever attempt to challenge the powers orchestrating the policies of the Federal Reserve System. This has guaranteed the elite families' rule over the entire country and economy for generations to come—as long as the Federal Reserve remains in its current form and is still standing.

This system, the "Federal Reserve System" is not federal, nor is it a reserve, it is a mirage of deceit which has merely allowed elite families to become the equivalent of 18th century pirates, using their cunning and lust for money to steal our nation's wealth and your children's' children's future. When you finish reading this book, you too, will likely be convinced of their true motives and demand change to be effected by contacting your local Congressman and Senator.

Congressmen Patman did not actually provide the original source for Mr. Edison's quote in this chapter's previously cited "69. If the Government can issue bonds, why can't it issue money and save the interest?" Many, many people on the Internet often quote this passage without reference.

Here is the actual quote taken from the New York Times quoting one of America's most famous inventors, Thomas A. Edison when he stated the matter this way in 1921:

> ***"If our nation can issue a dollar bond it can issue a dollar bill. The element that makes the bond good makes the bill good also....It is absurd to say that our country can issue $30 million in bonds and not $30 million in currency. Both are promises to pay: but one promise fattens the usurer and the other helps the people."***
> (Source: New York Times, December 6, 1921, "Ford Sees Wealth In Muscle Shoals...Edison Backs Him Up," as retrieved from http://query.nytimes.com/mem/archive-free/pdf?res=9C04E0D7103EEE3ABC4E53DFB467838A639EDE).

Historically, much has been written and complained about with respect to the Federal Reserve in America. This book certainly adds to the bonfire, but is most focused on the matter of the $30 Trillion heist and its impact on regular Americans. In the author's research for this book, he came across a couple of outstanding pieces of literature everyone should read (among the thousands of documents and video presentations this writer has read, viewed, or used in researching the subject, and in writing this book) on the subject of the Federal Reserve and the actual history of money and banking in the United States. They include:

1.) Our Money Wars: The Example and Warning of American Finance, by Samuel Leavitt, published in 1894, by the Boston Arena Publishing Company, Copley Square (see Chapter 17 of The $30 Trillion Heist---Scene Of The Crime? Volume II, "History Repeats Itself" for interesting excerpts from his scholarly work. It can be retrieved from https://archive.org/details/ourmoneywarsexa00leavgoog.

There is also a video on You Tube titled, the "The Money Masters," by Patrick S.J. Carmack and Bill Still, which is very well done, but seems to directly and frequently use the work originally written by Mr. Leavitt, which covers the history of money in our country up until 1894. This writer searched for a credit for Mr. Leavitt, but did not find one. Many of the sections in "The Money Masters" are eerily similar to Mr. Leavitt's work. Mr. Leavitt's work is one of the keys to understanding how the Federal Reserve was ever allowed to be established in the first place. Nevertheless, for the uninformed viewer, it is a good video you can watch to get better educated on the subject, with a simple search at www.youtube.com.

One of the most remarkable things learned from reading the history of money from Our Money Wars (Mr. Leavitt's work documents events from the year 1600 until the time of publication in the late 1800s, is extraordinarily detailed and it stands on the shelves of prestigious universities, worldwide) is in all this time, ***NOTHING much has changed in the world of finance,*** because the ***same powerful families still control the banking system.***

Until this fact changes, with the big banks broken up and the ill-obtained assets seized and given back to the people—restoring our great cities, like Detroit, Cleveland, Phoenix, etc. as well as the entire south, we are all doomed to become debt-enslaved surfs---just as the situation has been in England for CENTURIES.

2.) Another great book shedding modern-day light on the subject matter of The $30 Trillion Heist and its trilogy companions is Secrets of the Federal Reserve. This book was written by the late Mr. Eustace Mullins and was published in 1991. His original book, published under the title, Mullins On The Federal Reserve, was commissioned by the poet Ezra Pound in 1948.

Mr. Mullins spent most of his adult life directly researching the Federal Reserve in a finished work this writer believes was completed in a painstakingly, brilliant manner. While he was doing the research for his book, he was on the staff of the Library of Congress and was able to take great advantage of the resources at this institution, shedding important light on this very important subject. After learning of the content and subject of Mr. Mullin's book after he published his original work, the Library of Congress fired him.

Both of Mr. Mullin's books were written **LONG BEFORE** G. Edward Griffin wrote the more widely read and popularized, "The Creature from Jekyll Island" in 1994 and long, long before Mr. Patrick S.J. Carmack and Bill Still made the video, "The Money Masters," just to give credit where credit is due.

The advisor who originally tipped Mr. Mullins off about the story of the Federal Reserve, a Mr. Ezra Pound, was hated by the bankers and was held as the equivalent of a political prisoner for thirteen and a half years at St. Elizabeth's Hospital, in Washington, D.C. (which was a Federal institution for the mentally insane). His ultimate release was accomplished largely through the efforts of Mr. Mullins. Mr. Mullins was urged by Mr.

Pound to write the story of the Federal Reserve System, as if "it were a detective story."

This author has attempted to take the same approach with The Federal Reserve Trilogy.

Mr. Mullin's original work was published in 1952 by Kasper and Horton, in New York. Mullins On The Federal Reserve was the first nationally-circulated book which disclosed the secret meetings of the international bankers at Jekyll Island, Georgia on November 22, 1910, as well as the years preceding this fateful day in our nation's history.

As discussed elsewhere in The $30 Trillion Heist, Jekyll Island is the place where the draft of the ***Federal Reserve Act*** of 1913 was written by a group of men with undeniable ties to the world's richest families. They included Senator Nelson Aldrich, maternal grandfather to the Rockefellers; H. P. Davison of J.P. Morgan Company and Mr. Morgan's personal emissary; Paul Warburg of Kuhn, Loeb Company whose family was from Europe and owned banking interests with the Rothschilds and whose father worked for the Rothschilds directly; Frank Vanderlip of the National City Bank (controlled by the Rockefellers and Kuhn, Loeb); Charles D. Norton of the JP Morgan influenced First National Bank of New York (Mr. Norton went on to become a partner at J.P. Morgan--see New York Times article which follows), along with A. Piatt Andrew, Assistant Secretary of the Treasury. (see http://www.vho.org/aaargh/fran/livres9/mullins.pdf, or https://archive.org/details/EustaceMullins-SecretsOfTheFederalReserveTheLondonConnection1984 for additional information).

****

Thank you, Mr. Mullins for your tireless work on this subject. Your work does and always will, matter---may you rest in peace with God, above.

Mr. Mullins was also a Christian.

Who wrote the Federal Reserve Act and why the Federal Reserve even came into existence should be fully recognized and recognizable at this point. It was created to make money for the banks and the wealthy elite.

All you have to do today, is "follow the money" and it will lead you to the tallest buildings in every city---nearly every one of which is both owned and occupied by a bank, or has a mortgage owned by the banks and the wealthiest family empires in the world.

1913 Year of the Income Tax in America

Another interesting Constitutional event of even greater importance, happening in the same year as the advent of the Federal Reserve Act, was the passage of the 16th Amendment to the United States Constitution, which instituted the income tax.

The text of the 16th Amendment makes it clear even though the categories of direct and indirect taxation still exist, any determination income tax is a direct tax will be irrelevant because taxes on incomes, from salary or from real estate, are explicitly to be treated as indirect. The Congress passed this Amendment on July 2, 1909, and it was ratified on February 3, 1913. (Source: U.S. Constitution, http://www.usconstitution.net/constamnotes.html, and the Library of Congress, http://www.archives.gov/exhibits/charters/constitution_amendments_11-27.html).

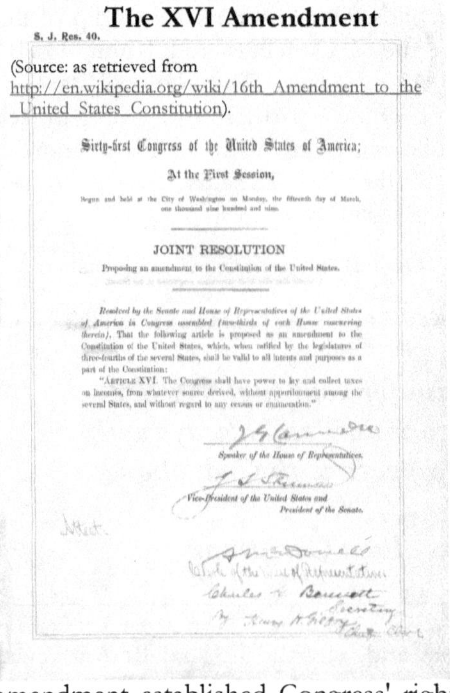
The XVI Amendment

(Source: as retrieved from http://en.wikipedia.org/wiki/16th_Amendment_to_the_United_States_Constitution).

S. J. Res. 40.

Sixty-first Congress of the United States of America;

At the First Session,

Begun and held at the City of Washington on Monday, the fifteenth day of March, one thousand nine hundred and nine.

JOINT RESOLUTION

Proposing an amendment to the Constitution of the United States.

Resolved by the Senate and House of Representatives of the United States of America in Congress assembled (two-thirds of each House concurring therein), That the following article is proposed as an amendment to the Constitution of the United States, which, when ratified by the legislatures of three-fourths of the several States, shall be valid to all intents and purposes as a part of the Constitution:

"ARTICLE XVI. The Congress shall have power to lay and collect taxes on incomes, from whatever source derived, without apportionment among the several States, and without regard to any census or enumeration."

Speaker of the House of Representatives.

Vice-President of the United States and President of the Senate.

With this final piece of the puzzle in place, the mighty families and bankers plotting the birth of the Federal Reserve System made haste and completed their draft of the Federal Reserve Act, which ultimately passed on December 23, 1913.

Prior to 1913, there was never a direct tax on Americans, except for an excise tax during the Civil War, which ultimately was repealed.

Passed by Congress on July 2, 1909, the 16th Amendment took until February 3, 1913, to be ratified by ¾s of the states (36 out of 48). The 16th amendment established Congress' right to impose a Federal income tax based upon a person's income, paving the way for the bankers and elite families to be assured they would be guaranteed their payment of principal and interest on the loans they made to the U.S. Government once their plan for the Federal Reserve was acted upon and passed by the House of Representatives later in the year on December 22, 2013. The Senate and President approved the bill on the following day, December 23.

Congress allowed the printing press of the Federal Reserve to be put in place because of the conniving ingenuity of the banking elite, along with the knowledge they could now spend their way into oblivion---without ever being held accountable for directly printing too much money.

Historically, Congress had some restraint and exhibited a bit of moral fiber and accountability to the people and did not run up extreme debts as we see today. They typically kept their spending in line with revenues, while actually balancing the budget nearly every single year, except in a time of war.

Unlimited Campaign Contributions = Corrupt Congress

Because the current members of Congress who support the banks (as well as many members before them) have been the benefactors of enormous campaign contributions from the banking industry and can now receive UNLIMITED campaign contributions (as upheld by the U.S. Supreme Court, but as of the writing of this book may be under further review/interpretation by this Court) from corporations and the wealthy elite---they, particularly, receive all the money they need for reelection.

This has caused many, many bankers and elite to purchase elections by backing BOTH sides of a major political struggle---just as they have done historically in times of war when they have backed both warring governments, with the victor guaranteeing the loser shall pay its debt to the bankers (the victor pays, also)!

History doesn't really change much—it just morphs into a new design from the same old template—it is up to the wise to figure out what is repeating and what is not.

The politicians, in the meantime, have gladly played right into the banker's hands, spending incomprehensibly, turning the other way when the Fed was up to dirty tricks and sacrificing the futures of all our children, while wrecking our country financially. Like the corrupt Roman Senate before them, Congressmen and Senators have homes and assets in Switzerland, Lichtenstein, Hong Kong, Singapore, Monaco, Aspen, South America, the Caribbean and all around the world. They are truly reminiscent of the ruling Roman Senate who had privileges and wealth, towering over the common man, which ultimately led to their own downfall.

With trillions of dollars taken from the American people and the absolute certainty of economic catastrophe hitting our nation, the troubling and important question of treason will be undoubtedly asked in years to come. The continued impoverishment and steady decline of our nation's working class and poor people, along with the true state of the economy, globally, will demand it.

Readers will be delighted to know if they wind up agreeing with many of the positions presented in this book and siding with our Founding Fathers by being against a centralized Federal Reserve System run by the private sector, they will be in good company. There have been many other wealthy and successful Americans who were against the establishment of the Federal Reserve System—or similar institutions, in our nation's history. These people are mentioned prominently throughout this book and in the trilogy. They not only include the likes of Thomas Edison and Henry Ford, but many others.

John Jacob Astor
July 17, 1763 – March 29, 1848
(Source: Astor library based on a portrait from Alonzo Chapell, as retrieved from http://en.wikipedia.org/wiki/Astor_Library).

John Jacob Astor IV
July 13, 1864-April 15, 1912
(Source: http://en.wikipedia.org/wiki/John_Jacob_Astor_IV).

In the Federal Reserve's first incarnation in the United States (where the bankers wanted control of the U.S. money supply) it was called the "Bank of the United States" and a very famous New Yorker, Jacob Astor, opposed it. As most readers know, the Waldorf-Astoria Hotel in New York is named after the family, and John Jacob Astor IV, the great-nephew, was the wealthiest man to die on the Titanic.

"**1820-A Valuable Client:** John Jacob Astor strongly opposed renewing the charter of the Bank of the United States in 1811. For reasons that are not entirely clear, the bank had closed his account and refused him further credit. Two decades later he was a customer and then, records suggest, rescuer of City Bank, by which time most of his fortune was in real estate. Astor also held shares in Farmers' Loan and Trust Co., which would become closely associated with City Bank as the century progressed. When it was published in 1845, three years before Astor's death, the sixth edition of Wealth and Biography of the Wealthy Citizens of New York City estimated Astor's wealth at $25 million." (Source: Citigroup web site as retrieved from; http://citigroup.com/citi/press/mobile/ir/html/timeline/index-com.html).

We all know "13" is a bad luck number and 1913 became the most unlucky year of all in the history of the United States. Upon passage of the Federal Reserve Act on December 23, 1913 ALONG WITH the passage of the legalization of an income tax upon American citizens' income earlier in the year, the people of the United States of America lost control of their financial freedom. A new era of taxing authority filled up our lives and as we are witnessing today, has inspired out-of-control spending by a corrupt Congress.

This was all made possible by the creation of a central bank too eager to supply the U.S. Government with all the money it desires---just as long as the principal and interest payments are guaranteed by the U.S. taxpayer—

and repaid to the elite. This system of Congress and the Federal Reserve working together defeats our Founding Fathers' intention of ridding Congress from the corruption which is a natural result of the delegation of direct government obligations, responsibility and power to a few people, who are controlled by private enterprise.

With our central bank incredibly influenced and controlled by private, wealthy citizens and a terrorizing banking cabal, the Congress in 1913 and every single Congress since, has succumbed to the powers of the money trust---powers our Forefathers fought against and KNEW was the road to trouble. They had experienced these problems, firsthand, with the Bank of England (controlled by the English Rothschilds) and the British Government. As our old history books tell us (the new ones have been white-washed away), men like Benjamin Franklin, Alexander Hamilton, James Madison and George Washington fought a war against England because of two major factors--both of which involved money!

Two Major Reasons for Revolutionary War With England

The first factor, of course, involved taxes. Prior to the Revolutionary War, England was taxing the American Colonies because the British government was deeply indebted to the bankers, thanks to England's distant forays into far-off lands and the lavish spending of government and monarchs. Because of its government's "overreach," the Brits didn't have enough money to pay for everything they wanted to "accomplish."

The result was a continued, heavy-handed rule over the American Colonies, with ever-increasing taxes on the American public. Ultimately, this led to the real Tea Party, where people took action and threw all the tea overboard in Boston Harbor, in protest of the high British taxes. This is why most Americans drink coffee instead of tea, even today!

The second factor involved grave concern the Colonies were printing their own money and paid NO INTEREST to anybody—avoiding English taxes and interest payments, altogether. This applied further pressure on the British, resulting in their financial mugging tactics and aggressive behavior toward the colonies.

These were the two principal causes of the war which led, ultimately, to U.S. independence.

The British lost the war, but spent millions of pounds doing so. As we have all seen from the history books, wars and government spending make bankers very rich. To this day, the Rothschild family, the principal family behind the Bank of England, is among the very wealthiest in the entire world.

The British people themselves, you might ask, how did they fair?

The spending and taxing of the people didn't do much for England or for the English people, as their empire crumbled before their very eyes over the very next century. The rich people either fled England, or ensconced themselves in the power hierarchy of the British government, assuring their family's thriving survival, no matter what the outcome would be for the English people, as a whole.

To win and succeed from Great Britain, our Founding Fathers spent hundreds of nights together---secretly keeping in the confines of private, smoke-filled conference rooms hidden away in pubs up and down the East coast of the United States. They met in Philadelphia and New York and New Hampshire and South Carolina---as well as many other cities and states. They planned NOT ONLY our independence from the British, but planned on a system of governance ensuring an oligarchical class of people would NEVER rule our country. They tried to guarantee rule would not only prevail politically via democratic elections, but also financially, by trying to ensure independence of government from the private sector.

Based upon what these men wrote and stated, you can probably imagine they are undoubtedly deeply disappointed with the people elected and running Congress since 1913. As for the bankers' actions, themselves, the Founding Fathers would not be surprised. They tried very hard to protect us from their clutches all the way back to 1776 with the writing of our Declaration of Independence and the writing and adoption of our Constitution, which began with deliberations at the Constitutional Convention in Philadelphia on May 25, 1787. The Continental Congress, on September 13, 1788, set the new Constitution into operation.

Central Banks Impose a Hidden Tax on the People

The oligarchs and the banking elite, truly a part of the ruling class, obtain their wealth because they keep, make and extract exorbitant taxes on the people "en masse."

The Queen of England's family has done this for centuries through taxation and pass-throughs to the "royal" family, while aggregating and controlling assets worldwide. The bankers, on the other hand, although not "royalty," created a system of financing which automatically places a tax on the people of the United States---it is called "interest" on government bonds and obligations. ***Additionally,*** when the Fed engages in outright "secret" bailouts, these monies are guaranteed by the taxpayer and must be repaid later by the American family, either causing enormous tax burdens on them for decades to come, OR creating tremendous inflation which will reduce the standard of living for everyone.

This always transpires because the Federal Reserve and government will print money in the hopes of inflating away their sins (see The $30 Trillion Heist---Follow The Money! Volume II, Chapter 2 subsection, "The Fed's Conflicts, Lack of Transparency & Control of The Business Cycle," as well as its Chapter 6, "Assflation™ and VaR—it's Déjà vu, All Over Again!"). Either way, a direct tax and outright heist from the people of their tax dollars and well-being has occurred.

Creating a central bank which is controlling, surreptitiously, the taxes of every single American merely creates a new, 21st Century form of oligarchy (accomplished by supplying Congress with all the money it wants to spend, while charging interest expense to the public and then dipping into the treasury when the bankers' investments go wrong).

The end result is the very same, as all the bankers' money and power comes off of the backs of labor---from the work, sweat and tears of other people, who become worse off because of increased taxes, inflation and the inefficient spending of the country's resources.

This is NOT applause for socialism or communism. This book firmly espouses the visions of our Forefathers and men like Henry Ford and Thomas Edison—both were dead set against paying interest on government debt to a group of private bankers.

Why borrow $30 Million and repay $60 Million, when you include the interest? The answer is we shouldn't be.

Two Biggest Mistakes in U.S. History

The violation of the Constitution's original intent of not allowing direct taxation on the people and not permitting the delegation of authority to coin money are two of the biggest mistakes ever made in the history of the United States and its people. The U.S Constitution, Article I, Section 9, Clause 4 states: "No Capitation, or other direct, Tax shall be laid, unless in Proportion to the Census or Enumeration herein before directed to be taken."

The U.S. Constitution, Article I, Section 8, states: "The Congress shall have power to lay and collect taxes, duties, imposts and excises, to pay the debts and provide for the common defense and general welfare of the United States; but all duties, imposts and excises shall be uniform throughout the United States; To coin money, regulate the value thereof, and of foreign coin, and fix the standard of weights and measures;..."

As the reader sees, the evidence piles up! Congress and the American people are going to have to take a long, hard look at distributing justice and recapturing assets stolen from all Americans by the banking elite. This is not about socialism---it is about fraud and regaining the stolen wealth taken from every hard-working American out there. The alternative is a debt or inflation encumbrance inflicting grievous harm on generations to come.

Chapter 8
Fractional Reserve Banking-Just the Tip of the Iceberg

Typically at the top of a credit bubble, or what the bankers like to call a "business cycle," is when banks PURPOSELY make credit easily available for nearly EVERYONE. When the time is right and the masses are in debt, the banks simply tighten the supply of credit, causing the bubble to burst, which forces the business cycle to go into a tail spin. With each "cycle" the bankers and wealthy elite know a certain percentage of the population will only be able to helplessly watch as the bank repossesses their property---stealing their hard-earned equity and assets away for pennies on the dollar.

"Steal" is harsh terminology, the author is aware of this; however, the "bubbles" and "cycles" are PURPOSELY created to take over coveted assets---AFTER other parties have invested significant amounts of capital in improving or creating the assets, during the upswing in the business cycle.

The bankers' ability to loosen and tighten the money supply can be accomplished in many ways, but among the simplest tools the bankers have to accomplish this goal is one they have used for centuries. It is the ability to use other people's money to make loans---and then simply not renew the loans, thereby tightening the supply of credit.

Bankers have made a lot of money through this practice in what is called in today's "Harvardized" terminology, "fractional reserve banking." This system allows bankers to receive your deposits, creating a liability for the bank. With each dollar you give them for safe keeping, they can lend out **at least** ten more dollars to other people---thereby creating credits in the borrowers' checking accounts and voila "money" (but not legal tender) out of thin air. These credits are available to the borrowers to spend with whoever will accept the draft of their checks, or if the bank will allow them, to withdraw funds. Fractional reserve banking is completely permissible under current law in the United States and Western Europe, as well as most Western countries.

The system is well known and older people will probably realize it is what caused the run on Jimmy Stewart's bank in the movie, "It's A Wonderful Life" in 1946, which recounted the hardships in America during the Great Depression in the 1930s. The fractional reserve system works for the bank IF all the depositors have confidence in the bank and the depositors don't all show up at once demanding their money.

Fractional reserve banking traditionally has created mega-wealth for the banks and the elite because when a person makes a deposit, the bankers can effectively earn not just 4%, 5%, 6% or 12% (or more) by loaning the depositor's money out, but they really earn at least 40%, 50%, 60% or 120% (or more), by simultaneously loaning the exact same deposit out to ten other people, thereby leveraging the loanable funds available to the bank by a factor of TEN! This is a great earnings stream on money which doesn't even belong to the banks!!!

Source: Still from "It's A Wonderful Life," 1946, filmed, produced and directed by Frank Capra. Jimmy Stewart and Donna Reed pictured--public domain image. Rko Pictures .

This power of fractional reserve banking is why the elite fight so hard to protect their interests in it. It is also why it is dangerous to write about.

Think about it, if you were a bank and somebody GAVE you money for FREE and you could lend out TEN TIMES THE AMOUNT. This means you wouldn't earn 3%, 4%, 5%, 10% or even 30% (like most credit cards charge, today!). Instead, with the power of fractional reserve banking, you would earn 30%, 40%, 50%, 100% and even up to 300% on the "deposit" which wasn't even yours to begin with.

> ***Is it no wonder why the banking elite want to keep control of the system and ensure they have absolute, effective control over the Federal Reserve?***

Banks Create Money Out of Thin Air

There are some very interesting accounting studies performed on the banks and how they actually book the debits and credits on loans and deposit transactions. The obvious potential conclusion is the banks may actually be committing fraud when they lend people money, as they are not giving people legal tender in exchange for the borrower's legal obligation to repay a loan. By making loans, literally created from the banks' liabilities, the validity of the original loan agreement is certainly put into question. This is an entirely different discussion and outside the purpose of this book; however, it is another interesting example of how the bankers have tried to legitimize what would be called fraudulent activity if anyone else were to try it.

The COMMITTEE ON BANKING AND CURRENCY, chaired by Wright Patman, agrees with the author and states:

> **Do private banks issue money today?**
> "Yes. Although banks no longer have the right to issue bank notes, they can create money in the form of bank deposits when they lend money to businesses, or buy securities. ***The important thing to remember is that when banks lend money they don't necessarily take it from anyone else to lend. Thus they 'create' it."*** (Source: COMMITTEE ON BANKING AND CURRENCY, HOUSE OF REPRESENTATIVES, SUBCOMITTEE ON DOMESTIC FINANCE, 88th Congress, 2nd Session, SEPTEMBER 21, 1964, by Wright Patman, Chairman, Chapter II, What Is Money?, 33.). Author's emphasis underlined, as retrieved from http://www.baldwinlivingtrust.com/pdfs/AllAboutMoney.pdf).

Fractional reserve banking, by itself, allows bankers to manipulate the supply of money and creates enormous wealth transfers in favor of the bankers and generally and ultimately creates economic turmoil for the general public. ***Why did we adopt this system?***

It is an important question and interesting to know how this system was ever invented, in the first place.

The Goldsmiths--How Fractional Reserve Banking Was Invented

Fractional reserve banking dates back to the era of the "goldsmiths" in medieval Europe (in the 1600s) when goldsmiths stored gold and silver in their vaults in exchange for a formal receipt, which was signed and sealed by the goldsmith where the property was stored. These receipts became popular as a currency because they weighed less than the actual gold and silver sitting in the goldsmith's vaults. One day, the goldsmiths realized they could make new receipts, with NO gold or silver backing them up, thereby committing fraud. They lent this new currency to other interested parties in exchange for the party's gold interest payments back to the goldsmiths. Thus, the goldsmiths collected specie (gold interest payments) payments in exchange for the issuance of pieces of paper they created without anything backing them up, eerily reminiscent of our current monetary system and the bank's fractional reserve banking system.

These men had discovered customers would leave their gold and silver in the vaults untouched—leaving the goldsmiths with plenty of deposits to handle any demands for gold or silver. Ultimately, the word got out and people were quite upset, ending the goldsmith's role as trusted keepers of wealth for society, but not before the goldsmiths had walked off with most of all the money and property over an approximate 100-year period of time!

This was the birthplace of the modern-day fractional banking system. (Source: ibid, page 41).

As uncovered by George Selgin, Professor of Economics at the Terry College of Business at the University of Georgia and published on March 30, 2010, he wrote of the goldsmiths:

> "Old-fashioned merchants complained bitterly that a class of men, who, thirty years before, had confined themselves to their proper functions, and had made a fair profit by embossing silver bowls and chargers, by setting jewels for fine ladies, and by selling pistols and dollars to gentlemen setting out to the Continent, had become the treasurers, and were fast becoming the masters, of the whole City. These usurers, it was said, played at hazard with what had been earned by the industry and hoarded by the thrift of other men. If the dice turned up well, the knave who kept the cash became an alderman: if they turned up ill, the dupe who furnished the cash became a bankrupt." (Source: The History of England, from the Accession of James the Second v. 4, London: Longman, Brown, Green, and Longmans page 514, as retrieved from http://www.english.gsu.edu/~mbrown/Texts/Misc/Macaulay_Hist_England_JamesII.pdf, page 1068).

Professor Selgin found this beautiful quote from a book by Thomas Babbington Macaulay, published in 1855, titled, The History of England, from the Accession of James the Second v. 4.

Usury—It Used to Be Bad

The practice of lending out currency and gaining interest on it is commonly known as "usury." Historically, usury was and still is outlawed by the Muslims, and was once outlawed by the Catholic Church. It is also forbidden in the Old Testament and Hebrew scriptures. The Jews even taught the word of God said any fellow Israelite you lent money to, if it is not repaid within seven years, should be forgiven because God wants his people to live in prosperity---not under the yoke and chain of debt (Source: The Bible, Deuteronomy 15, King James Version).

We know, as Christians, Jesus is the Messiah and God made a provision for all men to be saved through faith in Christ. This means we should also forgive those who have debts, thus allowing those debtors to live a life of prosperity and not a life of slavery caused by debt. This is Godly instruction, taken directly from God's instructions to the Jewish people and applies in principle exactly the same way to Christians.

It is interesting the world turned its back on the teachings of these age-old religions, particularly on a subject as important as money. As more of the evidence of wrong-doing in these pages accumulates, you will inevitably "feel" a certain sense of foreboding, or day of reckoning approaching, because based upon God's principles the system in place is clearly against His will.

By Complicating Terminology, the Fed Keeps its Secrets Hidden from Joe Six Pack

As discussed a few pages back, if you read Mr. Samuel Leavitt's work (Our Money Wars, as discussed in this book's Chapter 7, with some excellent excerpts from his work in The $30 Trillion Heist---Follow The Money! Volume II, Chapter 17, "History Repeats Itself"), you will discover our present-day bankers have merely "Harvardized" the same banking terminology which was used in the 1700s and 1800s.

This is a transparent and vain attempt by them to sound intelligent and beyond reproach when mere mortals might dare question their integrity and actions. You can see them complicate their speech and answers to direct questions whether they are testifying in front of Congress, whether they are speaking to reporters or whether they are just peering into a camera for benefit of a TV set.

Every chance they get bankers attempt to confuse anyone and everyone possible, using complicated words and structures in an attempt to hide their true activities and intentions. The elite have gone to great lengths to cover their tracks, even creating ingenious, innovative organizational names to hide their ownership interests and operational activities from the public's eye.

By using opaque names like the "Federal Reserve System," without using the word "bank" in the title of the original "Federal Reserve Act" and inventing words and terminology like "CDOs," "GMOs," "Futures," "Notional," "Quantitative Easing," "TARP," "SWAPS," "RESERVE," etc., while architecting a plan to have the Federal Reserve be run by the private sector, the bankers and the elite have tried to ensure their great deception has been kept secret from the American public.

Once again, please read these important comments and answers to questions from the work done by the COMMITTEE ON BANKING AND CURRENCY, HOUSE OF REPRESENTATIVES, SUBCOMITTEE ON DOMESTIC FINANCE, 88th Congress, 2nd Session, SEPTEMBER 21, 1964, by Wright Patman, Chairman, Chapter III, How is Money Created? Chapter 1, Preface, 10-15 (as retrieved from http://www.baldwinlivingtrust.com/pdfs/AllAboutMoney.pdf author's emphasis underlined):

> **10. Who really directs Federal Reserve operations?**
> Day-to-day operations in each of the 12 regional Federal Reserve banks are supervised by nine directors—six of them selected directly by privately owned commercial banks. <u>The most important monetary decisions for the system as a whole are made by the Open Market Committee, which is composed of 12 members.</u>
>
> **11. Do private bank interests influence Federal Reserve policy?**
> Yes. Of the 12 members of the Open Market Committee—the Committee which actually controls credit policy—5 are presidents of regional banks. These presidents are elected by the individual regional banks' nine-man board of directors with its preponderance of private commercial bank representatives. Further, all 12 of the regional bank presidents participate in the Open Market Committee's discussions, though only 5 can vote. The "discussion" Open Market Committee, then, has 19 members—12 regional bank presidents and the 7 members of the Federal Reserve Board.

12. Does it matter what amount of money is supplied the economy?
Yes, indeed. The money supply helps determine the general level of interest rates paid for the use of money, employment, prices, and economic growth. Many economists believe the money supply is the most important determinant of these variables.

13. Who determines the money supply?
The Federal Open Market Committee of the Federal Reserve System.

14. Why are interest charges important?
For many reasons. First, interest plays a large part in the cost of living. All business firms borrow to conduct their operations—some more than others. These include firms at every stage of production. So interest is a charge which is added on at each link of the production chain. This is a cost which must eventually be paid by the consumer. If it is not paid by consumers, output cannot be sustained. Thus, interest rates also are a determining factor of the level of business activity. Additionally, interest rates influence production because interest rates influence the amount business spends for investment in plant and equipment—the third largest amount of spending for the country's annual output. (Interest has this effect because a part of the country's annual investment is financed by borrowing.)

15. Do interest rate changes and tight money have other effects?
Yes. Consider what happens when the Government is restricting money and credit. Firms find loans difficult to obtain and investment tumbles. Small business is especially hard hit because the larger firms tend to have their credit needs catered to first. Further, when investment falls, firms which produce machinery or build factories find their orders slumping and lay off workers while cutting their own orders for goods. The economy pays for high interest in income not earned and in output not produced.

Federal Reserve Banks Are Not Owned By the Government

To keep their control of the Federal Reserve System, bankers have continued to mislead the general public and Congress ever since the Fed's founding in 1913. Many idiots, even today on CNBC, falsely believe the Federal Reserve is owned by the U.S. Government.

This author can still recall one of the most famous talking heads, a financial news reporter, proclaiming, "We have the greatest Central Bank in the whole world!" when the markets miraculously rose after the bank's self-engineered credit crisis hit.

The rise occurred, of course, because the fix was in and the $30 Trillion heist was on, as the Federal Reserve began secretly exchanging nearly $30 Trillion in U.S. taxpayer- and U.S. Government-backed electronic credits (and other cash-equivalents) for the worthless toxic securities on the books of the banks and elite.

It is remarkable how blind and utterly stupid some of the talking heads on TV are. Yes, even as a Christian, it is tough to sit and listen to sheer idiocy and not decry it.

"Quantitative Easing"—the Great Misnomer

There are many, many examples of the Federal Reserve's subterfuge, but one of this book's favorite mind-benders is the use of the phrase, "Quantitative Easing," or "QE3." Instead of plainly telling the public the Federal Reserve is using taxpayer-backed money via Fed credits (and/or U.S. cash and U.S. Treasury securities) to purchase worthless mortgage securities from the banks and government securities at auction because no one else will, the Fed attempts to disguise its true actions by creating the mesmerizing phrase, "Quantitative Easing." This terminology is designed to mislead the public and make it ***seem like*** the Federal Reserve is trying to help the economy!

In reality, the Fed is just giving the banks and rich people free money, as the securities they have been bringing to the Fed, in exchange for U.S. taxpayer-backed cash, are worthless, or worth only a fraction of their face value. With respect to its purchase of U.S. Government securities---this is purely inflationary and is a direct tax on the consuming public! As anyone on food stamps and anyone of the TRULY UNEMPLOYED (estimated at over 100,000,000 strong, now) understand, these bankers have done nothing to help the economy. They only realize they can't buy food for their families because costs keep rising and there are no jobs.

All the Federal Reserve and the bankers are doing is enriching the select by putting trillions of dollars into the pocketbooks of the banks—and the pocketbooks of their handlers---the elite owners of the Federal Reserve Banks.

Each word, every pronouncement and every incantation made by this den of vipers is carefully crafted to deceive and disguise their ongoing abuse of a typical American's natural good nature and trusting manner. Mr. Bernanke is a pro at using eloquent terms to diffuse and confuse, as he apparently learned well from the master of gibberish in banker-speak, his predecessor, Alan Greenspan.

This is the man who put the pieces in place to accomplish the grand heist by conditioning the public of the galactically stupid notion the Fed can't see a bubble forming and can't do anything about it…ergo, according to the Fed, artificially keeping rates low and exchanging good U.S. paper for toxic, bad paper has nothing to do with a bubble, or any other economic problem on the horizon! This, of course, is complete rubbish.

The utter nonsense which came out of this man's mouth, whether in front of Congress, the Queen of England or the general public is nothing short of stunning. It was even more stunning when uneducated Congressmen sat and became mesmerized by his arrogant gibberish, while he, in conspiracy with the Federal Reserve owners and members, set in motion the housing bubble and credit crisis.

As history reveals, it was Mr. Greenspan who initiated the major bailout of Wall Street during the Long Term Capital Management crisis and the NASDAQ collapse in 2000. This was accomplished by what Wall Street called the "Greenspan Put" and his easy money policies. He kept rates artificially too low and spent monies supporting markets---all in violation of the true spirit and workings of capitalism and the original intent of the Federal Reserve Act. Easy Al created the housing bubble through cheap interest rates and gushing flow of easy money in his effort to distort and artificially inflate the collapsing equity markets.

The Results of Mr. Greenspan's work was the raw destruction of millions of family's' wealth around the world, millions and millions of foreclosed homes and a very, very long unemployment line for the masses.

A couple of things which did increase, however, under the guidance of Mr. Greenspan, Mr. Bernanke and Ms. Yellen were the number of people on food stamps. This has become a real gusher for their legacy, as the food stamp population has grown to approximately 50 million people in the United States and real unemployment numbers are above great depression levels (see The $30 Trillion Heist---Follow The Money! Volume II, Chapter 15 "A Word on Unemployment").

To various elitist partners of the Fed Chairmen, however, this matters not. These elite were all ultimately taken care of through the actions of the Federal Reserve and recovered 100% of their toxic paper losses and went on to create Assflation™, allowing them to make money in their targeted and preferred asset classes.

Are Bankers the gods of Death?

George Clooney in the movie, "Michael Clayton," says: "I am Shiva, the god of death!" Mr. Greenspan's actions certainly caused a credit crisis and mortgage bubble which inflicted pain upon tens of millions of people and there is no question, in this author's mind, the actions of the current members of the Federal Reserve System have served only the interests of the banks and their elite and directly heisted nearly $30 Trillion secretly from the American Republic.

Are this book's words too harsh for this group of elitists?

Are they gods of death (or trying to be?)? Nearly every single war in history has been caused by economics, with even most religious wars started and fomented because of the poverty of the masses. Because bankers LEND money to governments (making wars possible to be fought even when tax receipts don't cover the war debt and payment for things like ammunition, tanks, planes and artillery!), bankers MAKE THE MOST MONEY when the government is at WAR.

Through the bankers' restriction of credit and manipulation of the money supply, they also create depressions and economic hardship, forcing millions out of work. Ultimately if pushed long and hard enough, people become violent and revolt, or set themselves against other nations in an attempt to survive and thrive in an austere economic climate.

The Rothschild banking family in Europe and the U.K. learned this secret back in the days of Napoleon and nothing has changed since then. The bankers have no interest in a debt-free America, or debt-free world. The more debt we have, the greater the interest payments will become. Because of the banking elite's love for money, they think NOTHING of causing, creating or supporting conflicts between governments around the world. As discussed in Chapter 7, "Our Constitution---Just a Quick Word---You Won't Be Bored!," they have often financed both sides of a war, ensuring the loser is forced by the winner to make payments on the debt incurred fighting it. Of course, the winner must pay as well!

To add kindling to the raging fire of fractional reserve banking and the system of the Federal Reserve controlled by the wealthy elite, bankers discovered late in the 20th Century a whole new way to make money. Because people in love with money can never get enough of it, getting rich on the fractional reserve banking system wasn't enough for these greedy monsters. They have now ventured, on a nearly COMPLETELY UNREGULATED BASIS, into the infinitely leveraged world of derivatives and swaps---betting, trading, selling and buying derivatives securities positions totaling close to ten times the **world's Gross Domestic Product.**

The derivative's system in place today, combined with the ongoing actions of the trading and selling regimes inside the banks, have placed the entire, civilized world at financial risk and has assured its doom. This is not an understatement. The evidence in these pages should overwhelmingly convince anyone of this fact. If this is not enough to convince you, then make sure you read D'Apocalypse™ Now!---The Doomsday Cycle. It describes, for everyone to understand, how and why derivatives will be the doom of the Western financial world.

This evidence should scare everybody---but it should especially scare the bankers and the ruling elite. Some of them might fear for their own salvations and even be saved, with the Holy Spirit convicting them, forcing their hearts to turn to God, instead of to self and seek His forgiveness.

Perhaps some will even have the courage to give away their wealth and truly follow the path of righteousness, before the greatest destroyer arrives.

We can all be assured of one thing, however: in the end times, no matter what system the bankers and the elite have in place, if anything, the greatest destroyer WILL arrive and demolish whatever they have built under their current schemes, completely. The sheer wake and impact of destruction, wiping out trillions of dollars instantly will be God's way of destroying the modern-day temples these men and women have built as shrines to themselves. It will be awesome and frightening to behold the pure power and impact of the destruction---trillion, by trillion, by trillion! This author cannot imagine what the Day of Judgment will be like for those who are not saved.

Wholesale Destruction of the Banking System by the D'Apocalypse™

The major subject of this book is not D'Apocalypse™ (the DEBT AND DERIVATIVES APOCALYPSE), but it does include a discussion about the wholesale destruction and compromise of the Western banking system as a result of a pre-planned debacle brought about by the banks and the elite.

When D'Apocalypse™ arrives and after they have caused enough pain, the bankers WILL bargain for global control over monetary policy and the money supply. Once this is accomplished, they will then reflate the system, in one form or another, to ensure future generations of elite families can continue to be served by the population of people around them.

The bankers will undoubtedly call in all their debt chips and threaten the politicians with continued economic doom if they are not bailed out on the backs of the taxpayer (once again), as they have many times before in history. This time, however, they will attempt to implement control on a centralized, world-wide basis, encouraging governments to consolidate the monetary system under one roof, for "better control, so this never happens again…."

It sounds incredible, but this is precisely what this book and trilogy expects they will attempt to do. To the outside world, it will appear their entire empire is collapsing around them, however, they will try to force a hard pivot and ***make the world*** bail them out---once again….this time not with a mere $30 Trillion, but ***with an infinite supply of cash*** supplied from their control over the world's printing presses!

The collapse should take place beginning in the mid-to-late part of 2015 (or, if the bankers cut the right deal with the next candidates for President, possibly right after the election in 2016, but this seems less likely) and the grasp for global monetary control to happen before 2020.

Their grab for power will only come after there is a lot of pain, suffering and hopelessness among the people---this is when the bankers and elite will strike. This could be any time after the market starts falling apart in 2015, but is more likely to be after a couple of years of economic agony, when 2017 begins.

Gold will be a great contrary indicator. The higher the price goes, the more out of control the system will be and the more likely the bankers will make their move for global monetary control.

Global Monetary Control—the End Game

The bankers believe this time, they will have such extensive leverage over politicians they can convince governments to deploy a newly created global, centralized banking system for the entire trading world. One of their tactics will be to feign magnanimity by offering to "forgive" some of the government debt (the bankers hold, or control, the debt of nations for nearly every major nation on earth) supposedly owed to them, in exchange for the elite's ability to run a new, global, centralized banking system.

This is the most likely scenario for how the banks and the wealthy elite will try to continue their scheme to defraud the people via the implementation of a global fractional reserve banking, monetary policy, money printing and a derivatives trading system they can ride rough shod over. They only care and want to ensure it is controlled by a handful of elite families and companies---this is the elite's dream and they are very close to making this dream a reality.

Their ultimate tactics may take a different form, but the damage which is going to be inflicted upon the wealth of nations and the common man, all over the world, will be TRAGIC when the derivatives collapse occurs.

God's Power Far Outweighs the Bankers

God's power far outweighs anything in the universe, as well as anything Wall Street, the bankers and the wealthy elite can throw at us and it is very likely, in their confidence and arrogance, they will underestimate what the response will be from the people, from God's people, all around the world.

As rioting and violence spreads from Greece, Brazil and Italy to the streets of America and the rest of Western Europe, with the youth unemployed, the middle class without jobs, crime skyrocketing and older people on fixed incomes finding the cost of bread and butter inflated beyond belief, the banks and the elite may have more on their hands than what they bargained for. This happened during the credit crisis and could easily happen again during D'Apocalypse™. Most wealthy people keep their heads buried in the sand, sipping their Margaritas, driving their Ferraris and steering their yachts. It is interesting the wealthy are playing, while the U.S. Government is arming itself to the teeth, apparently preparing itself for a domestic revolution.

Just as happened at the height of the credit crisis, there will be exceptional, elite casualties due to their over confidence and oversized egos---the size of the universe. Of course, it is not likely to be one of the families who helped found the Federal Reserve (or their heirs).

The playbook for our economy is a playbook which came straight out of hell, with Satan's puppets calling the signals. God is stepping in soon to try and teach those who are in love with money a very big lesson, as knowingly, or unknowingly, they are helping to implement the devil's master plan.

The culmination of this plan is a system where every transaction is controlled and the beast emerges, where, indeed, if you don't have a number you won't be able to buy, or sell, anything from the elite's newly privatized, centralized bank with global banking power and authority.

There is no shortage of the love for money on Wall Street. If what The Bible says is true---"The love of money is the root of all evil…"---then Wall Street and the banks are purely evil and are destined for a confrontation with God Himself.

We should all make preparations to protect ourselves and our loved ones now, spiritually and otherwise—but especially if you work on Wall Street, or for one of the banks.

You need to ask yourself "What would God say if I was earning a living from one of these institutions?" It doesn't matter if you are a secretary, trader, salesman, executive or flunky bean counter—the monies they pay you with are dirty monies taken surreptitiously off the backs of the taxpayer.

Every single large bank should have been bankrupted during the credit crisis.

Chapter 9
The $30 Trillion Heist

The Federal Reserve (and its member banks) in conjunction with other central banks around the world manipulate the supply of money and, as history proves, has caused great harm to the world's and nation's economies, including the Fed's own admission they caused the original Great Depression in the 1930s.

Of greater current and grave concern today, however, are the actions of the Federal Reserve during the credit crisis and the most recent facts uncovered indicating there may have been a heist of nearly $30 Trillion from the U.S. Treasury via the use of funds created by the Federal Reserve without the approval of Congress. These monies were used to secretly bailout banks, both internationally-based banks and domestic banks, along with other institutions and companies who have nothing to do with banking, or the Federal Reserve. It is an open question if the Fed bailed out certain wealthy, elite individuals.

The General Accounting Office, the official investigative unit of the U.S. Government, was empowered by Congress to initiate a partial audit of the Federal Reserve. The results were beyond troubling. Their report to Congress indicated nearly $30 TRILLION in secret bailout money was GIVEN to the banks and other large institutions---unbeknownst to the general public, federal government or Congress itself.

The sheer enormity of the heist is what is staggering. The entire U.S. GDP is only approximately $15 Trillion. This heist was nearly DOUBLE the national output of the entire country. Not only will the heist cause a massive increase in our national debt in the likely scenario U.S. cash, Fed electronic credits or U.S. treasury securities were issued in exchange for worthless securities (which to this day are very likely still sitting on the Fed's books), but ultimately, taxpayer's are on the hook for up to nearly $30 Trillion! Actually, it could be $30 Trillion PLUS INTEREST the taxpayers will pay to the banks, institutions and individuals who came running up to the Fed window to exchange their bad paper for good U.S. currency!!

There is only one word to describe this: ASTONISHING. It is astonishing in its size and it is astonishing in how brashly, secretly and connivingly the Federal Reserve, the banks and the elite took advantage of the American people.

The big problem is this heist and issuance of TRILLIONS of dollars in American Currency was done in secret, without Congressional approval. It represents the epitome in self-dealing---with no regard for being a good fiduciary, as the Fed's and banks' actions appear to be executed with utter contempt for the law. A good legal term for this kind of heinous activity is a "Capricious breach of fiduciary responsibility."

Others will call it plain, old fashioned piracy and thievery during the high tide of a rolling sea of digital currency.

There is a strong possibility and this book believes, the Fed and its co-conspirators **intentionally** violated the law, **intentionally** exceeded their authority, **intentionally** violated their oaths and commitments of office and **intentionally** abrogated their fiduciary responsibilities by sidestepping, **intentionally**, the approval of Congress in providing **additional, unapproved,** bailout monies to the banks and the elite.

They seized control of the money press and self-dealt to themselves because they could see the limits and difficulty with which Congress approved funds for the U.S. Treasury in the use of TARP (Troubled Asset Relief Program) funds to bail out bad loans at the banks.

This book postulates a theory the Fed, the banks and the elite ***knew*** the likelihood for additional bailout money from Congress was near ZERO and therefore decided to take matters into their own hands, burying the country in the process, by initiating a staggering set of secret bailouts totaling nearly $30 Trillion.

To accomplish this, they intentionally broke the law and intentionally abrogated and ignored their fiduciary responsibilities. The country will need either a court to decide this occurred, or force a full-unabridged and unrestricted audit of the Federal Reserve System and the member Reserve Banks, with no exceptions, internationally, or otherwise. This is the only way to find out what is buried in the vaults, records, facilities and hidden transactions of the Federal Reserve System and its member Federal Reserve Regional Banks.

TARP was a program approved by Congress for the government to purchase distressed assets and equity from financial institutions to strengthen the financial sector. It was signed into law by President George W. Bush on October 3, 2008.

It got approved because largely, then U.S. Treasury Secretary Henry Paulson (the ex-CEO of Goldman Sachs) and Ben Bernanke, Chairman of the Federal Reserve, scared the dickens out of everyone. When testifying before Congress after being questioned about the sheer magnitude (and shock!) of the $700 Billion request in TARP funds, Mr. Paulson responded, "…..we have a VERY BIG PROBLEM!"

In Mr. Paulson's book, On The Brink he discusses how approximately 7 months before the passage of the TARP bill he received a phone call on March 15, 2008 at his home from the CEO of Goldman Sachs, Lloyd Blankfein, with Mr. Blankfein providing Mr. Paulson a very detailed analysis of the growing credit crisis and market situation. Mr. Paulson indicates in his book Mr. Blankfein's conclusion was "apocalyptic." Over the course of the next several months, Mr. Blankfein's admonition and resulting scenario of financial doom began and started to shake things up in Washington.

The TARP program authorized expenditures of $700 billion. The Dodd–Frank Wall Street Reform and Consumer Protection Act reduced the amount authorized to $475 billion. By October 11, 2012, the Congressional Budget Office (CBO) stated that total disbursements would be $431 billion and estimated the total cost, including grants for mortgage programs that have not yet been made, would be $24 billion (Source: Congressional Budget Office "CBO REPORT ON THE TROUBLED ASSET RELIEF PROGRAM, October 2012").

The public was told the extent of the bailout was "only" the $700 Billion, as reduced by Dodd-Frank, per above. At least, this was the public's perception of what the total of the bailout SHOULD HAVE BEEN---as passed in accordance with law.

However, as presented and discovered in the GAO audit, it now appears the Federal Reserve System, the member banks and the Board of Governors may have schemed secretly to defraud the American public by engaging in secret bailouts, unauthorized by Congress and unauthorized in the original charter of the Federal Reserve Act of 1913.

The Federal Reserve issued up to nearly $30 TRILLION in electronic credits, U.S. Treasury securities or cash in exchange for worthless, near worthless or securities worth only a fraction of their face value, thereby robbing the American people. It is unknown how much of the nearly $30 Trillion may still be on the Fed's books because the Fed's special accounting standards allow it to use off-balance vehicles and the ability to list an asset at its "face" value, even though the security itself might be worthless. Only a full-blown, unrestricted audit will tell the tale of these shenanigans.

Under Mr. Bernanke's and Ms. Yellen's leadership and blessing, the New York Federal Reserve Bank, along with other member banks, exchanged trillions of dollars of cash-equivalent U.S. currency for toxic assets---all under the secret veil of silence with foreign banks, domestic banks, corporations, institutions, and even possibly wealthy individuals---without the knowledge or approval of Congress.

This is economic warfare against the people of the United States. It is warfare when anyone steals the entire Gross Domestic Product of a nation TIMES two! It is obviously in direct violation of the letter and spirit of the law as it was set forth in the Federal Reserve Act of 1913 and the spirit and intent of the TARP legislation approved by the President of the United States and Congress on October 3, 2008.

Among many restrictions, rules and regulations, the Federal Reserve Act sets forth limits on what the Federal Reserve can and cannot do, in Open Market Operations.

Open Market Operations are what takes place when the Federal Reserve is buying, selling or swapping securities with other member banks. The Act states specifically the Federal Reserve, in its Open Market Operations can ONLY involve itself in the purchase of U.S. Treasury Securities, banker's acceptances and commercial paper (see definitions, which follow in subsection "Fiduciary Breach," for the latter two types of securities). Any kind of transaction MUST be collateralized in a fashion which is beyond excellent, as our lawmakers wanted to make sure there wasn't any collusion going on with a renegade Fed exchanging AAA U.S. Treasury securities, Fed Credits or U.S. cash for other types of securities, which due to potential collusion, could be artificially inflated in price and of inferior grade. This is clearly defined in the Act in its large number of provisions speaking to the kinds, types and manner in which the Fed can engage in activities with the banks.

NOWHERE IN THE ORIGINAL ACT IS THE FEDERAL RESERVE AUTHORIZED TO PURCHASE, OR OTHERWISE SWAP FOR, PACKAGES OF TOXIC MORTGAGE POOLS AND DEBT SECURITIES, OR OTHER KINDS OF WORTHLESS DERIVATIVE SECURITIES, FROM FAILING, OR NON-FAILING INSTITUTIONS, WHILE FRAUDULENTLY VALUING THOSE TOXIC SECURITIES (IN COLLUSION WITH THE BANKS AND ELITE) AT PRICES SIGNIFICANTLY ABOVE FAIR MARKET VALUE.

THE FEDERAL RESERVE ACT WAS WRITTEN TO AVOID STICKING THE TAXPAYER WITH THE LOSSES FROM THIS KIND OF COLLUSION.

THIS IS THE KEY TO THE SUSPECTED FRAUD AND THE FOCUS OF THE THEORY OF THEFT IN THIS BOOK.

The Fed has relied on an amendment from 1968 allowing it to transact in agency paper of the federal government (e.g., FNMA, Freddie Mac, etc. are ground zero for the investment fraud the banking and ratings industry foisted on the American public) by utilizing them as collateral on loans for or from a commercial bank, or other party. The problem is these agency securities were fraudulently pooled and fraudulently valued by the ratings agencies---AS WAS WELL KNOWN TO THE GENERAL PUBLIC AND THE FEDERAL RESERVE during the time of the heist.

The Fed ignored this and inflated their values to provide TRILLIONS of dollars to the banks and the elite. It is possible the supposedly short-term loans the Fed made (by law, the Fed is only supposed to make short term loans, generally 90 days and no longer than 180 days, depending on the transaction) have continued to "rollover" to this very day, effectively creating a long-term loan and resulting in yet another potential direct violation of the Act. This would allow the banks and elite to ***keep*** the U.S. taxpayer-backed money, with the Fed winding up with worthless securities fraudulently valued on its books at exorbitantly high prices.

These unauthorized "long-term" interest-free loans could then just be parked in U.S. Treasury securities---getting the American public to pay banks interest on trillions and trillions of dollars given to them in exchange for their worthless paper! Here is an excerpt from the statute:

-STATUTE-
Subject to such limitations, restrictions, and regulations as the Board of Governors of the Federal Reserve System may prescribe, any Federal reserve bank may make advances to any individual, partnership, or corporation on the promissory notes of such individual, partnership, or corporation secured by direct obligations of the United States or by any obligation which is a direct obligation of, or fully guaranteed as to principal and interest by any agency of the United States. Such advances shall be made for periods not exceeding 90 days and shall bear interest at rates fixed from time to time by the Federal reserve bank, subject to the review and determination of the Board of Governors of the Federal Reserve System.

1968 - Pub. L. 90-505 added promissory notes secured by any obligation which is a direct obligation of, or fully guaranteed as to principal and interest by, any agency of the United States to the list of types of promissory notes on which federal reserve banks may make advances to individuals, partnerships, and corporations.
(Source: U.S. House of Representatives, 12 USC Sec. 347c, 01/015.2013 (112-90), TITLE 12 - BANKS AND BANKING, CHAPTER 3 - FEDERAL RESERVE SYSTEM, SUBCHAPTER IX - POWERS AND DUTIES OF FEDERAL RESERVE BANKS, Sec. 347c. Advances to individuals, partnerships, and corporations; security; interest rate, as retrieved from http://uscode.house.gov/view.xhtml?req=(title:12%20section:347c%20edition:prelim)%20OR%20(granuleid:USC-prelim-title12-section347c)&f=treesort&edition=prelim&num=0&jumpTo=true).

Unfortunately for our great nation, the Federal Reserve received and took in these fraudulently rated and fraudulently valued securities and did not swap them at fair market value, because most of them were likely worthless, or near worthless (why else would the banks rush to get them off their books, to the tune of nearly $30 TRILLION DOLLARS?).

The Fed GAVE the banks and the elite the U.S. cash-equivalent of 100% of the face value (or values far in excess of the toxic securities' fair market value) for the toxic securities being unloaded by the banks onto the Fed. This valued the toxic securities far in excess of their fair market value, with the U.S. taxpayer on the hook because the Fed exchanged taxpayer-backed Fed electronic credits, U.S. Treasury securities or outright cash for up to 100% of the face value of these worthless, or near worthless, pieces of paper.

This allowed the banks and the elite to purge themselves of all the horrid investments they made and become immediately profitable---thanks to the U.S. taxpayer and an unknowing Congress---because of the secrecy and veil of silence the Fed kept over these unapproved and secret bailouts.

If the Fed fraudulently allowed the true fair market value of these worthless securities to be falsely inflated back to their original "face" value, in order to somehow justify giving away the cash equivalent of nearly $30 Trillion in U.S. monies, God help them. There isn't a court in the land which would appreciate any fiduciary selling, or lending, prized assets (belonging to an owner, the U.S. taxpayer, for whom the fiduciary is responsible for making good investment decisions), in exchange for worthless property!!

A fiduciary in such a court room would be in jail for fraud and, if there was collusion among the other parties involved in the transaction, theft as well.

If the Fed played this game, as it appears it may have, it was literally as if someone had a $100 Monopoly bill (from the board game, "Monopoly") and walked up to the Fed and the Fed gave them $100 in U.S. Treasury securities---except the Fed did it with $30 TRILLION!

The heart of the problem lies in the fact the owners and members of the Board of Directors of the Federal Reserve Banks are working for the benefit of private companies (the Federal Reserve Banks and their members)---and represent the banks---not the people of the United States. This is where the collusion lies, along with the great conflicts of interest which exist at the Federal Reserve.

THIS BOOK ASKS THE IMPORTANT QUESTION IF THIS IS WHAT HAPPENED AND IS REALLY CONTINUING TO HAPPEN WITHIN THE BERNANKE AND YELLEN FEDERAL RESERVE SYSTEM??

The now published secret bailout activities are particularly infuriating because the worthless, or near worthless, derivatives and mortgage securities loaded on the books of thousands of banks were the securities these banks used as collateral for loans, or in selling transactions, with the Federal Reserve. Furthermore, these securities were delivered to the Fed from both foreign and domestic banks and institutions.

If these securities somehow remain hidden on the books of the Fed, in the future, the American public will not be able to sell these securities to offset the issuance of the electronic credits, U.S. cash, U.S. Treasury bills, notes and bonds issued in exchange for the worthless paper. This will lead to massive losses for the American taxpayer and will come out in future deficits and a massive inflation tax, with ominous economic implications for all.

This is the real dagger waiting to strike at the heart of America if the Federal Reserve is hiding, or has hidden, these kinds of transactions and their true value is not accounted for at fair market value on the books of the either the Federal Reserve, or the Federal Reserve Banks.

The Federal Reserve, operating under Ben Bernanke's and Ms. Yellen's direction, REIMBURSED AND GUARANTEED the LOSSES on the books of the bankers and the wealthy elite to the tune of nearly $30 TRILLION.

This is also the major reason why there has been NO economic recovery. The money didn't go to the economy and regular working people in the U.S. and Europe did not benefit—nearly 100% of the money went into the portfolios of the elite, who were able to recover all of their losses on their bad investments—courtesy of the U.S. taxpayer.

The partial GAO audit only covered the period between December 1, 2007-July 21, 2010, where plain as day they indicate over $26 Trillion in secret bailouts happened.

It makes one wonder what else has gone on at the Federal Reserve under the veil of secrecy and self-dealing. Some of the key GAO audit results are presented later in this chapter.

Fiduciary Breach

Aside from apparently breaching its fiduciary duty in the most appalling manner imaginable, the Fed apparently took the law into its own hands to please its owners and exceeded by a factor of 23 times (i.e., 2300%!) the legal authority Congress painstakingly granted the U.S. Treasury to purchase distressed securities under the $700 Billion TARP emergency legislation. Here are some of the key provisions of the original Federal Reserve Act of 1913. You be the judge if the suspicions, accusations and facts presented in this book are truth, falsities or conspiracy theories.

December 23, 1913. [H. R. 7837.] [Public, No. 43.]

CHAP. 6.—An Act To provide for the establishment of Federal reserve banks, to furnish an elastic currency, to afford means of rediscounting commercial paper, to establish a more effective supervision of banking in the United States, and for other purposes.

Federal Reserve Act.

Be it enacted by the Senate and House of Representatives of the United States of America in Congress assembled, That the short title of this Act shall be the "Federal Reserve Act."

Terms construed.

Wherever the word "bank" is used in this Act, the word shall be held to include State bank, banking association, and trust company, except where national banks or Federal reserve banks are specifically referred to.

Authority and powers of Board.

SEC. 11. The Federal Reserve Board shall be authorized and empowered:

Examination, etc., of reserve and member banks.

(a) To examine at its discretion the accounts, books and affairs of each Federal reserve bank and of each member bank and to require such statements and reports as it may deem necessary. The said board shall publish once each week a statement showing the condition of each Federal reserve bank and a consolidated statement for all Federal reserve banks. Such statements shall show in detail the

Published statements.

Doubtful assets.

(g) To require the writing off of doubtful or worthless assets upon the books and balance sheets of Federal reserve banks.

Open-market operations.

OPEN-MARKET OPERATIONS.

Federal reserve banks may deal in commercial paper, etc.

SEC. 14. Any Federal reserve bank may, under rules and regulations prescribed by the Federal Reserve Board, purchase and sell in the open market, at home or abroad, either from or to domestic or foreign banks, firms, corporations, or individuals, cable transfers and bankers' acceptances and bills of exchange of the kinds and maturities by this Act made eligible for rediscount, with or without the indorsement of a member bank.

Additional powers.

Every Federal reserve bank shall have power:

Gold transactions.

(a) To deal in gold coin and bullion at home or abroad, to make loans thereon, exchange Federal reserve notes for gold, gold coin, or gold certificates, and to contract for loans of gold coin or bullion, giving therefor, when necessary, acceptable security, including the hypothecation of United States bonds or other securities which Federal reserve banks are authorized to hold;

Bonds, notes, etc.

(b) To buy and sell, at home or abroad, bonds and notes of the United States, and bills, notes, revenue bonds, and warrants with a maturity from date of purchase of not exceeding six months, issued in anticipation of the collection of taxes or in anticipation of the receipt of assured revenues by any State, county, district, political subdivision, or municipality in the continental United States, including irrigation, drainage and reclamation districts, such purchases to be made in accordance with rules and regulations prescribed by the Federal Reserve Board;

Commercial exchange.

(c) To purchase from member banks and to sell, with or without its indorsement, bills of exchange arising out of commercial transactions, as hereinbefore defined;

(Source: Congressional Record, PUBLIC--No. 43--63rd CONGRESS, H.R. 7837, as retrieved from http://famguardian.org/TaxFreedom/Authorities/FedLaw/FedReserveAct-38Stat251-275,690-691.pdf).

For those non-financial students, here are the definitions of "bills of exchange" and "bankers acceptances."

> "**Bills of exchange** are similar to checks and promissory notes. They can be drawn by individuals or banks and are generally transferable by endorsements. The difference between a promissory note and a bill of exchange is that this product is transferable and can bind one party to pay a third party that was not involved in its creation. If these bills are issued by a bank, they can be referred to as bank drafts. If they are issued by individuals, they can be referred to as trade drafts." (Source: Investopedia, as retrieved from http://www.investopedia.com/terms/b/billofexchange.asp).

> "**Bankers Acceptance** is a short-term debt instrument issued by a firm that is guaranteed by a commercial bank. Banker's acceptances are issued by firms as part of a commercial transaction. These instruments are similar to T-Bills and are frequently used in money market funds. Banker's acceptances are traded at a discount from face value on the secondary market, which can be an advantage because the banker's acceptance does not need to be held until maturity. Banker's acceptances are regularly used financial instruments in international trade." (Source: ibid, as retrieved from http://www.investopedia.com/terms/b/bankersacceptance.asp).

The following key excerpts from actual audits, opinion letters, Senatorial findings and other key documents, including those involving off-balance vehicles, help to reveal how the bankers and Fed partners could accomplish a theoretical outright heist like this and explains, very well, the reasons for the continuing economic malaise in America and why the coming D'Apocalypse™ will occur.

The Fed's actions cause tremendous damage to the general economy because it takes money out of the people's hands and places the money into the hands of only a few very rich people, destroying cities, states and people's lives—all over the world.

Detroit---this is a major reason you are in trouble, along with profligate and out-of-control spending habits tied to exorbitant pension plans and other non-productive, social programs in your budget.

The following are the Federal Reserve's own auditor remarks from Deloitte & Touche dated March 5, 2013:

Deloitte.

Deloitte & Touche LLP
555 12th St. N.W.
Washington, DC 20004-1207
USA
Tel: +1 202 879 5600
Fax: +1 202 879 5309
www.deloitte.com

INDEPENDENT AUDITORS' REPORT

To the Board of Governors of the Federal Reserve System:

We have audited the accompanying financial statements of the Board of Governors of the Federal Reserve System (the "Board"), which are comprised of the balance sheets as of December 31, 2012 and 2011, and the related statements of operations, and cash flows for the years then ended, and the related notes to the financial statements. We also have audited the Board's internal control over financial reporting as of December 31, 2012, based on criteria established in *Internal Control—Integrated Framework* issued by the Committee of Sponsoring Organizations of the Treadway Commission.

Inherent Limitations of Internal Control Over Financial Reporting

Because of the inherent limitations of internal control over financial reporting, including the possibility of collusion or improper management override of controls, material misstatements due to error or fraud may not be prevented or detected and corrected on a timely basis. Also, projections of any evaluation of the effectiveness of the internal control over financial reporting to future periods are subject to the risk that the controls may become inadequate because of changes in conditions, or that the degree of compliance with the policies or procedures may deteriorate.

Deloitte & Touche LLP

March 5, 2013

(Source: 99th Annual Report 2012 Board Of Governors Of The Federal Reserve, page 322, as retrieved from http://www.federalreserve.gov/publications/annual-report/files/2012-annual-report.pdf).

As measured from December 1, 2007-July 21, 2010, the U.S. Government's General Accounting Office indicates, upon careful analysis and adding the bits and pieces together, **nearly $30 TRILLION** was secretly taken, courtesy of the U.S. taxpayers, in this 2 ½-year period!

Since the Federal Reserve Banks are private companies and the Federal Reserve System ***has never gone through a full audit---these amounts are also quite possibly, only the "tip of the iceberg."*** Needless to say, a demand and law requiring annual COMPLETE, UNABRIDGED, WITH NO LIMITS OF SCOPE audits of all activities and operations of the Fed should be implemented. Regardless of those results and because of the constant history of the Fed's actions in favor of only enriching and bailing out the banks and the elite at the expense of everyone else, the Fed should be simultaneously eliminated as an institution.

This first table shown in the GAO audit highlights (which you can see later on in this chapter, in subsection "The $26 Trillion as Reported by the GAO") proves over $16 TRILLION in "loans" were taken out from the Federal Reserve. The second table in subsection, "$10 Trillion Handed Out to Foreign Banks" of this chapter, shows an additional $10 TRILLION were taken out in foreign SWAPS. The Fed took in worthless, near worthless, or paper worth only a fraction of its face value—from both domestic and foreign institutions---and exchanged them for over $26 TRILLION in U.S. cash—electronically created right at the Fed's account for the institutions engaged in the transactions!

The entire United States Gross Domestic Product during 2012 was only $15.9 Trillion!!!

The Federal Reserve, on nothing but its own authority and in a massive breach of fiduciary responsibility, spent the equivalent of nearly two years-worth of the entire production of the United States to bail out the bankers and the elite families behind them.

Before discussing the Fed's ability to potentially HIDE (see Chapter 10, "Worthless Securities-How to Hide Them-Where They Go to Die!") the ultimate outcome of these "loans" and "swaps," suffice it to say there are GAPING holes in the Fed's accounting policies.

Even a cursory review of those policies will provide any reasonable person with extreme suspicion these transactions were NEVER repaid and remain in the state of "Neverland"---with the loans and swaps being automatically rolled over in favor of the bankers and elite---allowing them to use taxpayer cash against their worthless collateral which was iniquitously foisted onto the American Republic.

The Evidence

Here we will show how the Federal Reserve handed out $16 TRILLION (of the approximate $30 TRILLION the GAO audit exposes) in bailout money without a debate, without approval and without discussion with anyone else---except the Reserve Banks, the member banks and the owners hiding behind their board rooms. The result of this massive scheme was one of self-dealing to themselves, at the expense of everyone else in the United States.

According to the GAO's audit report, **the Fed unilaterally, without Congressional approval, CHANGED the kinds of securities** it would take in as collateral, and/or the kinds of securities it might purchase. The types of securities the Fed decided to deal in were once restricted under the very tight control of the original Federal Reserve Act, where the Fed was supposed to deal ONLY in U.S. Treasury securities (or transactions guaranteed by the U.S. Government), commercial paper and foreign exchange.

So what really happened? This book's interesting theory is the Fed saw Congress was going to provide NO MORE bail out money after Lehman Brothers went bust and they, along with the Reserve Banks, the member banks and the elite, apparently decided to change the law, on their own, and thereby accept virtually ANY KIND of worthless securities sitting on the banks' bankrupt balance sheets in exchange for taxpayer-backed cash and/or taxpayer-backed Federal Reserve credits to their accounts.

The theory has quite a bit of evidence to support it. It is also made in all sincerity because the mortgage pools and contracts the banks were dealing in and choking on were worthless, or nearly so, trading well below their face values. Most of the paper unloaded onto the Fed couldn't be traded at all, which should have caused the bankruptcy of every institution which made the poor business decisions to own the fraudulent paper in the first place. This included every single major bank in America!

No one wanted these securities because the ratings agencies had colluded with the mortgage and banking industry to fraudulently provide highly-graded ratings on worthless paper, with everyone playing along with Wall Street and the banks to defraud the general public. This only happened because they were being paid by the banks (i.e., bribe money!). Here is the GAO comment:

> "On March 11, 2008, the Federal Reserve Board announced the creation of the Term Securities Lending Facility (TSLF) to auction 28-day loans of U.S. Treasury securities to primary dealers to increase the amount of high-quality collateral available for these dealers to borrow against in the repurchase agreement markets. Through competitive auctions that allowed dealers to bid a fee to exchange harder-to-finance collateral for easier-to-finance Treasury securities, TSLF was intended to promote confidence among lenders and to reduce the need for dealers to sell illiquid assets into the markets, which could have further depressed the prices of these assets and contributed to a downward price spiral.26 TSLF auctioned loans of Treasury securities against two schedules of collateral.

Schedule 1 collateral included Treasury securities, agency debt, and agency MBS collateral that FRBNY **(Author's note: "FRBNY" is the Federal Reserve Bank of New York, which the Board of Governors designates as the agent to carry out its bidding in Federal Open Market Operations)** accepted in repurchase agreements for traditional open market operations with primary dealers.[27] Schedule 2 included schedule 1 collateral as well as a broader range of assets, including highly rated mortgage-backed securities.[28] **The Federal Reserve Board determined that providing funding support for private mortgage-backed securities through the schedule 2 auctions fell outside the scope of FRBNY's authority to conduct its securities lending program under section 14 of the Federal Reserve Act. Accordingly, for the first time during this crisis, the Federal Reserve Board invoked section 13(3) of the Federal Reserve Act to authorize the extension of credit, in this case in the form of Treasury securities, to nondepository institutions—in this case, the primary dealers.** (author's emphasis bold and/or underlined) As discussed later in this section, the Federal Reserve Board later expanded the range of collateral eligible for TSLF as the crisis intensified. TSLF closed on February 1, 2010. See appendix XIV for a more detailed explanation of this program.

[27]Before the crisis, FRBNY ran an overnight securities lending facility, the terms of which involved the lending of certain Treasury securities by FRBNY to primary dealers against other Treasury securities as collateral. Certain of the legal infrastructure for the traditional securities lending program was used for TSLF. Other legal and operational infrastructure had to be created specifically for TSLF.

[28]TSLF held separate auctions of Treasury securities against two different schedules of collateral to better calibrate the interest rate on TSLF loans to the level of risk associated with the collateral. The Federal Reserve Board set a higher minimum interest rate for schedule 2 TSLF auctions, which accepted riskier collateral types than schedule 1 auctions. For more information about how interest rates were determined for TSLF auctions, see appendix XIV."

(Source: **"FEDERAL RESERVE SYSTEM Opportunities Exist to Strengthen Policies and Processes for Managing Emergency Assistance, Report to Congressional Addressees,"** July 2011, hereinafter referred to as the

"GAO Audit," page 21-22, as retrieved from http://www.gao.gov/products/GAO-11-696).

Author's comment: PLEASE SEE DETAILED EXAMINATION OF SECTION 13(3) of The Federal Reserve Act in this chapter, which follows in subsection, "The Federal Reserve Act of 1913, Section 13." There is no basis, or authority granted, to accept private mortgage-backed securities according to the Act, in either its originally approved form, or in its current amended form.

Additionally, under Section 11(h) of the Act, the Board of Governors is required to suspend the operations of any Federal Reserve Bank in violation of the Act:

"SEC.11(h) The Federal Reserve Board shall be authorized and empowered: To suspend, for the violation of any of the provisions of this Act, the operations of any Federal reserve bank, to take possession thereof, minister the same during the period of suspension, and when deemed advisable, to liquidate or reorganize such bank."

The FRBNY is not authorized by the Act to deal in mortgage-backed and other forms of sketchy collateral, unless they are guaranteed by the United States government, or an agency of the United States government, and even then these securities must be handled with strong fiduciary responsibility, reasonable risk management practices and transactions must be exchange at FAIR MARKET VALUE when swapped, or otherwise traded, on the open market (i.e., the Fed isn't supposed to be able to purchase, or otherwise swap for, a rigged, inflated security and exchange it for U.S. cash!).

The letter and spirit of the Act from Section 13, paragraph ONE is quite clear on the types of securities the Fed can deal in. The Fed is also explicitly forbidden from supporting a failing institution which is another key requirement of the Act!

The GAO reported the following additional interesting, grave and concerning remarks regarding the Fed's unilateral actions during the credit crisis:

> "In September 2008, the bankruptcy of Lehman Brothers triggered an intensification of the financial crisis, and the <u>Federal Reserve Board modified the terms for its existing liquidity</u>

programs (author emphasis) to address worsening conditions. On September 14, 2008, shortly before Lehman Brothers announced it would file for bankruptcy, the Federal Reserve Board announced changes to TSLF (Term Securities Lending Facility-Auctioned loans of U.S. Treasury securities to primary dealers against eligible collateral-author's comment) and PDCF (Primary Dealer Credit Facility-Provided overnight cash loans to primary dealers against eligible collateral-author's comment) to provide expanded liquidity support to primary dealers. Specifically, the Federal Reserve Board announced that TSLF-eligible collateral would be expanded to include all investment-grade debt securities and PDCF-eligible collateral would be expanded to include all securities eligible to be pledged in the tri-party repurchase agreements system**, including noninvestment grade securities and equities.**[35] In addition, TSLF schedule 2 auctions would take place weekly rather than only bi-weekly. On September 21, 2008, the Federal Reserve Board announced that it would extend credit—on terms similar to those applicable for PDCF loans—to the U.S. and London broker-dealer subsidiaries of Merrill Lynch & Co. (Merrill Lynch), Goldman Sachs Group Inc. (Goldman Sachs), and Morgan Stanley to provide support to these subsidiaries as they became part of bank holding companies that would be regulated by the Federal Reserve System.[36] On September 29, 2008, the Federal Reserve Board also announced expanded support through TAF and the dollar swap lines. Specifically, the Federal Reserve Board doubled the amount of funds that would be available in each TAF auction cycle from $150 billion to $300 billion, and the FOMC authorized a $330 billion expansion of the swap line arrangements with foreign central banks.

Author's comment: There is no authority for the Fed to unilaterally change the Federal Reserve Act and EXPAND the kinds of eligible collateral it may receive! This is absolutely in violation of everything the Act stands for. It has NO AUTHORITY TO RECEIVE NONINVESTMENT GRADE SECURITIES AND EQUITIES!

[35]For TSLF, previously, only Treasury securities, agency securities, and AAA-rated mortgage-backed and asset-backed securities could be pledged. For PDCF, previously, eligible collateral had to have at least an investment-grade rating **(Author note: the**

ratings agencies were in on the fraud, slapping investment grade ratings to worthless pieces of paper)..."

"[36]Concurrently, the Federal Reserve Board announced that it had approved applications by Goldman Sachs and Morgan Stanley to become bank holding companies. In addition, Bank of America agreed to acquire Merrill Lynch, which would become part of a bank holding company pending completion of its merger with Bank of America, a bank holding company supervised by the Federal Reserve System upon completion of the acquisition. On November 23, 2008, in connection with other actions taken by Treasury, FDIC, and the Federal Reserve Board to assist Citigroup Inc., the Federal Reserve Board authorized FRBNY to extend credit to the **London-based broker-dealer of Citigroup** on terms similar to those applicable to PDCF loans..."(Source: GAO Audit, page 27).

"**In late 2008 and early 2009, the Federal Reserve Board again invoked its authority under section 13(3) of the Federal Reserve Act to authorize assistance to avert the failures of three institutions that it determined to be systemically significant:** (1) American International Group, Inc. (AIG); (2) Citigroup, Inc. (Citigroup); and (3) Bank of America Corporation (Bank of America)." (Source: GAO Audit, page 32, author's emphasis underlined).

With the Fed having secretly made these decisions in private, without consulting Congress, they EXTENDED the program to failed institutions even though the Federal Reserve Act **PROHIBITS BAILING OUT FAILING INSTITUTIONS and SECTION 13 of the Federal Reserve Act in its VERY FIRST PARAGRAPH, PROHIBITS "notes, drafts, or bills covering merely investments or issued or drawn for the purpose of carrying or trading in stocks, bonds, or other investment securities, except bonds and notes of the Government of the United States."**

KEY QUESTIONS NEEDING TO BE ASKED:

SHOULD CONGRESS BE PROSECUTING THESE PEOPLE THROUGH THE COURT SYSTEM???

HAVE THESE PEOPLE DECLARED ECONOMIC WAR ON THE UNITED STATES???

IF SO, SHOULD THESE PEOPLE BE TRIED FOR TREASON???

The Federal Reserve Act of 1913, Section 13

The following is the wording from the original Federal Reserve Act of 1913, Section 13:

The Federal Reserve Act of 1913
POWERS OF FEDERAL RESERVE BANKS.

SEC. 13. (Source: U.S. Congressional Record, as retrieved from http://archive.org/stream/congressionalrec51gunit#page/n681/mode/2up pages 1356-1357).

1356 CONGRESSIONAL RECORD—SENATE. DECEMBER 22.

1913. CONGRESSIONAL RECORD—SENATE. 1357

"Any Federal reserve bank may receive from any of its member banks, and from the United States, deposits of current funds in lawful money, national-bank notes, Federal reserve notes, or checks and drafts u on solvent member banks, payable upon presentation; or, solely for exchange purposes, may receive from other Federal reserve banks deposits of current funds in lawful money, national-bank notes, or checks and drafts upon solvent member or other Federal reserve banks, payable upon presentation. Upon the indorsement of any of its member banks, with a waiver of demand, notice and protest by such bank, any Federal reserve bank may discount notes, drafts, and bills of exchange arising out of actual commercial transactions; that is, notes, drafts, and bills of exchange issued or drawn for agricultural, industrial, or commercial purposes, or the proceeds of which have been used, or are to be used, for such purposes, the Federal Reserve Board to have the right to determine or define the character of the paper thus eligible for discount, within the meaning of this Act. **Nothing in this Act** contained shall be construed to prohibit such notes, drafts, and bills of exchange, secured by staple agricultural products, or other goods, wares, or merchandise from being eligible for such discount; **but such definition shall not include notes, drafts, or bills covering merely investments or issued or drawn for the purpose of carrying or**

> **trading in stocks, bonds, or other investment securities, except bonds and notes of the Government of the United States."**
> (Source: The Congressional Record, 1913, page 1356-1357 of The Federal Reserve Act, as retrieved from http://archive.org/stream/congressionalrec51gunit#page/n681/mode/2up).

The Federal Reserve Act from the Congressional Record of the 63rd Congress of December 22, 1913 provides MANY LIMITATIONS AND CLEARLY PROHIBITS THE FEDERAL RESERVE FROM ENTERING INTO TRANSACTIONS FOR NON-INVESTMENT GRADE SECURITIES AND DEFINITELY DOES NOT INCLUDE MORTGAGE-BACKED SECURITIES!

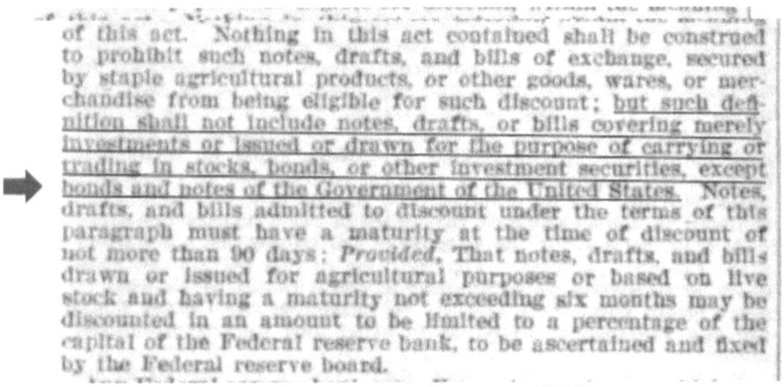
of this act. Nothing in this act contained shall be construed to prohibit such notes, drafts, and bills of exchange, secured by staple agricultural products, or other goods, wares, or merchandise from being eligible for such discount; but such definition shall not include notes, drafts, or bills covering merely investments or issued or drawn for the purpose of carrying or trading in stocks, bonds, or other investment securities, except bonds and notes of the Government of the United States. Notes, drafts, and bills admitted to discount under the terms of this paragraph must have a maturity at the time of discount of not more than 90 days: *Provided*, That notes, drafts, and bills drawn or issued for agricultural purposes or based on live stock and having a maturity not exceeding six months may be discounted in an amount to be limited to a percentage of the capital of the Federal reserve bank, to be ascertained and fixed by the Federal reserve board.

Source: ibid.

The provision the Federal Reserve and Mr. Bernanke is quoting for its authority, Section 13(3) of the Act, has NO BEARING OR RELATIONSHIP IN ANY WAY TO THE MANNER IN WHICH THE FEDERAL RESERVE ACTED TO BAIL OUT, SECRETLY, THE BANKS AND THE WEALTHY ELITE.

Additionally, even the Fed's reliance on Section 13(3) of the Act (as modified July 21, 1932) to accept non-U.S. government securities for discount appears to be AGAINST THE LAW---EVEN AS IT WAS REVISED IN 1932 and thereafter---clearly the securities the Fed was exchanging were investment securities!! They are clearly "verboten" in the Act!!

Before we quote Mr. Bernanke's testimony (on page 189), which provides the reader with the actual historic documentation of the Fed's claims and supposed reliance on the Federal Reserve Act, the following is the full Act in its CURRENT amended form.

This is the actual wording from Section 13, ***immediately preceding 13(3), which is the "cherry picked" section of the Federal Reserve Act*** which Mr. Bernanke relies upon. It is found under the U.S. House Code, 12 USC Sec. 343, Title 12, Chapter 3 Subchapter IX:

> 12 USC Sec. 343 01/05/2013 (112-90)
>
> -EXPCITE-
> TITLE 12 - BANKS AND BANKING
> CHAPTER 3 - FEDERAL RESERVE SYSTEM
> SUBCHAPTER IX - POWERS AND DUTIES OF FEDERAL RESERVE BANKS
>
> -HEAD-
> Sec. 343. Discount of obligations arising out of actual commercial transactions
>
> -STATUTE-
>
> ....Nothing in this chapter contained shall be construed to prohibit such notes, drafts, and bills of exchange, secured by staple agricultural products, or other goods, wares, or merchandise from being eligible for such discount, and the notes, drafts, and bills of exchange of factors issued as such making advances exclusively to producers of staple agricultural products in their raw state shall be eligible for such discount; ***but such definition shall not include notes, drafts, or bills covering merely investments*** or issued or drawn for the purpose of carrying or trading in stocks, bonds, or other investment securities, except bonds and notes of the Government of the United States. Notes, drafts, and bills admitted to discount under the terms of this paragraph must have a maturity at the time of discount of not more than ninety days, exclusive of grace.
>
> (Source: U.S. Congress, retrieved from 12 USC § 343 - Discount of obligations arising out of actual commercial transactions, as retrieved from: http://uscode.house.gov/view.xhtml?req=Discount+of+obligations+arising+out+of+actual+commercial+transactions%2C&f=treesort&fq=true&num=1&hl=true&edition=prelim&granuleId=USC-prelim-title12-section343).

The Heart of the Problem: Section 13 of the Federal Reserve Act as Amended by Dodd-Frank

The following is the full text of section 13 of the code for the Federal Reserve Act. ***It is a bit boring, but notice at the end (see arrow) how they snuck in the amendments from Dodd-Frank legislation to NOW ALLOW ANY INDIVIDUAL, PARTNERSHIP OR CORPORATION to use the Fed Window!!***

This is really bamboozling the public in such a shameless way it would seem absolutely unbelievable, except it is true. This is how they bail out rich, elite individuals and companies who have NO BUSINESS being at the Fed Window taking American tax dollars in exchange for worthless securities and allowing these groups to gamble with taxpayer monies.

-CITE-
12 USC Sec. 343 1/15/2013

-EXPCITE-
TITLE 12 - BANKS AND BANKING
CHAPTER 3 - FEDERAL RESERVE SYSTEM
SUBCHAPTER IX - POWERS AND DUTIES OF FEDERAL RESERVE BANKS

-HEAD-
Sec. 343. Discount of obligations arising out of actual commercial transactions

-STATUTE-
Upon the indorsement of any of its member banks, which shall be deemed a waiver of demand, notice and protest by such bank as to its own indorsement exclusively, any Federal reserve bank may discount notes, drafts, and bills of exchange arising out of actual commercial transactions; that is, notes, drafts, and bills of exchange issued or drawn for agricultural, industrial, or commercial purposes, or the proceeds of which have been used, or are to be used, for such purposes, the Board of Governors of the Federal Reserve System to have the right to determine or define the character of the paper thus eligible for discount, within the meaning of this chapter. ***Nothing in this chapter*** contained shall be construed to prohibit such notes, drafts, and bills of exchange, secured by staple agricultural products, or other goods, wares, or merchandise from being eligible for such discount, and the notes, drafts, and bills of exchange of factors issued as such making advances exclusively to producers of staple agricultural products in their raw state shall be eligible for such discount; but such definition ***shall not include*** notes, drafts, or bills covering merely investments or issued or drawn for ***the purpose of carrying or trading in stocks, bonds, or other investment securities***, except bonds and notes of the Government of the United States. Notes, drafts, and bills admitted to discount under the terms of this paragraph must have a maturity at the time of discount of not more than ninety days, exclusive of grace.

Author Note: As plain as day, Section 3 (A) is subject to the preamble of Section 13—which clearly forbids dealing in investments!

(3)(A) (1) In unusual and exigent circumstances, the Board of Governors of the Federal Reserve System, by the affirmative vote of not less than five members, may authorize any Federal reserve bank, during such periods as the said board may determine, at rates established in accordance with the provisions of section 357 of this title, to discount for any participant in any program or facility with broad-based eligibility, notes, drafts, and bills of exchange when such notes, drafts, and bills of exchange are indorsed or otherwise secured to the satisfaction ***of the Federal reserve bank***: Provided, That before discounting any such note, draft, or bill of exchange, ***the Federal reserve bank*** shall obtain evidence that such participant in any program or facility with broad-based eligibility is unable to secure adequate credit accommodations from other banking institutions. All such discounts for any participant in any program or facility with broad-based eligibility shall be subject to such limitations, restrictions, and regulations as the Board of Governors of the Federal Reserve System may prescribe.

Author note: The Federal Reserve Banks ARE OWNED and controlled at the board level by the COMMERCIAL BANKS and the ELITE!! This is truly a case of the fox watching the hen house!!!

It is an impossible conflict of interest to allow the Federal Reserve Banks to secure to their satisfaction collateral and securities tendered to them by the commercial banks, partnerships, corporations and individuals (Dodd-Frank legislation amended the Federal Reserve Act to allow this change---see the end of this Section 13 of the Act) in exchange for U.S. taxpayer-backed Federal Reserve Credits, U.S. Treasury securities or other cash-equivalents!! This is the key to the believed fraud this book describes as the heart of the problem of the Federal Reserve.

(B)(i) As soon as is practicable after July 21, 2010, the Board shall establish, by regulation, in consultation with the Secretary of the Treasury, the policies and procedures governing emergency lending under this paragraph. Such policies and procedures shall be designed to ensure that any emergency lending program or facility is for the purpose of providing liquidity to the financial system, and not to aid a failing financial company, and that the security for emergency loans is sufficient to protect taxpayers from losses and that any such program is terminated in a timely and orderly fashion. The policies and procedures established by the Board shall require that a Federal reserve bank assign, consistent with sound risk management practices and to ensure protection for the taxpayer, a lendable value to all collateral for a loan executed by a Federal reserve bank under this paragraph in determining whether the loan is secured satisfactorily for purposes of this paragraph.

(ii) The Board shall establish procedures to prohibit borrowing from programs and facilities by borrowers that are insolvent. Such procedures may include a certification from the chief executive officer (or other authorized officer) of the borrower, at the time the borrower initially borrows under the program or facility (with a duty by the borrower to update the certification if the information in the certification materially changes), that the borrower is not insolvent. A borrower shall be considered insolvent for purposes of this subparagraph, if the borrower is in bankruptcy, resolution under title II of the Dodd-Frank Wall Street Reform and Consumer Protection Act [12 U.S.C. 5381 et seq.], or. any other Federal or State insolvency proceeding

(iii) A program or facility that is structured to remove assets from the balance sheet of a single and specific company, or that is established for the purpose of assisting a single and specific company avoid bankruptcy, resolution under title II of the Dodd-Frank Wall Street Reform and Consumer Protection Act, or any other Federal or State insolvency proceeding, shall not be considered a program or facility with broad-based eligibility.

(iv) The Board may not establish any program or facility under this paragraph without the prior approval of the Secretary of the Treasury.

(C) The Board shall provide to the Committee on Banking, Housing,
and Urban Affairs of the Senate and the Committee on Financial Services of the House of Representatives -

(i) not later than 7 days after the Board authorizes any loan or other financial assistance under this paragraph, a report that includes -

(I) the justification for the exercise of authority to provide such assistance;

(II) the identity of the recipients of such assistance;

(III) the date and amount of the assistance, and form in which the assistance was provided; and

(IV) the material terms of the assistance, including -

(aa) duration;

(bb) collateral pledged and the value thereof;

(cc) all interest, fees, and other revenue or items of value to be received in exchange for the assistance;

(dd) any requirements imposed on the recipient with respect to employee compensation, distribution of dividends, or any other corporate decision in exchange for the assistance; and

(ee) the expected costs to the taxpayers of such assistance; and

(ii) once every 30 days, with respect to any outstanding loan or other financial assistance under this paragraph, written updates on -

(I) the value of collateral;

(II) the amount of interest, fees, and other revenue or items of value received in exchange for the assistance; and

(III) the expected or final cost to the taxpayers of such assistance.

(D) The information required to be submitted to Congress under subparagraph (C) related to -

(i) the identity of the participants in an emergency lending program or facility commenced under this paragraph;

(ii) the amounts borrowed by each participant in any such program or facility;

(iii) identifying details concerning the assets or collateral held by, under, or in connection with such a program or facility,

shall be kept confidential, upon the written request of the Chairman of the Board, in which case such information shall be made available only to the Chairpersons or Ranking Members of the Committees described in subparagraph (C).

(E) If an entity to which a Federal reserve bank has provided a loan under this paragraph becomes a covered financial company, as defined in section 201 of the Dodd-Frank Wall Street Reform and Consumer Protection Act [12 U.S.C. 5381], at any time while such loan is outstanding, and the Federal reserve bank incurs a realized net loss on the loan, then the Federal reserve bank shall have a claim equal to the amount of the net realized loss against the covered entity, with the same priority as an obligation to the Secretary of the Treasury under section 210(b) of the Dodd-Frank Wall Street Reform and Consumer Protection Act [12 U.S.C. 5390(b)].

-SOURCE-

(Dec. 23, 1913, ch. 6, Sec. 13 (pars.), 38 Stat. 263; Sept. 7, 1916, ch. 461, 39 Stat. 752; Mar. 4, 1923, ch. 252, title IV, Sec. 402, 42 Stat. 1478; July 21, 1932, ch. 520, Sec. 210, 47 Stat. 715; Aug. 23, 1935, ch. 614, title II, Sec. 203(a), title III, Sec. 322, 49 Stat. 704, 714; Pub. L. 102-242, title IV, Sec. 473, Dec. 19, 1991, 105 Stat. 2386; Pub. L. 111-203, title XI, Sec. 1101(a), July

21, 2010, 124 Stat. 2113.)

-REFTEXT-

REFERENCES IN TEXT

This chapter, referred to in the first par., was in the original "this Act", meaning act Dec. 23, 1913, ch. 6, 38 Stat. 251, known as the Federal Reserve Act. For complete classification of this Act to the Code, see References in Text note set out under section 226 of this title and Tables.

The Dodd-Frank Wall Street Reform and Consumer Protection Act, referred to in par. (3)(B)(ii), (iii), is Pub. L. 111-203, July 21, 2010, 124 Stat. 1376. Title II of the Act is classified principally to subchapter II (Sec. 5381 et seq.) of chapter 53 of this title. For complete classification of the Act to the Code, see Short Title note set out under section 5301 of this title and Tables.

-COD-

CODIFICATION

Section is comprised of the second par. and par. (3) of section 13 of act Dec. 23, 1913. Act Mar. 4, 1923, split the second par. of section 13, as amended in 1916 (39 Stat. 752), into two pars., the first of which constitutes the first par. of this section and the second of which constitutes section 344 of this title. Act July 21, 1932, added the second par. of this section which was designated to follow the second par. of section 13. Pub. L. 111-203, Sec. 1101(a)(1), designated the second par. as par. (3). For classification to this title of other pars. of section 13, see Codification note set out under section 342 of this title.

-MISC1-

AMENDMENTS

2010 - Pub. L. 111-203, Sec. 1101(a)(1)-(4), designated second par. as par. (3)(A), substituted "any participant in any program or facility with broad-based eligibility" for "any individual, partnership, or corporation", "bill of exchange," for "bill of exchange for an individual or a partnership or corporation", and "such participant in any program or facility with broad-based eligibility" for "such individual, partnership, or corporation".

Author Note: ***Notice how the Federal Reserve and the Dodd-Frank Act now legally allow INDIVIDUALS to come to the Fed Window, along with Partnerships and Corporations---they have changed the Fed into a banker- and elite-controlled investment bank---placing taxpayer money at risk every day of every week---with no accountability!***

Par. (3)(A). Pub. L. 111-203, Sec. 1101(a)(5), which directed substitution of "for any participant in any program or facility with broad-based eligibility" for "for individuals, partnerships, corporations", was executed by making the substitution for "for individuals, partnerships, or corporations", to reflect the probable intent of Congress.

Par. (3)(B) to (E). Pub. L. 111-203, Sec. 1101(a)(6), added subpars. (B) to (E).

1991 - Pub. L. 102-242 struck out "of the kinds and maturities made eligible for discount for member banks under other provisions of this chapter" after first reference to "bills of exchange" in second par.

1935 - Act Aug. 23, 1935, Sec. 322, substituted words immediately preceding proviso for "indorsed and otherwise secured to the satisfaction of the Federal reserve bank."

1932 - Act July 21, 1932, added second par.

(Source: ibid)

The following is Mr. Bernanke's actual testimony before Congress on February 10, 2009 (author emphasis underlined), notice how he ignores the preamble to Section 13(3) of the Act, as you just saw, above. Also notice how he decides because of an institution's systemic importance, The Federal Reserve and the Board of Governors could apparently just ignore the law, with respect to aiding failing institutions. This is something strictly forbidden in the original Act and in the Dodd-Frank amended legislation:

The Use of Authorities Under Section 13(3) of the Federal Reserve Act

"Section 13(3) of the Federal Reserve Act authorizes the Federal Reserve Board to make secured loans to individuals, partnerships, or corporations in "unusual and exigent circumstances" and when the borrower is "unable to secure adequate credit accommodations from other banking institutions." This authority, added to the Federal Reserve Act in 1932, was intended to give the Federal Reserve the flexibility to respond to emergency conditions. Prior to 2008, credit had not been extended under this authority since the 1930s.[1] However, responding to the extraordinarily stressed conditions in financial markets, the Board has used this authority on a number of occasions over the past year.

Following the Bear Stearns episode in March 2008, the Federal Reserve Board invoked Section 13(3) to make primary securities dealers, as well as banks, eligible to borrow on a short-term basis from the Fed.[2] This decision was taken in support of financial stability, during a period in which the investment banks and other dealers faced intense liquidity pressures.[3] The Fed has also made use of the Section 13(3) authority in its programs to support the functioning of key credit markets, including the commercial paper market and the market for asset-backed securities. In my view, the use of Section 13(3) in these contexts is well justified in light of the breakdowns of these critical markets and the serious implications of those breakdowns for the health of the broader economy. As financial conditions improve and circumstances are no longer "unusual and exigent," the programs authorized under Section 13(3) will be wound down, as required by law. Other components of the Federal Reserve's credit programs, including our lending to depository institutions, liquidity swaps with other central banks, and purchases of agency securities, make no use of the powers conferred by Section 13(3).

In a distinct set of activities, the Federal Reserve has also used its Section 13(3) authority to support government efforts to stabilize systemically critical financial institutions

(Author's note: the Federal Reserve Act specifically, under ALL conditions, both in its modified form over the years and in its original form PROHIBITS the rescuing, aiding, abetting or bailing out of failing institutions—regardless of whether, or not, they are "systemically critical"!! This is what causes the entire problem to get worse---the Federal Reserve using taxpayer money to prop up failed institutions and rewarding bad behavior and mal investment---precisely what the Act is designed to PREVENT).

The Federal Reserve collaborated with the Treasury to facilitate the acquisition of Bear Stearns by JPMorgan Chase & Co. and to prevent the failure of the American International Group (AIG), and we worked closely with the Treasury and the Federal Deposit Insurance Corporation to help to stabilize Citigroup and the Bank of America. In the cases of Bear Stearns and AIG, as part of a strategy to avoid impending defaults by the companies, the Federal Reserve made loans against pools of collateral.

Activities to stabilize systemically important institutions seem to me to be quite different in character from the use of Section 13(3) authority to support the repair of credit markets. The actions that the Federal Reserve and the Treasury have taken to stabilize systemically critical firms were essential to protect the financial system as a whole, and, in particular, the financial risks inherent in the credits extended by the Federal Reserve were, in my view, greatly outweighed by the risks that would have been faced by the financial system and the economy had we not stepped in. However, many of these actions might not have been necessary in the first place had there been in place a comprehensive resolution regime aimed at avoiding the disorderly failure of systemically critical financial institutions. The Federal Reserve believes that the development of a robust resolution regime should be a top legislative priority. If the specification of this regime were to include clear expectations of the Federal Reserve's role in stabilizing or resolving systemically important firms--a step we very much support--then the contingencies in which the Fed might need to invoke emergency authorities could be tightly circumscribed."

(Source: Ben Bernanke Congressional Testimony, February 10, 2009, as retrieved from http://www.federalreserve.gov/newsevents/testimony/bernanke20090210a.htm).

What becomes VERY clear is Mr. Bernanke IGNORES the paragraph which precedes Section 13(3). The preamble of Section 13 states "Nothing in this chapter" in the code and "Nothing in this Act" in the original Act. Its rule of law applies to the ENTIRE ACT. As you saw, already in the actual code from the House of Representatives, THE AMENDED ACT READS AS FOLLOWS:

"SECTION 13(2). Discount of commercial, agricultural, and industrial paper

Upon the indorsement of any of its member banks, which shall be deemed a waiver of demand, notice and protest by such bank as to its own indorsement exclusively, any Federal reserve bank may discount notes, drafts, and bills of exchange arising out of actual commercial transactions; that is, notes, drafts, and bills of exchange issued or drawn for agricultural, industrial, or commercial purposes, or the proceeds of which have been used, or are to be used, for such purposes, the Board of Governors of the Federal Reserve System to have the right to determine or define the character of the paper thus eligible for discount, within the meaning of this Act. **Nothing in this Act** contained shall be construed to prohibit such notes, drafts, and bills of exchange, secured by staple agricultural products, or other goods, wares, or merchandise from being eligible for such discount, and the notes, drafts, and bills of exchange of factors issued as such making advances exclusively to producers of staple agricultural products in their raw state shall be eligible for such discount; **but such definition shall not include notes, drafts, or bills covering merely investments or issued or drawn for the purpose of carrying or trading in stocks, bonds, or other investment securities, except bonds and notes of the government of the United States. Notes, drafts, and bills admitted to discount under the terms of this paragraph must have a maturity at the time of discount of not more than 90 days, exclusive of grace."**

[12 USC 343. As amended by act of Sept. 7, 1916 (39 Stat. 752), which completely revised this section; and by act of March 4, 1923 (42 Stat. 1478). As used in this paragraph the phrase "bonds and notes of Government of the United States" includes Treasury bills or certificates of indebtedness. (See act of June 17, 1929, amending section 5 of Second Liberty Bond Act of Sept. 24, 1917). As to eligibility for discount under this paragraph of notes representing loans to finance building construction, see this act, section 24).] (Source: Federal Reserve, retrieved from http://www.federalreserve.gov/aboutthefed/section13.htm and can also be seen here http://uscode.house.gov/view.xhtml?req=Discount+of+obligations+arising+out+of+actual+commercial+transactions%2C&f=treesort&fq=true&num=1&hl=true&edition=prelim&granuleId=USC-prelim-title12-section343). Author's emphasis bold and/or underlined).

Even in the subsequent amendment to the Act in 1932, Congress had the foresight to PREVENT the Fed and its member banks from entering into INVESTMENT BANKING activities and **RESTRICTED THEM FROM DEALING IN NOTES, DRAFTS OR BILLS COVERING MERELY INVESTMENTS OR ISSUED OR DRAWN FOR THE**

PURPOSE OF TRADING IN STOCKS, BONDS OR OTHER INVESTMENT SECURITIES, EXCEPT BONDS AND NOTES OF THE GOVERNMENT OF THE UNITED STATES.

What was Mr. Bernanke's response to Congress?
"In my view, the use of Section 13(3) in these contexts is well justified in light of the breakdowns of these critical markets and the serious implications of those breakdowns for the health of the broader economy....Activities to stabilize systemically important institutions seem to me to be quite different in character from the use of Section 13(3) authority to support the repair of credit markets."

Perhaps this is Mr. Bernanke's view, but it certainly does not appear to be THE LAW. What looks like really happened here was a complete disregard and abuse of the law and the previous paragraphs of Section 13 of the Act, which allowed the greatest heist in our history to take place.

The Fed's actions have bankrupted America in the process. This is a far more serious problem than bailing out institutions who Mr. Bernanke believed were "systemically important." As this book makes the point---as does the trilogy---it would have been far, far better to allow the "systemically important financial institutions" to FAIL and guarantee the DEPOSITORS their money!! This would have punished the elitists who own the stocks and the bonds of Fed-backed banks who have ALSO BEEN siphoning TRILLIONS OF DOLLARS out of America for over a century---causing all manner of inflation and debt explosion by the Congress, Senate and many Administrations.

Any one of a large number of wealthy businessmen would have loved to have taken over JP Morgan Chase, Citibank, Goldman Sachs, Morgan Stanley, Bear Stearns, Bank of America, AIG, Lehman Brothers, etc...the insiders at the commercial banks, their minions at the Federal Reserve Board of Governors and the elitists who own them would not allow this to happen. They would have lost the keys to the golden goose if they had!

America needs to TAKE BACK what these pirates have stolen from us.

What is entirely shocking and disgraceful is nearly no one in Congress or the Senate seems to have actually READ the Federal Reserve Act---particularly Section 13, in its entirety.

Look once again at key sections of the Federal Reserve Act taken directly from the Congressional Record for the SIXTY-THIRD CONGRESS, Congressional Record Book on December 23, 1913 and follow the blue arrows. Anyone can immediately see there are gross violations of the letter, intent and spirit of the original Act:

CHAP. 6.—An Act To provide for the establishment of Federal reserve banks, to furnish an elastic currency, to afford means of rediscounting commercial paper, to establish a more effective supervision of banking in the United States, and for other purposes.

December 23, 1913.
[H. R. 7837.]
[Public, No. 43.]

Be it enacted by the Senate and House of Representatives of the United States of America in Congress assembled, That the short title of this Act shall be the "Federal Reserve Act."

Federal Reserve Act.

Wherever the word "bank" is used in this Act, the word shall be held to include State bank, banking association, and trust company, except where national banks or Federal reserve banks are specifically referred to.

Terms construed.

SEC. 11. The Federal Reserve Board shall be authorized and empowered:

Authority and powers of Board.

(a) To examine at its discretion the accounts, books and affairs of each Federal reserve bank and of each member bank and to require such statements and reports as it may deem necessary. The said board shall publish once each week a statement showing the condition of each Federal reserve bank and a consolidated statement for all Federal reserve banks. Such statements shall show in detail the

Examination, etc., of reserve and member banks.

Published statements.

Doubtful assets.

(g) To require the writing off of doubtful or worthless assets upon the books and balance sheets of Federal reserve banks.

Open-market operations.

OPEN-MARKET OPERATIONS.

Federal reserve banks may deal in commercial paper, etc.

SEC. 14. Any Federal reserve bank may, under rules and regulations prescribed by the Federal Reserve Board, purchase and sell in the open market, at home or abroad, either from or to domestic or foreign banks, firms, corporations, or individuals, cable transfers and bankers' acceptances and bills of exchange of the kinds and maturities by this Act made eligible for rediscount, with or without the indorsement of a member bank.

Additional powers.

Every Federal reserve bank shall have power:

Gold transactions.

(a) To deal in gold coin and bullion at home or abroad, to make loans thereon, exchange Federal reserve notes for gold, gold coin, or gold certificates, and to contract for loans of gold coin or bullion, giving therefor, when necessary, acceptable security, including the hypothecation of United States bonds or other securities which Federal reserve banks are authorized to hold;

Bonds, notes, etc.

(b) To buy and sell, at home or abroad, bonds and notes of the United States, and bills, notes, revenue bonds, and warrants with a maturity from date of purchase of not exceeding six months, issued in anticipation of the collection of taxes or in anticipation of the receipt of assured revenues by any State, county, district, political subdivision, or municipality in the continental United States, including irrigation, drainage and reclamation districts, such purchases to be made in accordance with rules and regulations prescribed by the Federal Reserve Board;

Commercial exchange.

(c) To purchase from member banks and to sell, with or without its indorsement, bills of exchange arising out of commercial transactions, as hereinbefore defined;

(Source: U.S. Congressional Record, SIXTY-THIRD CONGRESS. SEss. II. CHs. 4-6. 1913. Pages 251, 262, 263 & 264, as retrieved from http://famguardian.org/TaxFreedom/Authorities/FedLaw/FedReserveAct-38Stat251-275,690-691.pdf).

Making the situation even more outrageous, the Federal Reserve Board has AN OBLIGATION TO FORCE THE BANKS TO WRITE OFF ANY DOUBTFUL OR WORTHLESS ASSETS!

Section 11(g) of the Federal Reserve Act requires:
SEC. 11 . The Federal Reserve Board shall be authorized and empowered:
(g)- To require the writing off of doubtful or worthless assets upon books and balance sheets of Federal reserve banks." (Source: ibid).

SEC. 11. The Federal Reserve Board shall be authorized and empowered: Authority and powers of Board.

Doubtful assets. (g) To require the writing off of doubtful or worthless assets upon the books and balance sheets of Federal reserve banks.

Suspension of reserve banks. (h) To suspend, for the violation of any of the provisions of this Act, the operations of any Federal reserve bank, to take possession thereof, administer the same during the period of suspension, and, when deemed advisable, to liquidate or reorganize such bank.

(Source: ibid, page 262).

As you can see, the FEDRAL RESERVE ACT STRICTLY limits the risk AND the KINDS OF TRANSACTIONS any Federal Reserve Bank can enter or which the Federal Reserve Board can even authorize. It also requires the write off of doubtful or worthless assets! It does NOT say the Federal Reserve Bank of New York can take in worthless mortgage securities and then exchange them for U.S. Treasury securities, Federal Reserve banking credits, or cash!

Setting America Up to be the Patsy, Once Again

Time after time in the Act, you can see limitations on maturities and the restrictions on securities transactions written into the law, which were designed to PREVENT the kinds of unauthorized actions taken by this Fed, according to what was published and reported in the GAO audit.

After the Dodd-Frank Wall Street Reform and Consumer Protection Act [12 U.S.C. 5390(b)] was passed on July 21, 2010 (conveniently the same date as the GAO audit was completed), the Fed and its Congressional minions inserted language which should strike fear into the hearts and minds of every American. The amended legislation now permits individuals, corporations and partnerships to come to the Fed Window!

Dodd-Frank Allows INDIVIDUALS AND CORPORATIONS To Take Advantage of the American Taxpayer

Among the many loopholes among this outrageously weak legislation, are the following: further amendments to Section 13(3) in the Amended Act:

(3)(A) (1) In unusual and exigent circumstances, the Board of Governors of the Federal Reserve System, by the affirmative vote of not less than five members, may authorize any Federal reserve bank, during such periods as the said board may determine, at rates established in accordance with the provisions of section 357 of this title, to discount for **any participant** in ***any program or facility*** with broad-based eligibility, notes, drafts, and bills of exchange when such notes, drafts, and bills of exchange are indorsed or otherwise secured to the satisfaction of the Federal reserve bank: Provided, That before discounting any such note, draft, or bill of exchange, the Federal reserve bank shall obtain evidence that such participant in any program or facility with broad-based eligibility is unable to secure adequate credit accommodations from other banking institutions. All such discounts for any participant in any program or facility with broad-based eligibility shall be subject to such limitations, restrictions, and regulations as the Board of Governors of the Federal Reserve System may prescribe.

(Author's note: *This section was amended by the Dodd-Frank Act and now allows individuals and corporations to come to the Fed's window---clearly against all guides of history and any notion of sound practice for a central bank!!):*

As amended: (3)(A), substituted "any participant in any program or facility with broad-based eligibility" for "**any individual, partnership, or corporation**", "bill of exchange," for **"bill of exchange for an individual or a partnership or corporation**", and "such participant in any program or facility with broad-based eligibility" for "**such individual, partnership, or corporation**". (Source: Dodd-Frank Wall Street Reform and Consumer Protection Act [12 U.S.C. 5390(b)], the Amended Federal Reserve Act).

Clearly the Fed and their Congressional buddies have rigged the game to CONTINUE to bail out wealthy individuals and corporations---things this Fed did during the credit crisis which were strictly against the law at the time.

The highlights cited in this section of the book (above and below) exemplify general areas subject to corruption and collusion because of nonsensical legislation. There are many, many others as reported in this book.

Dodd-Frank Allows a Failing Institution to "Self-Proclaim" Solvency

In the following recitation from the Dodd-Frank legislation, the reader will learn how our brilliant lawmakers inserted language to allow a failing institution to avoid the tag of being "insolvent" by merely having the failing company's CEO provide a letter stating it isn't insolvent!

To allow a CEO (who by any reasonable opinion should not be allowed to issue such an opinion because of conflicts of interests) be the person to sign an affidavit to save his, or her, failing company by simply certifying it isn't insolvent, smacks of collusion with corporate America in a very dark and sinister way. It is simply outrageous legislation.

In the crude parlance of America…it stinks like a pile of manure!

The legislators who passed this law are setting America up to be the patsies, once again, when the great collapse of D'Apocalypse™ arrives. Ben Bernanke and the rest of the Federal Reserve System, the member banks and the elite appear to be just hoping they can avoid personal prosecution by hiding behind weak legislation designed to rob the public.

It is highly likely the people will not buy the attempts to mask over larceny with after-the-fact proclamations of "legality," made possible through corrupt legislation. People will demand real justice when what seems to be outright fraud is exposed and the apparent collusion is uncovered, when the collapse occurs. It will be then the people rise up.

Dodd-Frank Requires "Sound Risk Management Practices"--an Utter Failing of This Fed

Dodd-Frank, like the original Act, requires the use of sound risk management practices:

> "(B)(i) As soon as is practicable after July 21, 2010, the Board shall establish, by regulation, in consultation with the Secretary of the Treasury, the policies and procedures governing emergency lending under this paragraph. Such policies and procedures shall be to ensure that any emergency lending program or facility is for the purpose of providing liquidity to the financial system, and not to aid a failing financial company, and that the security for emergency loans is sufficient to protect taxpayers from losses and that any such program is terminated in a timely and orderly fashion. The policies and procedures established by the Board shall require that a Federal reserve bank assign, **consistent with**

> **sound risk management practices** and to ensure protection for the taxpayer, a lendable value to all collateral for a loan executed by a Federal reserve bank under this paragraph in determining whether the loan is secured satisfactorily for purposes of this paragraph." (Source: ibid).

Under Dodd-Frank, or under the Act prior to Dodd-Frank, no one at the Fed was using ***"sound risk management practices,"*** because the sheer volume of U.S. taxpayer-backed transactions, at TWICE THE SIZE OF THE U.S. Gross Domestic Product would be out of the bounds of reason for nearly anyone, anywhere, around the world—***except for those being secretly bailed out through the Fed's nefarious actions.***

> "(ii) **The Board shall establish procedures to prohibit borrowing programs and facilities by borrowers that are insolvent**. Such procedures may include a **certification from the chief executive officer (or other authorized officer) of the borrower,** at the time the borrower initially borrows under the program or facility (with a duty by the borrower to update the certification if the information in the certification materially changes), **that the borrower is not insolvent.** A borrower shall be considered insolvent for purposes of this subparagraph, if the borrower is in bankruptcy, resolution under title II of the Dodd-Frank Wall Street Reform and Consumer Protection Act [12 U.S.C. 5381 et seq.], or any other Federal or State insolvency proceeding." (Source: ibid).

The clear letter of the law is quite restrictive and was designed to PREVENT FREE-WHEELING HANKY PANKY INVESTMENT BANKING ACTIVITIES by the Federal Reserve and its Reserve Banks in collusion with the member banks and owner-elites controlling them.

Federal Reserve Act Requires Only Short Term Loans, Limited by a Bank's Capital

Furthermore, the Act requires the Fed to only commit to lending practices for the short term. These are less than 180 days, with most of the terms requiring 90 days. You can see "acceptances" in Section 13 of the ACT are restricted to the ***import or export of goods having a maturity date no longer than 90 days and must be endorsed by one member bank, with the aggregate amount not exceeding 10% of the bank's capital and no bank can accept notes exceeding more than ½ of a bank's paid up capital and surplus.***

Section 13 also elicits another exception which states national banking associations shall not to be indebted for any amounts in excess of its paid up capital stock, undiminished by losses, or otherwise, except for demands for bills of exchange or drafts drawn against monies actually on deposit to the credit of the association, or due thereto.

Bear Stearns Deal Should Not Have Even Been Entered Into

The clear language of the ACT causes absolute astonishment the Fed could even approve the merger of Bear Stearns with JP Morgan Chase bank, ***given the fact Bear Stearns was a failing institution whose liabilities stemming from derivatives and its balance sheet were in the TRILLIONS of dollars***---dwarfing JP Morgan Chase's very own capital!!

THIS IS IN DIRECT VIOLATION OF SECTION 13 OF THE FEDERAL RESERVE ACT, as you just read. Just because the banks keep the derivatives off their balance sheets by using off-balance sheet techniques and clever accounting policies, doesn't mean these transactions are not direct liabilities of the banks. In fact, they are.

AIG Was Not a Bank and Not a Fed Participant!

Another important event bringing into question the Fed's motives and legality of its actions is how could the Fed unilaterally support AIG when it wasn't and isn't a bank—which is another requirement of the Act at the time of the secret bailouts when the Fed bailed out this ***insurance*** company?

We know WHY they did this, of course. Goldman Sachs was completely exposed to the transactions in collateralized-debt obligations and mortgage-backed securities they had entered into with AIG. Goldman had horrific exposure in the derivatives area and was (and is) a long-standing member of the club on Wall Street. Additionally, Henry Paulson, ex-CEO of Goldman Sachs, owned a great deal of Goldman Sachs stock and used his authority and influence at the U.S. Treasury Secretary's position to paper over his, and Goldman's own bad bets, as well as their own atrocious activities when they created the AIG problem in the first place!

"What can we make of 'two dozen' conversations between treasury secretary Henry Paulson and Goldman's Lloyd Blankfein last September during the AIG rescue? ...Paulson's office calendar...reveals that he spoke to Goldman's boss, Lloyd Blankfein, two dozen times during the September week in which the treasury bailed out the troubled insurer AIG. That's "far more frequently" than Paulson talked to any other Wall Street executive.

"Hank" Paulson U.S. Treasury Secretary 2006-2009 prior to this time was CEO of Goldman Sachs 1999-2006
(Source: as retrieved from http://en.wikipedia.org/wik/Henry_Paulson).

Two dozen times? That's more than three times a day. More often than I speak to the Guardian's business editor. It's more often than many courting couples communicate. It's almost stalker-like behaviour. On 17 September alone, Paulson and Blankfein apparently spoke five times.

Paulson, as we know, was Goldman Sachs's chief executive for eight years before moving into government and Goldman, as has been widely documented, was the biggest counterparty to the ill-considered financial insurance policies which drove AIG to the brink of collapse."
(Source: "How close are Goldman Sachs's connections with the US treasury?", by Andrew Clark, August 10, 2009, The Guardian, retrieved from http://www.guardian.co.uk/business/andrew-clark-on-america/2009/aug/10/goldman-sachs-aig-treasury).

Mr. Bernanke's Testimony Self-Serving

The Fed was clearly worried about violating the law and specifically referenced Section 13 of the Act during Mr. Bernanke's testimony to Congress on February 10, 2009. You read his self-serving speech earlier in the chapter when he attempted to justify his actions in **"The Use of Authorities Under Section 13(3) of the Federal Reserve Act."**

The Fed was worried about this because, in reality, Section 13 of the Act, despite Mr. Bernanke's posturing otherwise, seems to clearly OUTLAW the actions taken by the Fed to save the banks and the elite. The LAW CLEARLY states the Federal Reserve Banks ***only*** have the power to deal in gold coin and bullion, exchange Federal Reserve Notes for gold, gold coin, or bullion, when ***given acceptable*** security, including hypothecation of United States bonds, to buy and sell bonds and notes of the UNITED STATES, and bills, notes, revenue bonds and warrants with limited maturity dates. This did not and does not include 30-year worthless mortgages!

Because of this concern, Mr. Bernanke attempted to twist the law into his own favor by "cherry picking" certain sections of the law and then appeared to add his own law---e.g., some institutions were systemically critical to the system---thereby justifying his actions!

This is not the law.

In fact, it is the direct problem with this Federal Reserve---supporting and propping up failed and failing institutions which have now put our entire system in jeopardy---with nowhere to run, as D'Apocalypse™ cometh!

The truth is and this book believes, the facts do not support Mr. Bernanke's twist and interpretation of the law.

Section 13 of the Federal Reserve Act and the amended code, when read in their ENTIRETY and not cherry-picked, as Mr. Bernanke did, clearly OUTLAWS the actions taken by the Fed to save the banks and elite.

The act and amended code also clearly state the Federal Reserve Banks ***only*** have the power to deal in gold coin and bullion and can ***only exchange*** Federal Reserve Notes for gold, gold coin, bullion, or when the Fed is given acceptable security. This includes hypothecation of United States bonds to buy and sell bonds and notes of the UNITED STATES, and bills, notes, revenue bonds and warrants with a ***maturity from the date of purchase NOT EXCEEDING SIX MONTHS*** ISSUED IN ANTICIPATION OF THE COLLECTION OF TAXES, OR IN ANTICIPATION OF THE RECEIPT OF ASSURED REVENUES BY ANY STATE, COUNTY, DISTRICT, POLITICAL SUBDIVISION OR MUNICIPALITY IN THE CONTINENTAL UNITED STATES, along with the ability to deal in U.S. Government securities and agency paper (as collateral for loans), backed by the United States.

All the kinds of securities the Federal Reserve deals with, moreover, ***REQUIRE fair market value*** be assigned to the assets being exchanged, bought or sold---and the securities are SHORT TERM in nature, as is abundantly defined in the Federal Reserve Act:

SIXTY-THIRD CONGRESS. Sess. II. Ch. 6. 1913. 265

hypothecation of United States bonds or other securities which Federal reserve banks are authorized to hold;

(b) To buy and sell, at home or abroad, bonds and notes of the United States, and bills, notes, revenue bonds, and warrants with a maturity from date of purchase of not exceeding six months, issued in anticipation of the collection of taxes or in anticipation of the receipt of assured revenues by any State, county, district, political subdivision, or municipality in the continental United States, including irrigation, drainage and reclamation districts, such purchases to be made in accordance with rules and regulations prescribed by the Federal Reserve Board; Bonds, notes, etc.

(c) To purchase from member banks and to sell, with or without its indorsement, bills of exchange arising out of commercial transactions, as hereinbefore defined; Commercial exchange.

(d) To establish from time to time, subject to review and determination of the Federal Reserve Board, rates of discount to be charged by the Federal reserve bank for each class of paper, which shall be fixed with a view of accommodating commerce and business; Discount rates.

(e) To establish accounts with other Federal reserve banks for exchange purposes and, with the consent of the Federal Reserve Board, to open and maintain banking accounts in foreign countries, appoint correspondents, and establish agencies in such countries wheresoever it may deem best for the purpose of purchasing, selling, and collecting bills of exchange, and to buy and sell with or without its indorsement, through such correspondents or agencies, bills of exchange arising out of actual commercial transactions which have not more than ninety days to run and which bear the signature of two or more responsible parties. Foreign accounts and agencies.

GOVERNMENT DEPOSITS. Government deposits.

Sec. 15. The moneys held in the general fund of the Treasury, except the five per centum fund for the redemption of outstanding national-bank notes and the funds provided in this Act for the redemption of Federal reserve notes may, upon the direction of the Secretary of the Treasury, be deposited in Federal reserve banks, which banks, when required by the Secretary of the Treasury, shall act as fiscal agents of the United States; and the revenues of the Government or any part thereof may be deposited in such banks, and disbursements may be made by checks drawn against such deposits. Use of reserve bank as fiscal agents, etc.

No public funds of the Philippine Islands, or of the postal savings, or any Government funds, shall be deposited in the continental United States in any bank not belonging to the system established by this Act: *Provided, however*, That nothing in this Act shall be construed to deny the right of the Secretary of the Treasury to use member banks as depositories. Deposit of public funds restricted. Proviso. Use of member banks as depositories.

NOTE ISSUES. Federal reserve notes.

Sec. 16. Federal reserve notes, to be issued at the discretion of the Federal Reserve Board for the purpose of making advances to Federal reserve banks through the Federal reserve agents as hereinafter set forth and for no other purpose, are hereby authorized. The said notes shall be obligations of the United States and shall be receivable by all national and member banks and Federal reserve banks and for all taxes, customs, and other public dues. They shall be redeemed in gold on demand at the Treasury Department of the United States, in the city of Washington, District of Columbia, or in gold or lawful money at any Federal reserve bank. Issue authorized. Receivability. Redemption.

Any Federal reserve bank may make application to the local Federal reserve agent for such amount of the Federal reserve notes hereinbefore provided for as it may require. Such application shall Applications for, by reserve banks. Collateral required.

(Source: U.S. Congressional Record, SIXTY-THIRD CONGRESS. SEss. II. CHs. 4-6. 1913. Page 265, as retrieved from: http://famguardian.org/TaxFreedom/Authorities/FedLaw/FedReserveAct-38Stat251-275,690-691.pdf).

Any fiduciary should NEVER overpay for an asset. An entity, like the Fed, ***IF it were in collusion with the banks***, would fraudulently ***inflate*** the value of the toxic mortgage securities and effect the cash transaction using U.S. taxpayer-backed money at fraudulently higher valuation levels. This would allow the banks to obtain valuable U.S. taxpayer cash, or cash-equivalents, in exchange for worthless securities and/or securities of a toxic nature---totally ripping off the taxpayer. On top of the potential skullduggery involved, this kind of activity would certainly fall under the category of the requirement for the Federal Reserve to use "reasonable risk management practices." The Federal Reserve, it seems, obviously knowingly and recklessly ignored this rule of the law.

As already shown the reader at the very beginning of Section 13, ***the Fed is prohibited from dealing in investment securities—in both the amended Act and original Act.***

The Federal Reserve Act prohibits the dealing in notes, drafts or bills covering merely investments or issued or drawn for the purpose of carrying or trading in stocks, bonds or other investment securities, except bonds and notes of the Government of the United States (or those guaranteed by the United States).

With this more specific understanding of the restrictions clearly defined and inscribed in the Halls of Congress in the Federal Reserve Act of 1913 and the amended Act, following are three distinct tables which summarize some of Mr. Bernanke's Federal Reserve Bank transactions, uncovered during the partial audit of the Fed for the period December 1, 2007 and July 21, 2010 by the General Accounting Office of the United States Government. Collectively, they total over $26 TRILLION!!

These transactions should cause astonishment and righteous indignation for every American.

Have the Fed, the Federal Reserve Banks and elite Declared Economic War on America?

None of the authorizations contained in the Act include provisions or the ability for the Board of Governor's to approve transactions involving securities not specifically referenced in the Act.

It definitely would prohibit any member Reserve Bank, or the Board itself, from transacting in worthless derivative securities, worthless mortgage-backed bonds and other questionable collateral approved by the Fed. Furthermore, any transactions entered into by the Federal Reserve require reasonable risk management practices and the utmost in fiduciary responsibility. All transactions initiated by the Federal Reserve are required to be purchased in the open market at fair market value.

The Fed's dubious exchanges and transactions were ***NOT*** exchanged in this manner. As everyone in the world knew and knows, most of the securities transactions, represented in the tables which follow, are and were worthless, or worth only a fraction of their face value.

Sound risk management practice was ***not*** used by this Federal Reserve—another apparently clear violation of the intent and letter of the law.

What really transpired was a complete refund to the banks and the wealthy elite---allowing them to save both their banks and their portfolios, while remaining in control over the monetary policy system and authority of the United States of America.

The kinds of restrictions in the ACT and clear rules for member banks and the Board of Governors create many questions and grave concerns over the practices instituted by the Bernanke Federal Reserve. These actions appear to have enabled a grand theft from taxpayers, a secret bailout of the rich and a treasonous poisoning and bankrupting of America. The taking of nearly $30 Trillion of taxpayer-backed monies is abominable and should have never, ever been allowed to transpire.

This book believes the actions of this Federal Reserve, the banks and the elite appear to be a clear, viscous, deliberate and conscious act of

ECONOMIC WARFARE AND SABOTAGE AGAINST THE PEOPLE OF THE UNITED STATES OF AMERICA.

Only a full-blown audit will tell the true story.

Using the United States Treasury to Bankroll Bad Bets

You will now see how the Fed secretly gave $16 Trillion to the top 25 Commercial banks and another $10 Trillion to foreign banks, receiving all kinds of securities in exchange which were likely NOT authorized in the Federal Reserve Act and/or were valued at fraudulently high valuations.

You will also see in the notes to the Financial Statements in chapter 10 of this book (as well as in the second book of the trilogy, The $30 Trillion Heist---Follow The Money! Volume II, Chapter 12, "Honesty and Integrity of the Federal Reserve") some of the many ways in which the Fed eviscerated the heart and soul of the Federal Reserve Act by dealing in unapproved securities our forefathers had outlawed. They had written the Act trying to protect us from unscrupulous bankers who might use the U.S. Treasury to bankroll their bad banking bets:

The $26 Trillion as Reported by the GAO

The tables, which follow, are in $ BILLIONS
(e.g., Citigroup was given $2,513,000,000,000 ($2.513 Trillion!).

Table 8: Institutions with Largest Total Transaction Amounts (Not Term-Adjusted) across Broad-Based Emergency Programs (Borrowing Aggregated by Parent Company and Includes Sponsored ABCP Conduits), December 1, 2007 through July 21, 2010

(Source: "FEDERAL RESERVE SYSTEM Opportunities Exist to Strengthen Policies and Processes for Managing Emergency Assistance," GAO-11-696 Federal Reserve System, page 131).

Dollar in billions

Borrowing Parent Company	TAF	PDCF	TSLF	CPFF	Subtotal	AMLF	TALF	Total loans
Citigroup Inc.	$110	$2,020	$348	$33	$2,511	$1	-	**$ 2,513**
Morgan Stanley	-	1,913	115	4	2,032	-	9	**2,041**
Merrill Lynch & Co.	0	1,775	166	8	1,949	-	-	**1,949**
Bank of America Corporation	280	947	101	15	1,342	2	-	**1,344**
Barclays PLC (United Kingdom)	232	410	187	39	868	-	-	**868**
Bear Stearns Companies, Inc.	-	851	2	-	853	-	-	**853**
Goldman Sachs Group Inc.	-	589	225	0	814	-	-	**814**
Royal Bank of Scotland Group PLC (United Kingdom)	212	-	291	39	541	-	-	**541**
Deutsche Bank AG (Germany)	77	1	277	-	354	-	-	**354**
UBS AG (Switzerland)	56	35	122	75	287	-	-	**287**
JP Morgan Chase & Co.	99	112	68	-	279	111	-	**391**
Credit Suisse Group AG (Switzerland)	0	2	261	-	262	0	-	**262**
Lehman Brothers Holdings Inc.	-	83	99	-	183	-	-	**183**
Bank of Scotland PLC (United Kingdom)	181	-	-	-	181	-	-	**181**
BNP Paribas SA (France)	64	66	41	3	175	-	-	**175**
Wells Fargo & Co.	159	-	-	-	159	-	-	**159**
Dexia SA (Belgium)	105	-	-	53	159	-	-	**159**
Wachovia Corporation	142	-	-	-	142	-	-	**142**
Dresdner Bank AG (Germany)	123	0	1	10	135	-	-	**135**
Societe Generale SA (France)	124	-	-	-	124	-	-	**124**
All other borrowers	1,854	146	14	460	2,475	103	62	**2,639**
Total	**$3,818**	**$8,951**	**$2,319**	**$738**	**$15,826**	**$217**	**$71**	**$16,115**

Source: GAO analysis of Federal Reserve System data

As retrieved from http://www.gao.gov/products/GAO-11-696, page 131.

"To place $16 trillion into perspective, remember that GDP of the United States is only $14.12 trillion. The entire national debt of the United States government spanning its 200+ year history is "only" $14.5 trillion. The budget that is being debated so heavily in Congress and the Senate is "only" $3.5 trillion. Take all of the outrage and debate over the $1.5 trillion deficit into consideration, and swallow this Red pill: There was no debate about whether $16,000,000,000,000 would be given to failing banks and failing corporations around the world.

In late 2008, the TARP Bailout bill was passed and loans of $800 billion were given to failing banks and companies. <u>That was a blatant lie considering the fact that Goldman Sachs alone received 814 billion dollars.</u> (author's emphasis)

As, it turns out, the Federal Reserve donated $2.5 trillion to Citigroup, while Morgan Stanley received $2.04 trillion. The Royal Bank of Scotland and Deutsche Bank, a German bank, split about a trillion and numerous other banks received hefty chunks of the $16 trillion."

(Source: "Audit of the Federal Reserve Reveals $16 Trillion in Secret Bailouts," by Iam1ru1-2, unelected.org, 12/27/2011, retrieved from http://www.freerepublic.com/focus/f-news/2825696/posts).

$10 Trillion Handed Out to Foreign Banks

An additional $10 Trillion was handed out to foreign banks (Source: "FEDERAL RESERVE SYSTEM Opportunities Exist to Strengthen Policies and Processes for Managing EmergencyAssistance" GAO-11-696, page 205, as retrieved from http://www.gao.gov/products/GAO-11-696):

Table 24: Foreign Central Banks' Use of Dollar Swap Lines by Aggregate Dollar Transactions

Dollars in billions

Rank	Central bank	Number of transactions	Aggregate dollar transactions	Percent of total
1	European Central Bank	271	$8,011	79.7%
2	Bank of England	114	919	9.1
3	Swiss National Bank	81	466	4.6
4	Bank of Japan	35	387	3.9
5	Danmarks Nationalbank (Denmark)	19	73	0.7
6	Sveriges Riksbank (Sweden)	18	67	0.7
7	Reserve Bank of Australia	10	53	0.5
8	Bank of Korea (South Korea)	10	41	0.4
9	Norges Bank (Norway)	8	30	0.3
10	Banco de Mexico	3	10	0.1
Total		**569**	**$10,057**	**100.0%**

Source: GAO analysis of Federal Reserve Board data.

Note: Foreign central banks not included in this table did not draw dollars under their swap line agreement with FRBNY. Aggregate dollar transactions represent the sum of all dollars drawn under the swap line arrangements and have not been adjusted to reflect differences in the terms over which the dollar draws were outstanding.

Use of Dollar Swap Lines by Foreign Central Banks

Table 24 lists the foreign central banks in order of the aggregate amount of dollars drawn under the swap line arrangements with FRBNY. The European Central Bank received the largest amount of dollars under the swap line arrangements. Banco do Brasil, Bank of Canada, Monetary Authority of Singapore, and the Reserve Bank of New Zealand did not draw on their swap lines. The European Central Bank accounted for about 80 percent of total dollars drawn under the swap lines.

Page 204 GAO-11-696 Federal Reserve System

Adding insult to injury, our Federal Reserve Bank, also took in $738 BILLION in highly questionable commercial paper in exchange for $738 BILLION in good-as-gold, U.S. cash. As you can see, most of these exchanges were with FOREIGN banks, controlled by the Rothschild cabal of bankers and elite in Europe.

These were the largest commercial paper exchangers:

Table 20: Top 25 Largest CPFF Borrowers

Dollars in billions

Rank	Issuer of unsecured commercial paper or sponsor of ABCP issuer	ABCP	Unsecured commercial paper	Issuer total	Percent of total CPFF issuance
1	UBS AG (Switzerland)	$0.0	$74.5	$74.5	10.1%
2	American International Group	36.3	24.0	60.2	8.2
3	Dexia SA (Belgium)	0.0	53.5	53.5	7.2
4	Hudson Castle	53.3	0.0	53.3	7.2
5	BSN Holdings (United Kingdom)	42.8	0.0	42.8	5.8
6	The Liberty Hampshire Company	41.4	0.0	41.4	5.6
7	Barclays PLC (United Kingdom)	0.0	38.8	38.8	5.3
8	Royal Bank of Scotland Group PLC (United Kingdom)	24.8	13.7	38.5	5.2
9	Fortis Bank SA/NV (Belgium)	26.9	11.6	38.5	5.2
10	Citigroup Inc.	12.8	19.9	32.7	4.4
11	Natixis (France)	4.7	22.3	27.0	3.7
12	General Electric Co	0.0	16.1	16.1	2.2
13	Ford Credit	15.9	0.0	15.9	2.1
14	Bank of America Corporation	0.0	14.9	14.9	2.0
15	State Street Corporation	14.1	0.0	14.1	1.9
16	GMAC LLC	13.5	0.0	13.5	1.8
17	KBC BANK NV (Belgium)	9.0	2.3	11.3	1.5
18	ING Groep NV (Netherlands)	0.0	10.9	10.9	1.5
19	Dresdner Bank AG (Germany)	5.1	4.9	10.0	1.4
20	Northcross (United Kingdom)	8.6	0.0	8.6	1.2
21	WestLB (Germany)	8.2	0.0	8.2	1.1
22	Merrill Lynch & Co	0.0	8.0	8.0	1.1
23	Allied Irish Bank (Ireland)	0.0	6.6	6.6	0.9
24	Bayerische Motoren Werke AG (Germany)	0.0	6.2	6.2	0.8
25	Handelsbanken (Sweden)	0.0	6.0	6.0	0.8
	All Others	24.9	61.8	86.7	11.8%
Total		**$342.3**	**$395.9**	**$738.3**	**100.0%**

Source: GAO analysis of Federal Reserve Board data.

(Source: ibid, page 196).

Note: In the above figure, total amounts borrowed represent the sum of all loans. Total borrowing is aggregated at the parent company level and generally includes borrowing by branches, agencies, subsidiaries, and sponsored ABCP conduits that we could identify. Total borrowing for each parent company consolidates amounts borrowed by acquired institutions as of the date the acquisition was completed. The country of domicile is shown in parentheses for companies based outside the United States.

Millions More Handed Out to Key Wall Street Players

Leave it to the brilliant men and women running the Federal Reserve System and its member banks to leave no stone unturned. One more important detail relating to the GAO's audit is conflicts of interest extend beyond the banks themselves into key industry corporations, enlisted as VENDORS to the Fed, thereby going onto the Fed's and banks' payrolls.

These entities work directly for the Federal Reserve and receive millions and millions of taxpayer-backed dollars, as taken from the Fed's balance sheet, to "service" the needs of the Fed, its member banks and the wealthy elite.

By analyzing "Maiden Lane LLC," an entity shell corporation founded by the Fed to receive worthless assets from the banks (see The $30 Trillion Heist---Follow The Money! Volume II, Chapter 11, "The Crystal Ball and the Acquisition of Giants," under subsection, "Bear Stearns" for additional information on this transaction) you can see over one hundred million dollars going out the door to vendors, as documented by the General Accounting Office:

Key Vendors for Maiden Lane LLC

FRBNY used a number of vendors to help manage and administer Maiden Lane LLC. Table 17 lists Maiden Lane LLC vendors that have received more than $1 million in fees.

Table 17: Vendors for Maiden Lane LLC that Earned Fees Greater than $1 Million, 2008–2010

Vendor	Services provided	Contract date	Awarded competitively?	Total fees paid (2008–2010)
BlackRock	Investment manager	9/9/2008	No	$107,648,136
Ernst & Young	Due diligence	4/15/2008	No	$11,657,764
State Street Corporation	Administrator, custodian	6/26/2008	Yes	$9,182,946
EMC	Primary servicer	6/1/2008	No	$8,455,193
NationStar	Special servicer	2/5/2010	Yes	$3,456,150
Clayton	Servicer surveillance, advisory services	7/8/2009	Yes	$2,739,711
Cleary Gottlieb Stein & Hamilton	Legal services	9/13/2008	No	$2,422,169
Deloitte & Touche	Audit services	9/1/2008	N/A	$1,725,586
Axiom	Legal services	11/19/2008	No	$1,413,821
Wells Fargo	Primary servicer	6/1/2008	No	$1,300,949
Simpson Thacher & Bartlett	Legal services	3/24/2008	No	$1,147,617
Kelley Drye & Warren	Legal services	9/22/2009	No	$1,001,123

Sources: GAO presentation of FRBNY information.

(Source: ibid, page 184).

Figure 5: Comparison of the Transaction Structures for Maiden Lane LLC, Maiden Lane II LLC, and Maiden Lane III LLC

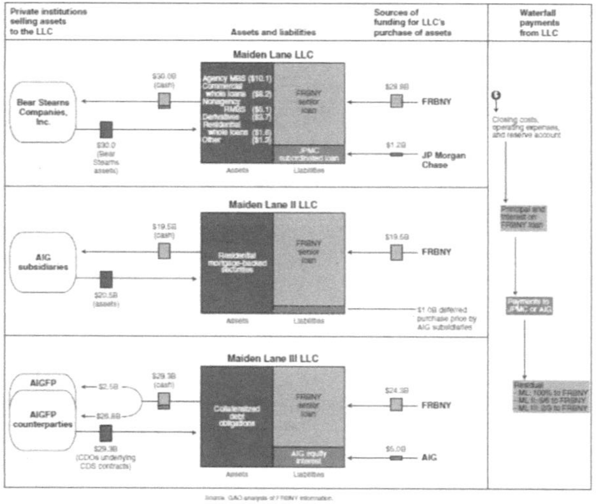

For the assistance provided to Citigroup and Bank of America, FRBNY and FRBR, respectively, coordinated with Treasury and FDIC to negotiate similar types of loss protections. In contrast to the Maiden Lane transactions, FRBNY and FRBR agreed to provide loans under certain

(As retrieved from: http://www.gao.gov/products/GAO-11-696).

Figure 2: Financial Reporting of the Federal Reserve's Emergency Programs

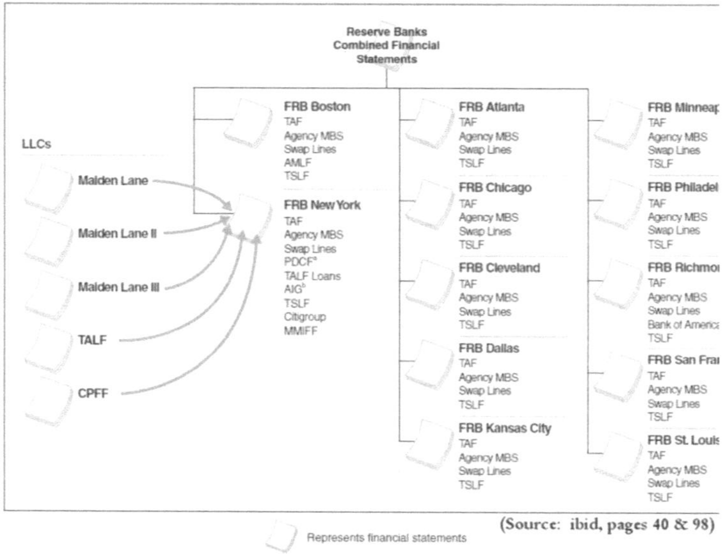

(Source: ibid, pages 40 & 98)

Scrutiny of Record Shows Conflicts of Interest Abound

After reviewing and reading even just some of the exerpts in this book, ***how*** could the Fed, the banks and the elite accomplish the degree of manipulation and power it required to allow the SECRET transfer of nearly $30 TRILLION of U.S. taxpayer-backed dollars to the banks and the elite---without Congressional approval???

As is obvious by now, these transfers required autonomous control over monetary policy and the money supply----all made possible through the Federal Reserve. This is directly what allowed secret multi-trillion-dollar-pass-throughs to be given to the elite and their banks.

Is the Fed acting in the public's interest---or, as this book and trilogy suggests, the Fed is acting solely for the elite and the banks?

The public ownership records provide some clues, however, in an important congressional investigation, which built upon the late Chairman Wright Patman's exploration of the inner workings of the Federal Reserve, the 1976 Congress compiled an exhaustive report detailing the conflicts of interest at the Federal Reserve and Federal Reserve Banks. The Chairman of this Committee, Henry S. Reuss from Wisconsin, in his forward to the 120-page report stated:

> "I transmit herewith a staff study of the corporate, banking and trade association relationships of the directors of the 12 Federal Reserve Banks.
>
> This Committee has observed for many years the influence of private interests over the essentially public responsibIlities of the Federal Reserve System.
>
> As the study makes clear, it is difficult to imagine a more narrowly-based board of directors for a public agency than has been gathered together for the twelve banks of the Federal Reserve System.
>
> Only two segments of American society – banking and big business-have any substantial representation on the boards, and often even these become merged through interlocking directorates.
>
> The study raises a substantial question about the Federal Reserve's oft-repeated claim of "independence". One might ask, independent from what? Surely not banking or big business, if we are to judge from the massive inter-locks revealed by this analysis of the district boards.
>
> The big business and banking dominance of the Federal Reserve System cited in this report can be traced, in part, to the original Federal Reserve Act, which gave

member commercial banks the right to select two-thirds of the directors of each district bank But the Board of Governors in Washington must share the responsibility for this imbalance. They appoint the so-called "public" members of the boards of each district bank, appointments which have largely reflected the same narrow interests of the bank-elected members.

The parochial nature of the boards affects the public interest across a wide area, ranging from monetary policy to bank regulation These are the directors, for example, who initially select the presidents of the 12 district banks—officials who serve on the Federal Open Market Committee, determining the nation's money supply and the level of economic activity. The selection of these public officials, with such broad and essential policymaking powers, should not be in the hands of boards of directors selected and dominated by private banking and corporate interests.

* The nation would be better served by making the Federal Reserve System truly independent of big business and banking, freed of its built-in conflicts of interest, and more open in its activities for example.

* Voting membership, on the Federal Open Market Committee should be restricted to officers appointed by the President of the United States.

* The three Class A directors, who by law must be bankers, should be prohibited from participating in decisions bearing directly or indirectly on bank or holding company regulatory matters....

...Until we have basic reforms, the Federal Reserve System will be handicapped in carrying out its public responsibilities as an economic stabilization and bank regulatory agency. The System's mandate is too essential to the nation's welfare to leave so much of the machinery under the control of narrow private interests. Concentration of economic and financial power in the United States has gone too far. We should celebrate our Bicentennial by reversing the trend away from Thomas Jefferson."

Henry S. Reuss

HENRY S. REUSS, *Chairman,*
Banking, Currency and Housing Committee
Of the U.S. House of Representatives.

(Source: "Federal Reserve Directors: A Study of Corporate and Banking Influence, Staff Report for the Committee on Banking, Currency and Housing," House of Representatives, 94th Congress, Second Session, August 6, 1976, pages III & IV, as retrieved from http://adabyron.net/FederalReserveDirectors.pdf).

The report provides a treasure chest of information from nearly 40 years ago regarding the detailed makeup and inherent conflicts of interest of the members and directors of the Federal Reserve System, as well as their ownership and relationship interests with major companies and elite families around the world.

These conflicts carry forward to this very day (see Senator Bernie Sanders comments on conflicts in The $30 Trillion Heist---Follow The Money! Volume II, Chapter 2, "The Fed's Conflicts, Lack of Transparency & Control of The Business Cycle") and their ingrown presence RESULTED in the manipulation of Congress and the American people to the tune of nearly $30 Trillion over a two-and-a-half year period (and ***God*** only knows how many more trillions have been taken since 1913…).

Allowing a system of conflicts to exist simply inspires subterfuge in the ongoing operations of the Federal Reserve System.

Chairman Reuss' report focused on only the direct links of the Federal Reserve directors to the banking and corporate community and did not attempt to detail all of the massive conflicts which occur through secondary interlocks. Many of the directors of the Federal Reserve Banks are chief operating officers and chairmen of companies whose boards, in turn, have major links among other industrial and financial giants.

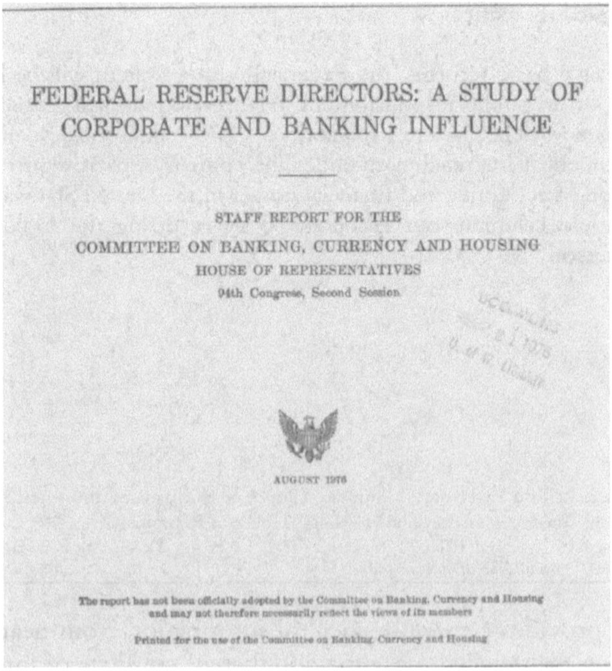

FEDERAL RESERVE DIRECTORS: A STUDY OF CORPORATE AND BANKING INFLUENCE

STAFF REPORT FOR THE

COMMITTEE ON BANKING, CURRENCY AND HOUSING

HOUSE OF REPRESENTATIVES

94th Congress, Second Session

AUGUST 1976

The report has not been officially adopted by the Committee on Banking, Currency and Housing and may not therefore necessarily reflect the views of its members

Printed for the use of the Committee on Banking, Currency and Housing

As the report shows and tells us:

> "The tabular charts clearly show that substantial segments of corporate/banking power have a channel of communication and influence into the Federal Reserve Bank of New York—easily the most important of the district banks, with substantial roles in monetary policy and international operations of the entire Federal Reserve System. While these secondary links spread out through the twelve district banks like an international cobweb, this study does not determine the extent to which these links influence Federal Reserve directors. However, they are, at a minimum, additional evidence of the dominance of big corporations and big banking institutions in the backgrounds and the day-to-day lives of the great majority of Federal Reserve directors."
> (Source: ibid, page 56, underline, author's emphasis).

Here are the conflicts, interrelationships and interests as Congress saw them. The Fed is entangled with rich owners who do not serve the American public's interests---these people only serve their own.

Chart 2-A

District Two

FEDERAL RESERVE BANK OF NEW YORK
Class A Directors

DAVID ROCKEFELLER	STUART MC CARTY	HARRY J. TAW
Chase Manhattan Corporation, Chairman , (Holding company for nine banks, including Chase Manhattan Bank, N.A.) $57.8 billion/assets, Holding Company Rank: 2 -Chase Manhattan Bank, N.A., New York, New York, Chairman, $33.8 billion, Rank: 3. -Chase Manhattan Bank, (Switzerland), Director. -Chase International Investment Corporation, Chairman, (wholly- owned foreign financing subsidiary of the Chase Manhattan Bank, N.A.) -Chase Manhattan Bank Foundation, Chairman. -Rockefeller Brothers Fund, Trustee, Vice-Chairman and Member of Executive Committee, Chairman, nominating Committee. -Rockefeller Family Fund, Trustee, member of Executive Committee. -Rockefeller Center, Inc., Director& Member, Finance Comm.	First-City National Bank of Binghamton, N.Y., President, $231 million, Rank: 395. -Lincoln Firstbanks, Inc., Dir. And Vice-President (bank holding company which owns above bank). $2.6 billion/assets; Holding Company Rank: 28 -Crowley Foods, Inc., Director. -Systems Manufacturing Company, Director. -Security Mutual Life Insurance Company, Director. -New York State Bankers Association, Member, Government Relations Committee, September, 1974- . -Comptroller of the Currency's Regional Advisory Commission for the 2nd National Bank Region, Member, 1968-1969.	-First National Bank of Cortland, N. Y., President, $53.5 million, Rank: 1,782. -Cortland County Development Corporation, Vice-President. -Independent Bankers Assoc. New York State, Director., 1975-1976. -New York State Bankers Assoc. Treasurer and Member Board of Directors. -New York State Bankers Assoc. Member at Large, Council of Administration, 1969. -Comptroller of the Currency's Regional Advisory Commission, Member, 1970-1971.

49
Tabular Chart A

David Rockefeller Chairman of the Board Chase Manhattan Corp

Chase Manhattan Corp. Officer & Director Interlocks

Private Investment Co. for America	Allied Chemical Corporation (2)	American Express Co. (2)	AT&T	United Sates Steel Corp.
Firestone Tire & Rubber Company	General Motors	Hewlett-Packard	Pacific North-western Bell Co.	Richardson Merrill Inc
Orion Multinational	Rockefeller Family & Associates	FMC Corporation	BeachviLime Ltd.	Metropolitan Life Insurance Co
ASARCO, Inc. (2)	Chrysler Corp. (2)	Utah Int'l Inc.	Eveleth Expansion Company	Private Investment Co
Southern Peru copper Corp.	Int'l Basic Economy Corp	Exxon Corporation	Fidelity Union Bancorporation	May Department
Industrial Miners Mexico S.A.	Selected Risk Investment	International Nickel/ Canada	Cypress Woods Corporation	Norton-Simon Inc.
Continental Co.	R. H. Macy & Co.	Equitable Life Assurance Soc.	International Minerals &	Sperry Rand Corporation
Honeywell, Inc.	Selected Risk Investment & Co.	Federated Capital Corporation	Burlington Industries	Stone-Webster Inc.
Northwest Airlines, Inc.	Omega Fund, Inc.	Federated Dept. Stores	Wachovia Corporation	San Salvador Development Company
Northwestern Bell Telephone Co.	Squibb Corporation	General Electric	Jefferson Pilot Corporation	Standard Oil of Indiana
Minnesota Mining & Mfg. Co	Olin Corporation	American Petroleum Institute	Private Investment Co. for America	
	Mutual Benefit Life Ins. Co. of New Jersey (2)	Scott Paper Co.	R. J. Reynolds Industries, Inc	
		American Petroleum Institute		

50
Tabular Chart B

William S. Sneath President, Union Carbide Corporation

Chase Manhattan Corp. Officer & Director Interlocks

Private Investment Co. for America	Canadian Pacific Steamships, Ltd	ASARCO	Morgan Guaranty Trust Company	J. C. Penney
Firestone Tire & Rubber Company	Pacific Logging Co.	American Title Insurance Co.	J. P. Morgan Company	Great American Reserve Insurance Co.
Orion Multinational Services Ltd	Marathon Realty Co., Inc	Chrysler Corporation	Depository Trust Company	
ASARCO, Inc. (2)	Soo Line Railroad Co.	Continental Corporation	Metropolitan Life Insurance Company	
Southern Peru copper Corp.	Great Lake Paper Company	Continental Insurance Company	Canadian Pacific Investments, Ltd	
Industrial Miners Mexico S.A.	Trans-Canada Piple Lines, Ltd	Security Reinsurance Corp., Ltd	Canadian Pacific Securities, Ltd	
Continental Co.	Canadian Marconi Co.	Putnam Trust	Chase Manhattan Corp. (Member, International Advisory Board)	
Honeywell, Inc.	Canadian Fund, Inc	Toronto Dominion Bank & Trust	The Royal Bank of Canada	
Northwest Airlines, Inc.	Great American Reserve Insurance Company	National Reinsurance Corporation	Sun Life Assurance Company of Canada	
Northwestern Bell Telephone Co.	Manufacturers Hanover Trust Co. (Former Chief Exec. Officer)	Chemical Bank (Member, East Side Advisory Board)	Canadian Investment Fund	
	American Century Mortgage Investors			

51
Tabular Chart C

Jack B. Jackson
President, J. C. Penney Co.,

J. C. Penney Co., Inc., Officer and Director Interlocks

- Protection Mutual Insurance Company
- Great American Reserve Insurance Company (2)
- Educator & Executive Insurers, Inc. (2)
- Educator & Executive Life Insurance Co.
- J. C. Penney Financial Corporation (2)
- J. C. Penney Insurance Co. (3)
- J. C. Penney Life Ins. Co. (3)
- Sarma (Belgium) S.A. (2)
- Discount Corp. of N. Y.
- United Mutual Savings Bank

- Grumman Corporation
- Inmont Corporation
- JCP Realty, Inc.
- New York Telephone Company
- Ball Corp.
- Bankers Trust Co.
- Bankers Trus New York Corporation
- Bristol Myers Co. (2)
- Union Dime Savings Bank
- Thiokol Corporation

- Simplicity Pattern Co.
- Kennecot Copper Corp.
- 1st Fed'l Savings & Loan Association
- United States Trust Company
- N. Y. Stock Exchange
- Citicorp
- Citibank (FNCB, N.Y.)
- General Electric
- FNCB-Waltons Corporation
- Rand Corporation

- Wackenhut Corporation

52
Tabular Chart D

Maurice F. Granville, Chairman of the Board, Texaco, Incorporated

Texaco Officer & Director Interlocks

- Arabian American Oil Company
- Brown Brothers Harriman & Co.
- Brown Harriman & International Bks. Ltd
- American Express
- American Express Int'; Bkg. Corp.
- Anaconda
- Rockefeller Foundation
- Owens-Corning Fiberglass
- National City Bk. (Cleveland)
- Sun Life Assurance Co.
- General Reinsurance.
- General Electric.

- St. John d'el Ray Mining Co., Ltd.
- National Steel Corporation
- Massey-Ferguson, Ltd.
- Mutual Life Insurance Co.
- Mass Mutual Income Investors
- United Services Life Ins Co.
- Fairchild Industries
- Blount, Inc.
- William Wrigley, Jr., Co
- Natonal Blvd. Bk. Of Chicago
- Lykes Youngstown Corporation
- Inmont Corporation

- Ligget & Myers, Inc.

53
Tabular Chart E

Alan Pifer, President, Carnegie Corporation of New York

Carnegie Corporation Officer & Director Interlocks

- Rockefeller Center, Inc.
- The Cabot Corporation
- Federal Reserve Bank of Boston
- Owens, Corning Fiberglass
- New England Telephone Co.
- Fisher Scientific Company
- Mellon National Corporation
- Equitable Life Assurance Society
- Twentieth Century Fox Corporation
- J. Henry Schroder Banking Corporation

- J. Henry Schroder Trust Company
- Paul Revere Investors, Inc.
- Qualpeco, Inc.

54
Tabular Chart F

Robert H. Knight, Partner, Shearman & Sterling, Attornerys, N.Y.C.

Law Firm represents:

- The First National City Corporation, N.Y.
- The Bank of Nova Scotia Trust Company of New York
- The Canadian Bank of Commerce Trust Co. (N.Y.)
- The Fuji Bank and Trust Company, N.Y.C.

55
Tabular Chart G

Frank R. Milliken, President, Kennecott Copper Corporations

Kennecott Copper Officer & Director Interlocks

- Marine Midland Bank
- Zion's Utah Bancorporation
- Beneficial Life
- Affiliated Bankshares
- Atlantic Mutual Co.
- Citibank (FNCB) (2)
- Centennial Insurance Co.
- Omega Fund
- CIT Financial Corp.
- Madison Fund

- Guaranty Bank & Trust Co.
- J. P. Morgan & Co.
- Morgan Guaranty Trust Co. (2)
- Imperial Life Assurance Company of Canada
- Roy West Banking Corporation
- Trust Corporation of the Bahamas
- Braden Copper Co. (subsidiary of Kennecott) (5)
- Kennecott Refining Corporation

- Goodyear Tire and Rubber Co.
- Goodyear Canada Inc.
- Lykes-Youngstown Corporation
- Wards Foods, Inc.
- Chubb Corporation
- Eastern Airlines
- W. R. Grace & Co. (2)
- Zions First National Bank
- Hotel Utah
- Utah Portland Cement Company
- Heber J. Grand Co.
- Denver & Rio Grande and Western Railway (2)
- Mountain Fuel Supply Company

- Rio Grande Industries (2)
- Broadmoor Hotel, Inc.
- 1st Nat'l Bk. Of Colorado Springs
- Manitou & Pikes Peak Railway Co.
- Mountain States Telephone & Telegraph Co.
- S. S. Kresge Co.
- Bristol Myers
- United Mutual Savings Bank
- Simplicity Patterns
- 1st Federal Savings and Loan Association
- United States Trust Company
- J. C. Penney

- New York Stock Exchange
- Continental Can Company
- Citicorp (2)
- General Motors
- Ingersoll Rand Co.
- Stone & Webster
- Deering Milliken
- Pacific Tin Consolidated Corporation
- Alex Brown & Sons
- McGraw Hill, Inc.
- Kuhn, Loeb & Co.
- Los Angeles and Salt Lake Railroad
- Westinghouse
- Uniroyal, Inc.

- Getty Oil Company
- Chase Brass & Copper
- Norton Company
- Merck & Company
- Montreal Trust Company
- Great Atlantic & Pacific Tea Co.

(Source for the preceeding charts, ibid, pages 9, 49-55)

"***A 1975 study of the expense vouchers of Federal Reserve district banks revealed relatively heavy expenditures for entertainment, dinners and other functions, including joint meetings between the Federal Reserve district banks and the commercial bankers associations.*** The same expense reports contain a substantial number of outlays for dues and fees to various private organizations—at least some of which apparently fall within the 'public relations' area.[7] At the national level, some of the activities of the Federal Reserve directors are masked behind their corporate shields, and it is often difficult to distinguish the lobbying generated by the Federal Reserve banks from that of the corporate-banking lobby.

Throughout 1975, directors of Federal Reserve district banks flooded the Congress with letters urging the defeat of the audit legislation. For example, Malcolm T. Stamper told the Congress he was opposing the legislation 'in my capacity as president of the Boeing Company and as Chairman of the Seattle Federal Reserve' branch. Since that time Mr. Stamper has been promoted. He is now a class B director at the San Francisco Federal Reserve Bank.

Crown Zellerbach was another major corporation which lobbied against the audit bill. Its president—Charles Dahl—is another Class B director on the Federal Reserve Bank in San Francisco. Similar letters opposing the audit bill came from Dresser Industries, an energy industry manufacturing conglomerate, whose chairman was a Class C director of the Federal Reserve District Bank of Dallas.

This was the pattern across the country, with the Federal Reserve calling on its corporate-banking directors to lead the lobbying campaign. In some cases, former directors were enlisted in the battle. At least one of these former directors—from the Federal Reserve branch in El Paso, TX—Informed the Banking Committee of attempts by the president of the Federal Reserve Bank of Dallas to have him join the letter-writing campaign.

This type of lobbying activity is not limited to the audit proposals, but is available to the Federal Reserve on a wide range of banking, regulatory and legislative issues. In addition, these boards of prestigious businessmen serve as an on-going public relations front for the entire System.......While Corporate America has wide representation—through director interlocks—with all twelve banks in the Federal Reserve System, analysis of each district bank and cross-checking one district bank with the others reveals not only the narrow pool of talent but the "club" nature of the system.

This "club" approach leads the Federal Reserve to consistently dip into the same pools—the same companies, the same universities, the same bank holding companies—to fill directorships. This is particularly true in connection with those positions where the Board of Governors and/or the distinct banks have the right of appointment—the Class C directorships on the district boards and the various branch director positions:"

[7] *"The Federal Reserve System: Accountability or Waste"*, Staff Report of the Subcommittee on Domestic Monetary Policy. Committee on Banking, Currency and Housing. U.S. House of Representatives. 94th Congress. 1st Session. July, 1975, 41 Pages.
(Source: "Federal Reserve Directors: A Study of Corporate and Banking Influence, Staff Report for the Committee on Banking, Currency and Housing," House of Representatives, 94th Congress, Second Session, August 1976, page 56-57, 62, Henry S. Reuss, Chairman, author's emphasis underlined, as retrieved from http://adabyron.net/FederalReserveDirectors.pdf)

The Federal Reserve System of the United States is hopelessly conflicted and needs to be dissolved. The Congress needs to take back the authority to control the United States' money supply and monetary policy. This is the only solution which will help save the country from a continuing explosion in the number of poor people and an overall reduction in the standard of living for the vast majority of Americans.

It is only logical these travesties would happen to the masses when an elite group is literally siphoning off trillions and trillions of dollars from taxpayer's pockets---forcing them to pay more taxes and live with higher inflation costs to pay for the greed, avarice and malevolent intentions of the Federal Reserve, the banks and the elite.

Chapter 10
Worthless Securities-How to Hide Them-Where They Go to Die!

Unfortunately for all of us, we are left holding the bag. The Federal Reserve grossly and egregiously breached its fiduciary duties by actively purchasing worthless, near worthless, fraudulently valued or otherwise unauthorized securities in nearly $30 Trillion of secret transactions during the mortgage and credit crisis, pursuant to the GAO audit. As the audit confirms, the money was undisputedly secretly given directly to the banks and the elite to reimburse them for their bad bets made during the mortgage and credit crisis. This enabled what this book and the trilogy labels, "The $30 Trillion Heist"---the most vile, skullduggerous act in the history of our nation.

Never before in the history of mankind has so few…inflicted so much damage…on so many people.

A staggering **$30 Trillion Dollars has been HEISTED from the U.S. taxpayer, with over $26 Trillion of it taken over only a 2 ½ year period between December 1, 2007 and July 21, 2010.** The balance is from the publicly announced "QE" programs of the Fed, which will total approximately $4 Trillion when they are completed.

The suspect and toxic securities are believed to be held at the Fed and the Federal Reserve Member Banks in an array of on- and off-balance sheet vehicles, as collateral on never-to-be-repaid loans and concealed purchases, as most of the swaps, purchases and bridges transacted upon are likely worthless today (or worth only a fraction of the value exchanged for them). The American taxpayer will likely NEVER be repaid.

The Fed and the Federal Reserve Banks Do NOT follow GAAP

The Fed and Wall Street will undoubtedly say, "This is impossible!" They will look right into the camera and say, ***"…but we were audited!"*** Indeed they were, but the ***partial*** GAO audit and Federal Reserve annual reports reveal a dirty little secret which most people don't realize:

The Fed does not have to obey Generally Accepted Accounting Principles!

Why not, you ask? For the incredible reason the Fed has instituted *its own* set of accounting standards which in fact, permit off-balance vehicles and assets, among some other very questionable and suspicious accounting standards susceptible to manipulation and potentially fraud! The Federal Reserve, apparently, considers itself above the law of the land and instituted its own accounting standards for the benefit of its elite owners.

Critical to understanding this smoke screen is the fact the Fed has granted itself the authority, via its self-promulgated accounting rules, to value worthless securities AT THEIR FACE VALUE.

This means even worthless securities you couldn't sell to anybody on planet earth, can be valued by the Fed at 100% of their original issuance price, or PAR value (see, later in this chapter, "Reserve Banks Record Worthless Securities at Face Value—Not Market Value!," as well as The $30 Trillion Heist---Follow The Money! Volume II, Chapter 12, "Honesty and Integrity of the Federal Reserve," subsection, "How They Actually Take the Money to Buy the Ferrari"), instead of their fair market value---which was likely worthless!

Just imagine the "ye protest too much" responses from the bankers when they are confronted by these facts! We can almost see and hear CNN now, capturing a reincarnated Mr. Bernanke in Ms. Yellen, and their co-conspirators, indignantly (at least pretending to be) saying:

"But, the Board of Governors is independent, we are not controlled by the banks!"

"There is no collusion!"

"All valuations were done in accordance with accounting standards!"

"We do not operate for the banks, we operate for the American people!" etc., etc.

It is enough to make a knowledgeable person want to vomit.

The decision of the Federal Open Market Committee ("FOMC") and the Board of Governors to SECRETLY allow worthless (or near worthless, or otherwise fraudulently valued) securities to be exchanged with failing institutions, not authorized in the Federal Reserve Act of 1913, for U.S. cash and U.S. Treasury securities is just plain wrong.

The Federal Open Market Committee's decisions are implemented by the New York Federal Reserve Bank, whose experience is heavily relied upon in the FOMC meetings and as a result, is heavily weighted in favor of the operating banks. The New York Federal Reserve Bank (which is a private company OWNED by its member banks and their elite owners) owns a permanent seat on the Committee--the only Reserve Bank member to do so.

Board of Governors Guaranteed Big Pay Days

As is no secret, the Board of Governors (Mr. Bernanke, Mr. Greenspan in his day and the other directors) are all guaranteed, through Wall Street's oldest traditions, of rich payoffs as soon as they leave the Fed.

They have to wait a couple of years to work directly for a bank, but in the interim two-year period, they are all hired to give speeches and consult with banking entities, or affiliated companies, all over the globe at exorbitant rates---as directed by the member banks and the elite. As a result, these people can never be objective and they will always play ball with and for the banks first, with the American people a very distant second or third place, if you count the fact the Fed bailed out Europe, as well during the credit crisis---using U.S. taxpayer-backed dollars to make the save!

Mr. Bernanke, Ms. Yellen and the Fed seem to have gotten away with his sleight of hand in raiding the U.S. Treasury, at least to date. This has happened, despite the fact it appears his Fed unilaterally ignored the laws and provisions of the Federal Reserve Act by electing to secretly aid and abet a select group of citizens and companies using trillions of U.S. taxpayer-backed dollars.

As a result, Mr. Bernanke's and Ms. Yellen's Fed continues to use good-as-gold, U.S. taxpayer-backed Fed credits and other cash-equivalents to create trillions of more dollars "out-of-thin-air" through "QE" programs to aid, abet and assist the member banks, the elite and the institutions which serve them.

It is highly likely the toxic securities taken in by the Fed are sitting on its books, with a gigantic loss having been hidden from the public. This is only made possible because the Federal Reserve is protected by its opaque accounting standards and its refusal to be honest with the American public.

In the Fed's "QE3" program, or some call it "QE Infinity," Mr. Bernanke turned the green light on, yet again, for a major party to be held at the banks, as the Federal Reserve was purchasing a total of $85 Billion of potentially worthless paper a month---$40 Billion A MONTH until mid-2015 and another $45 Billion A MONTH through "Operation Twist." Ms. Yellen has recently announce some cutbacks in the amount of quantitative easing---which, ultimately will cause interest rates to rise---and bring about D'Apocalypse™.

These total an additional $1.02 TRILLION dollars/year in giveaways for through 2015, from the date of Mr. Bernanke's announcement on September 13, 2012. Despite Mr. Bernanke's indications the Fed may "taper off," the damage is already done. Mr. Bernanke's problem is the market he pushed up through Assflation™ is in a bubble and will continue to inflate until it bursts. It is completely out of his control at this point in time.

Despite May 2013 comments by Federal Reserve of Philadelphia's President, Charles Plosser, (i.e., the Fed could end "QE" in 2013 if the employment situation improved"), **the die is cast.**

Combined with the $26 Trillion given away from December 1, 2007-July 21, 2010, the total amount of heisted money using U.S. taxpayer-backed cash and cash-equivalents will hit nearly $30 Trillion by 2015, DOUBLE THE ENTIRE UNITED STATES GROSS DOMESTIC PRODUCT.

In testimony before Congress on May 22, 2013, Mr. Bernanke said the Fed plans to continue its $85 billion-a-month purchases in Treasury and mortgage bonds until the job market improves substantially. Of course Mr. Bernanke, under pressure from the likes of Congressman Kevin Brady, Chairman of the Joint Economic Committee (a panel composed of members from both the Senate and the House of Representatives), hedged his bets for the sound bite and indicated the Fed could increase OR decrease purchases, depending on how the economy performs and if inflation shows any sign of rearing its ugly head.

Translation: the Fed will do EVERYTHING it can to help the banks first until they have sold back every single worthless security, in every off-balance vehicle they have under their control---back to the American public!

Without Complete Access & Regular Full-Blown Audits, the Worst Must Be Assumed

Some may find this interpretation a bit cynical of the author, however, the facts argue otherwise. Without full access to ALL aspects of the Federal Reserve operations and without a TRULY independent audit, a reasonable person MUST expect the worst case scenario and assume as a country we are sitting on a $30 Trillion bombshell.

The Fed and Federal Reserve Bank's Off-Balance Sheet Vehicles Hide the Truth

The following excerpts from Federal Reserve Annual Reports and GAO reports to Congress ***highlight the problems with the banks AND the Federal Reserve using off-balance vehicles.*** Underlining has been added to highlight important disclosures regarding this ongoing, monstrous issue.

As discussed and produced through evidence in this book, the Federal Reserve System is not subject to GAAP (Generally Accepted Accounting Principles) and does not have to report off-balance vehicles and can ignore the true value of securities when valuing them for purposes of its balance sheet.

As an example and to make this point crystal clear, the Fed can count a worthless security at its original issuance price of $10,000,000.00 instead of at its proper fair market value of "$0.00," in the case, let's say, of a toxic mortgage pool. The Fed pays the banks and elite $10,000,000.00 in U.S. taxpayer-backed cash. The loss of the $10,000,000.00 will then ultimately and over time, be foisted onto the American public.

Using the Fed's accounting rules, the loss can be amortized over a 30-year mortgage bond's life, it can also be hidden completely in an off-balance vehicle---with the write-off happening 30 years from now, long after Mr. Bernanke and his cohorts are in the grave. Alternatively, the Fed could decide to NEVER even surface the off-balance sheet vehicle, keeping the transactions buried FOREVER, brushing them under the carpet of history. This small example was with only ten million dollars. Imagine the magnitude of the potential fraud with $30 TRILLION in secret transactions----twice the size of the U.S. Gross Domestic Product!

America will and is suffering because the losses come back through taxation pressure, a weakened U.S. balance sheet and serious inflation---all debilitations with serious ramifications on the way of life for all Americans.

The other evil aspect of these activities is potentially worse than even these grim points. Reimbursing the rich and elite for their $30 Trillion in losses provides socialism for the rich and extreme hardship for everybody else.

This is exactly the strategy the Spanish deployed when they conquered most of South America---and then lost it. They plundered nations, took the spoils and left the masses with NOTHING. This worked out well, initially, for the monarchs and elite, as they grew rich. Over time, of course, the sun set on the Spanish Empire, as every single nation rejected its rule. Today the country of Spain has horrendous debt problems, as is well known. Without serious political and economic reform, Spain will get much worse and will not be alone. The United States will not be far behind.

This kind of action—the empowered few for the elite rich, surreptitiously robbing the nation of its wealth---creates vast differences between classes of people. This is something America has never had to deal with before, on a relative basis, in its entire history. America has always been known as the "great middle class."

By design, however, the Fed has made it very difficult to trace back the questioned transactions to the Fed, the banks and the elite without help from books like this one and a massive campaign to our Congressmen and Senators. Reform is urgently needed, as we head straight for D'Apocalypse™.

The following are some of the Notes to the Financial Statements, as mentioned previously:

Notes to the Combined Financial Statements of the Federal Reserve Banks 2007:

> "The Federal Reserve has supervisory and regulatory authority over a variety of financial institutions and activities. It plays an important role as umbrella supervisor of bank holding companies, including financial holding companies. And it is the primary federal supervisor of state banks that are members of the Federal Reserve System....Liquidity and capital were strained as some BHCs (author comment: Bank Holding Companies) brought certain off-balance-sheet exposures onto their books....persisting problems in the commercial paper market that had sparked draws on back-up lines of credit, and more recently, consolidation of

assets of off-balance-sheet affiliates onto banks' balance sheets….the FRBNY (author's comment: Federal Reserve Bank of New York) may enter into transactions that contain varying degrees of off-balance-sheet market risk that result from their future settlement and counter-party credit risk." (Source: 94th Annual Report 2007, Board of Governors of the Federal Reserve, page 265, 362).

From the 2011 Annual Report of the Federal Reserve:

"Regulatory capital ratios of bank holding companies rose further as large institutions prepared to meet future requirements that are expected to be more stringent than those currently in place. The Basel III framework agreed to by the governors and heads of supervision of countries represented on the Basel Committee on Banking Supervision will raise required capital ratios, tighten the definition of regulatory capital, and increase the risk weights assigned to some assets and off-balance-sheet exposures." (Source: 98th Annual Report of the Board of Governors of the Federal Reserve, 2011, pg. 72, as retrieved from http://www.federalreserve.gov/publications/annual-report/files/2011-annual-report.pdf).

Author's comment: As you can read in the Fed's own notes to its financial statements, bank holding companies can ***STILL*** own off-balance sheet vehicles—even after the credit crisis debacle proved they were a land mine!! The banks merely have to apply a computer model to them and assign a given portfolio a risk variable and calculate the "theoretical" loss—they do this under a fancy process called "VaR," or Value at Risk.

VaR is a widely used risk measure of theoretical loss on a specific portfolio of financial assets, probability and time horizon. This kind of thinking led to the downfall of Long Term Capital Management and the onset of the Credit Crisis, where seemingly "valuable" portfolios wound up being worthless. All the variables in such models are subject to the control of the banks and the attitude of "What could possibly go wrong??" is NEVER covered by these blind models.

These models mask the real risk from the public's eyes, while allowing the banks to INFINITELY LEVERAGE THEIR CAPITAL CREATING THE WORST CASE SCENARIO FOR THE COUNTRY AND WORLD THROUGH A DERIVATIVES COLLAPSE—CALLED D'APOCALYPSE™!

"China continued to tighten its monetary policy, extending reserve requirements to a wider range of bank liabilities as it attempted to rein in off-balance sheet lending by its banks." (Source: ibid, pg. 268).

(**Author's comment:** Derivatives risk is a GLOBAL risk, involving nearly every country.)

"In connection with its foreign currency activities, the FRBNY may enter into transactions that are subject to varying degrees of off-balance-sheet market risk and counterparty credit risk that result from their future settlement. The FRBNY controls these risks by obtaining credit approvals, establishing transaction limits, receiving collateral in some cases, and performing daily monitoring procedures." (Source: ibid, pg. 396).

"The FRBNY enters into commitments to buy and sell federal agency and GSEMBS (author comment: "Government Sponsored Enterprise Mortgage Backed Securities") and records the related securities on a settlement-date basis. As of December 31, 2011, the total purchase price of the federal agency and GSEMBS under outstanding purchase commitments was $41,503 million, of which $513 million was related to dollar roll transactions. As of December 31, 2011, the total sales price of the federal agency and GSEMBS under outstanding sales commitments was $4,430 million, all of which was related to dollar roll transactions. These commitments, which had contractual settlement dates extending through February 2012, are for the purchase and sale of TBAMBS (author comment: "To Be Announced Mortgage Backed Security") for which the number and identity of the pools that will be delivered to fulfill the commitment are unknown at the time of the trade. As of December 31, 2011, the fair value of federal agency and GSEMBS purchases and sales, net under outstanding commitments was $41,873 million and $4,473 million, respectively. These commitments are subject to varying degrees of off-balance-sheet market risk and counterparty credit risk that result from their future settlement. (Source: ibid, pg. 394).

The GAO Report to Congressional Committee July 27, 2011:

"***The financial crisis also has raised concerns about the management of and capital treatment for risks associated with certain off-balance sheet assets, including contingent liquidity and reputation risks. Many large financial institutions created SPEs (author comment: SPE = "Special Purpose Enterprise") to buy and hold mortgage-related securities and other assets that were previously on their balance sheet***....SPEs also are known as off-balance sheet entities, because they generally are structured in such a way that their assets and liabilities are not required to be consolidated and reported as part of the overall balance sheet of the financial institution that created them. According to federal banking regulators, when a bank committed to provide contingent funding support to an SPE, it generally would have been required to hold a small amount of capital against such a commitment. [92] ***For some types of SPEs, such as structured investment vehicles, banks provided no such contingent commitments and were subject to no capital charge.*** Nevertheless, some institutions retained significant reputation risk associated with their structured investment vehicles, even if they were under no legal obligation to provide financial support."[93]

[92]Contingent funding support includes liquidity facilities and credit enhancements. Liquidity facilities are the assurance of a loan or guarantee of financial support to back up an off-balance sheet entity. Credit enhancements are defined as a contractual arrangement in which a bank retains or assumes a securitization exposure and, in substance, provides some degree of added protection to the parties to the transaction.

[93]Reputation risk is the potential for financial loss associated with negative publicity regarding an institution's business practices and subsequent decline in customers, costly litigation or revenue reductions.

(Source: GAO Report to Congressional Committees, July 27, 2009, "FINANCIAL MARKETS REGULATION, Financial Crisis Highlights Need to Improve Oversight of Leverage at Financial Institutions and across System", page 56, as retrieved from http://www.gao.gov/new.items/d09739.pdf).

Figure 9: Example of an Off-Balance Sheet Entity

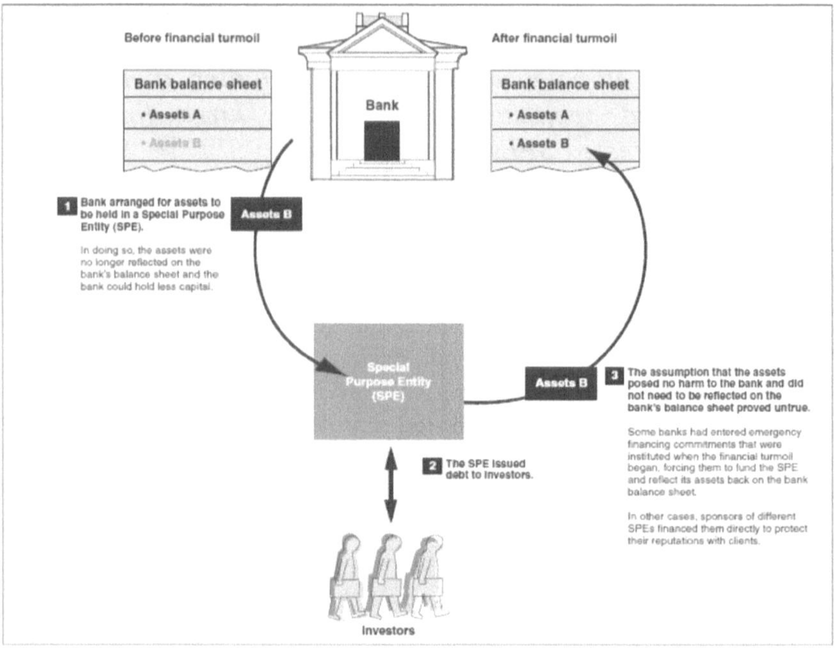

Source: GAO

(Source: ibid, page 58).

Fed Made Up Its Own Accounting Rules—Does Not Follow GAAP!

As also discussed in The $30 Trillion Heist---Follow The Money!, Volume II (Chapter 12, "Honesty and Integrity of the Federal Reserve," subsection "How the Fed Set Up the Rules to Hide Trillions…") the Federal Reserve does not use GAAP and has, even with the new Dodd-Frank legislation, numerous ways to hide and camouflage its activities, in and around Variable Interest Entities and other on- and off-balance sheet vehicles. From the 2012 Annual Report of the Fed:

"(3) Significant Accounting Policies

> ***Accounting principles for entities with the unique powers and responsibilities of the nation's central bank have not been formulated by accounting standard-setting bodies. The Board of Governors has developed specialized accounting principles and practices that it considers to be appropriate*** for the nature and function of a_central bank. These accounting principles and practices are documented in the Financial Accounting Manual for Federal Reserve Banks (FAM), which is issued by_the Board of Governors." (Source: 99th Annual Report

2012 Board of Governors of the Federal Reserve System, page 350, as retrieved from http://www.federalreserve.gov/publications/annual-report/files/2012-annual-report.pdf, author's emphasis underlined).

Reserve Banks Record Worthless Securities at Face Value—Not Market Value!

The Fed leans feebly on its self-proclamation of special status to allow itself to ***not record securities it receives in exchange for taxpayer cash at fair market value!*** This allows, as we saw in the $10,000,000.00 example previously in this chapter, the receipt of a worthless debt security to be recorded at its fraudulently higher original face value, permit the Fed to reimburse its member banks 100% for their loss—and carry the worthless security on the books of taxpayers forever!

This loss gets foisted deliberately on the American people and is amortized over the life of the worthless asset (i.e., a 30-year mortgage bond could be amortized over a 30-year period!), or otherwise hidden from view, as discussed. "SOMA" (referred to in the following excerpt is the "System Open Market Account") is perhaps the main vehicle for the Reserve Banks to move good U.S. Cash to the member banks and elite, in exchange for worthless debt and questionable collateral. Again, citing the 2012 Annual Report of the Federal Reserve Board of Governors, as it relates to the twelve Federal Reserve Banks:

> "Limited differences exist between the accounting principles and practices in the FAM and accounting principles generally accepted in the United States of America (GAAP), due to the unique nature of the Reserve Banks' powers and responsibilities as part of the nation's central bank and given the System's unique responsibility to conduct monetary policy. ***The primary differences are the presentation of all SOMA securities holdings at amortized cost and the recording of all SOMA securities on a settlement-date basis."*** (Source: ibid, page 351).

Accounting Vehicles Disguise Transactions and Mask Worthless Securities

Also, reading along in the 2012 Annual Report footnotes, the alert reader discovers in order for the Fed to acquire trillions and trillions and trillions of dollars in worthless and/or questionable securities from even only the KNOWN vehicles used by the Fed (in this case, the "Maiden Lane" Variable Interest Entities set up by the Fed), ***the Federal Reserve banks***

have ELIMINATED INTERCOMPANY BALANCES AND TRANSACTIONS!

The effect and intent of this, of course, is to potentially and massively ***understate*** the amount of securities involved in the transactions on the balance sheets. Again, from the 2012 Annual Report:

> "a. Consolidation
> The combined financial statements include the accounts and results of operations of the Reserve Banks as well as several variable interest entities (VIEs), which include Maiden Lane LLC (ML), Maiden Lane II LLC (ML II), Maiden Lane III LLC (ML III), and TALF LLC. The consolidation of the VIEs was assessed in accordance with Financial Accounting Standards Board (FASB) Accounting Standards Codification (ASC) Topic 810 (ASC 810) Consolidation, which requires a VIE to be consolidated by its controlling financial interest holder. Intercompany balances and transactions have been eliminated in consolidation. See Note 6 for additional information on the VIEs." (Source: ibid, page 352)

No Cash Flow Statements for Federal Reserve Banks

And, finally, the Federal Reserve Banks do not report, or publish, a basic cash flow statement---absolutely a must in any conscionable set of financial statements for any company!!

Even the Board of Governors of the Federal Reserve provides a cash-flow statement for its operations! The banks, where the action is, DO NOT!! This is beyond suspicious and it smacks of intent to deceive, with the sole intention to hide the true activities of the Federal Reserve Banks!

> "***In addition, the Reserve Banks do not present a Combined Statement of Cash Flows as required by GAAP because the liquidity and cash position of the Reserve Banks are not a primary concern given the Reserve Banks' unique powers and responsibilities as a central bank.*** Other information regarding the Reserve Banks' activities is provided in, or may be derived from, the Combined Statements of Condition, Income and Comprehensive Income, and Changes in Capital, and the accompanying notes to the combined financial statements. Other than those described above, there are no significant differences between the policies outlined in the FAM and GAAP." (Source: ibid, page 351, author's emphasis underlined).

A couple of key points to notice. It is obvious the Fed doesn't have to play by the same rules as anyone else and can value securities and hold them in nearly any manner it sees fit---even if they are invisible to the likes of the general public, Congress and auditing personnel.

What is also interesting is in the Fed's own 2011 Annual Report, it indicates under the BASEL III accord the Fed would"...increase the risk weights assigned to some assets and off-balance-sheet exposures." By definition, this means the ***banks can still hold off-balance vehicles with all the exposure they entail.***

Founding Father's Rolling in Their Graves

This pillaging of America's wealth, indebting it to bankers to the additional tune of nearly $30 Trillion (on top of the other trillions they have taken out of the system since the foundation of the Fed in 1913---just as reported by Congressman Lindbergh back in 1917, as discussed in more detail later in this chapter, subsection "1917 Impeachment Speech By Congressman Charles Lindbergh"), is truly the most historic, horrific and astonishing heist EVER committed in the history of mankind and has our founding fathers' rolling in their graves.

It is a particularly grave concern because while the Fed acted **WITHOUT AUTHORITY** in creating $30 Trillion and secretly giving it away to the banks and the elite, **CONGRESS DOES HAVE THE AUTHORITY** to print the same $30 trillion and could use it to refund taxes back to the middle class, the working poor, the upper class!

If they had done this, it would have ***definitely kick started*** the economy and provided for DIRECT AND IMMEDIATE help in every city under attack in America!

This would be NO LESS INFLATIONARY than the Fed's current policy because the Fed is just giving away cash, cash equivalents and treasury securities in exchange for toxic assets from the banks and elite!

The big difference is the Fed is giving $30 Trillion to rich people and this book suggests a far better way would be to spread it around to all Americans.

We would be far better off ***giving the people*** a direct infusion of money, on a massive scale, and setting up incentive, enterprise zones in those areas hardest hit by the mortgage and credit crisis debacle. This would solve the unemployment problem and go back to a system where and how America once flourished---there was no self-appointed oligarchy over the citizens and rich people didn't socialize their losses on the poor, middle class, well off, weak and innocent!

Unfortunately the banks, the elite and the uber rich are robbing everyone blind. The real ramifications of Bernanke's and Ms. Yellen's Fed issuing nearly $30 Trillion in U.S. cash include:

1) A dramatic increase in our government's debt position; and
2) A flooding of the rich with reimbursement money, causing Assflation™, where only the elite's asset classes appreciate in value, while damaging the rest of the economy; and
3) Escalation of the costs of everything, as the wealthy use their newly acquired wealth to drive asset, commodity, food, real estate and other prices to rise dramatically; and
4) A Massive destruction to the jobs base for the common man in both domestic and international markets as the $30 Trillion is hoarded and not reinvested in economy; and
5) Absolute havoc for over forty-million taxpayers, as they were thrown out of their homes and onto the streets; and
6) An economic firestorm, called D'Apocalypse™, set to engulf nations in economic flames beginning in the latter part of 2015.

The real and severe impact of the Fed's foolhardy decisions will be felt AFTER Mr. Bernanke leaves his Chairman's post at the Fed. Rumor has it, he couldn't wait to go! With Janet Yellen the new Chairperson, Mr. Bernanke can only pray the world turns its attention on her, who will undoubtedly be left holding the bag.

Mr. Bernanke hopes his exit will allow him to pull an "Alan Greenspan" and he will attempt to use subterfuge and banker-speak to tell the world (just like his predecessor Mr. Greenspan tried to explain away his direct responsibility for the mortgage crisis):

⇒ ***"We had no way of expecting a bubble to come as a result of our actions to 'save' the economy";***

⇒ ***"The debt was repaid and we made a profit";***

⇒ ***"We didn't cause the derivatives market to blow up!";***

⇒ ***"We didn't cause a loss of jobs!";***

⇒ ***"We did not act solely with the interests of our owners at heart;"***

⇒ ***"We did not cause Assflation™!";***

⇒ ***"We did not cause D'Apocalypse™!"; and***

⇒ ***"It makes no difference if the Fed issues the debt, or the U.S. issues it directly, because you have to pay interest anyway!"***

You can imagine the words which will pour forth to try and cover his tracks and misdirect.

All of these theoretical statements likely to be said are lies. As any half-educated person knew, bubbles existed in the real estate market leading up to the credit crisis, there was a bubble of gigantic proportions which caused the NASDAQ crash back in 2000 and there is a current, ongoing bubble being blown throughout the credit crisis, caused by the issuance of debt securities and the pumping of money through the banks into their proprietary trading accounts—on a scale of enormity defying imagination! This is Assflation™, caused completely by the Bernanke and Yellen Fed.

Of all the theoretical statements which Mr. Bernanke could make, one of the biggest whoppers we can imagine him stating is the last one, "It makes no difference if the Fed issues the debt, or the U.S. issues it directly, because you have to pay interest anyway!"

This last lie is crucial to understand because we, as a nation, do not have to promise to pay interest to anyone! The U.S. Government can issue currency by express authority in the U.S. Constitution with its full faith and credit---at NO INTEREST!

Abraham Lincoln did just this when he issued "Greenbacks" to pay for the Civil War! They can even be pledged with collateral, as our U.S. Notes were backed by a gold reserve, at one point in time!

(Source: National Numismatic Collection at the Smithsonian Institution, as retrieved from http://www.dreamoutloud.com/2011/01/02/abraham-lincoln-issues-the-greenback/).

(Source: Antique Bank Notes retrieved from: http://www.antiquebanknotes.com/Gold-Certificate/Series-1882.aspx).

Fed Transactions Disguised and Hidden-Need Full Independent Audits

We know also, thanks to the GAO's audit and the accounting rules the Fed has granted to itself, thousands of the Fed's transactions ***are hidden off-balance sheet, being eliminated from scrutiny through "Intercompany transactions" and have been disguised and camouflaged underneath a canopy of vehicles and strategies to prevent the truth from being told.***

The Fed NEVER intends for these transactions to see the light of day, whether, or not, the loans were repaid (or are merely accounted for as fully collateralized assets with phony face values affixed to toxic securities and sketchy collateral made possible through a scandalous accounting gimmick designed to trick the American public), we won't know.

That is, we won't know until there is a full, complete physical audit of all assets, operations, buildings and personnel of the Federal Reserve and its member banks, without restrictions of any kind. This book does not advocate going to a gold standard, but any audit should also include the drilling of every single gold bar in the Federal Reserve System and Fort Knox to ensure they are not filled with Tungsten. This will answer a number of questions for the American people who have a right to know the true story on the country's gold and how much it actually owns.

Is There Outright Theft and Skullduggery at the Federal Reserve Banks?

What has been happening under the Bernanke and Yellen Fed may appear to many as an outright theft. It would be very easy to agree with this suspicion if apparent skullduggery was also taking place to hide such a crime. Do the following activities appear to be skullduggerous to you?

1) Burying the evidence through on- and off-balance sheet vehicles to intentionally veil holdings; and

2) Allowing what would be fraudulent accounting in any other company, by not conforming with Generally Accepted Accounting Principles, as is REQUIRED FOR ANY OTHER CORPORATION. This accounting gimmick allows the Fed to value securities at their face value instead of at their true, fair market value—allowing worthless securities to be exchanged for U.S. cash at the toxic securities full, face value; and

3) Plotting, perhaps intentionally, to allow TENS OF YEARS to pass by before the worthless securities come due before they are written off---or simply buried forever; and

4) Granting of "loans" at nearly zero percent interest rates, the parties and terms of which are unknown; and

5) Intentionally violating the law by circumventing the letter and spirit of the Federal Reserve Act of 1913 in both its original and amended form; and

6) Conspiring with the member banks, as well as domestic and international potential economic enemies of America to loot the American Treasury, SECRETLY, and then attempt to disguise the extent of the subterfuge and sabotage of the economy to avoid public scrutiny and punishment.

The question remains---do these activities point to skullduggery? Only each reader can decide for him, or herself.

If you agree there is skullduggery, then this CALLS FOR AN IMPEACHMENT petition to hit the floor of Congress, just as Congressman Charles Lindbergh did in 1917 against the Board of Governors of the Federal Reserve.

Such an impeachment petition should also demand a repeal of the Federal Reserve Act IN ITS ENTIRETY and a full criminal investigation of ALL PARTIES who have enriched themselves at the expense of the American people since the inception of the Federal Reserve in 1913. The Statute of Limitations should be waived because of the fraud involved.

If there is skullduggery and Congress does not act on this, there should be a revolt in the voting booths by the people of the United States and every single Congressman and Senator and elected official should be voted out of office.

1917 Impeachment Speech By Congressman Charles Lindbergh

".....that the increase in the aggregate sum of interest paid to the banks (by the U.S. Government—author's comment) upon the said inflated bank credits and ***the increase caused by the said inflation in the speculative values upon commodities required to supply the necessities of life for the people has been many billions of dollars, which have been added to the cost of living for the people to pay; that said increase in the cost of living is mainly the profits that the conspirators have added to their individual fortunes to the equivalent loss of the people*** generally and to the Government as well."

---Congressman Charles Lindbergh, Februrary, 12, 1917

(Source: Congressman Lindbergh's address to the U.S. House of Representatives, February 12, 1917, Second Session of the Sixty-Fourth Congress, Volume LIV, Congressional Record, pages 3126 - 3128). Author's emphasis bold italics.

U.S. Congressional Record 1917

3128 CONGRESSIONAL RECORD—HOUSE. FEBRUARY 12,

and the country from time to time such facts and occurrences relating to banking and currency as affect the business of the people in trade and commerce exchanges, domestic and foreign, so that Congress should receive information that would give to Congress the facts upon which to base any necessary amendments to the act in order to make it responsive to the general welfare; that, contrary to the spirit of the Federal Reserve act, the aforesaid five active working members of the Federal Reserve Board have willfully failed to keep the public and Congress informed of the inflation of bank credits and the effect of it that has taken place under the "administration" of the said act, and in violation of the spirit thereof said members have conspired with the members of the Federal reserve advisory council and their business associates hereinbefore named and have aided and abetted in a conspiracy to a systematic inflation of bank credits for the benefit of the said conspirators and against the public welfare; that in consequence of said unlawful acts and misfeasance in office of the said members of the Federal Reserve Board the banks have, for private gain, increased the bank credits of the country since the passage of said act approximately seven thousand millions of dollars and without effecting a corresponding reduction in the interest rate, thus increasing the aggregate amount of interest paid by the people to the said banks equal to that charged upon said sum; that the effect of the inflation of bank credits has been and is to also increase speculative credits enormously more than equal to the inflation of bank credits, and that such increase since the Federal reserve act took effect has been billions of dollars; that the increase in the aggregate sum of interest paid to the banks upon the said inflated bank credits and the increase caused by the said inflation in the speculative values upon commodities required to supply the necessities of life for the people has been many billions of dollars, which have been added to the cost of living for the people to pay; that said increase in the cost of living is mainly the profits that the conspirators have added to their individual fortunes to the equivalent loss of the people generally and to the Government as well.

12 Federal reserve banks, there to form a basis upon which to issue still more Federal-reserve notes and further inflate credit without causing a reduction of interests that in the aggregate would equal the charge made on the inflated currency, but serving mainly as a guaranty to reenforce the conspirators hereinbefore named in exploiting of the people for private gain.

Eleventh. That the Federal reserve act obligates the United States to redeem in gold at the United States Treasury all Federal reserve notes, and as a part of the said conspiracy and in furtherance of the same, and to extend the speculation of the operators and perpetrators of the said conspiracy to include Europe and other foreign territory, they, most of them being international as well as domestic bankers, seek to dominate the relations of the United States with foreign countries and to selfishly influence the same by means of the control of finances, and in furtherance of said branch of their speculations have conspired with the said five active working members of the Federal Reserve Board to secure aid from the Federal Reserve System for said selfish purposes and not in the interest of the public, the conspirators in connivance with the said five active working members of the Federal Reserve Board had the said board select and appoint, through the Federal reserve bank of New York, the so-called Bank of England as its agent, thus putting the credit of the Government of the United States back of this foreign corporation, organized for private gain, which is no longer able to make payments in gold and fails to give a statement of its true conditions; that said Federal Reserve Board is threatening to permit and also to render aid to the international bankers in America who dominate the banking system, to enter into further entangling alliances with bankrupt countries of Europe at the very time this Government contemplates issuing hundreds of millions of dollars of interest-bearing bonds upon the credit of the people of the Nation to meet the Government expenses.

Twelfth. That during the Civil War the Government of the United States issued money commonly called "greenbacks"; the same being issued upon the credit of the people of the Na-

(Source: Congressional Record 1917, page 3126-3129, Second Session of the Sixty-Fourth Congress, Volume LIV, as retrieved from: http://archive.org/stream/congressionalrec54dunit#page/n1585/mode/1up).

The Fed Only Acts in the Interest of the Banks and the Elite Families

As you can see from reading excerpts of Congressman Lindbergh's speech, NOTHING has changed with respect to the actions of the Federal Reserve---EXCEPT TODAY, THE AMOUNTS ARE TRILLIONS OF DOLLARS AND NOT BILLIONS OF DOLLARS, as Congressman Lindbergh complained about in 1917!

The Fed ONLY acts in the interests of the banks and the elite families! Congressman Lindbergh really goes on a tear in 1917---taking up a number of pages in the Congressional Record is a hard thing to do since the type font is SMALL and the pages are large!

In his impeachment presentation he lists the usual suspects of JP Morgan, Paul Warburg and others who he accuses of manipulating the Fed for their own benefit at the expense of taxpayers and the government. He even informs Congress of the fact the members of the policy-making body on the Federal Reserve Board own shares of common stock in National City Bank (Now Citigroup) and the First National Bank of New York (i.e., Bank of New York, now called Bank of New York Mellon, another major Fed member bank and owner).

Unfortunately, the potential fraud of the Greenspan and Bernanke banking eras goes way beyond anything man has ever seen before. Trillions and trillions of dollars have been handed out involving a swap of taxpayer-backed cash, cash-equivalents and U.S. Treasury securities in exchange for ***toxic securities, likely bearing very long maturities (e.g., 30-year mortgage bonds grouped in pools which were defaulted upon and now are absolutely worthless or worth only a fraction of their face value)*** and other worthless assets.

Mr. Bernanke, the Board of Governors of the Federal Reserve, the Federal Reserve Regional Banks and the Open Market Committee of the Federal Reserve knowingly allowed this "Monopoly Money" to be exchanged for U.S. taxpayer-backed dollars in order to bail out the banks and the elite families of the world—and could have cared less about the American public.

The subject securities and records of their transactions are likely sitting in a vault until their long-term maturity date arrives and they are ultimately written off.

Their plan appears to be to keep these apparently fraudulent transactions hidden from the public's and Congress' prying eyes until long after Bernanke's and his co-conspirator's deaths. By this time, a new set of Congressmen will be in power, once again---all clueless as to how the Fed is stealing America's heart and soul.

However, it will be business as usual at the Federal Reserve, the member banks and of course, the wealthy elite!

New York Federal Reserve Bank
By Irving Underhill, 1930s
As retrieved from http://nyc-architecture.com/?p=1925

BY PERHAPS KEEPING WORTHLESS SECURITIES IN A DARK, HIGHLY SECURE VAULT, MULTIPLE STORIES UNDERGROUND, GUARDED BY THE FED'S OWN PRIVATE ARMY, WITHIN THE BOWELS OF THE FORTRESS KNOWN AS THE NEW YORK FEDERAL RESERVE BANK, MR. BERNANKE AND THE OTHER PARTIES TO THE $30 TRILLION HEIST MAY HAVE PLANNED TO LET THESE SECURITIES SILENTLY REST UNTIL ALL THE CO-CONSPIRATORS ARE LONG GONE AND IN THE GRAVE---SIX FEET UNDER.

IF THIS STATEMENT IS EVEN CLOSE TO BEING TRUE, IT MIGHT PERMIT THE GREATEST THEFT EVER KNOWN TO MANKIND TO BE SIMPLY BRUSHED ASIDE---SWEPT AWAY UNDER THE CARPET OF HISTORY---WITH THE ELITE LAUGHING ALL THE WAY TO THE BANK... LITERALLY!!!

Federal Reserve Illustration Popular Mechanics Magazine 1931

HOW UNCLE SAM GUARDS HIS MILLIONS IN VAULTS OF FEDERAL RESERVE BANKS

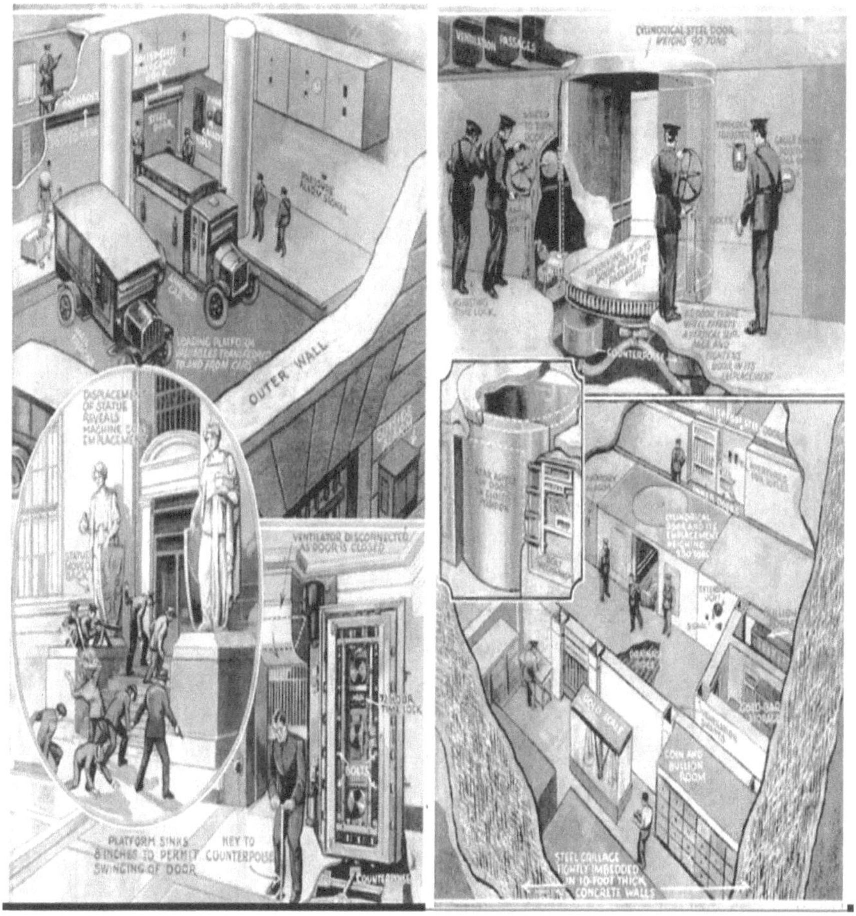

(Source: ***Popular Mechanics March* 1931**, page 458 & 459, copyright expired - not renewed. Public domain image, as retrieved from http://books.google.com/books?id=S-QDAAAAMBAJ&printsec=frontcover&source=gbs_ge_summary_r&cad=0#v=onepage&q&f=false).

Chapter 11
Is There a Case For Treason?

Congress ONLY AUTHORIZED $700 Billion in bailout money via the Troubled Asset Relief Program (TARP) to be used to purchase distressed assets.

The Fed and the co-conspirators apparently and capriciously violated multiple sections of the Federal Reserve Act, including, but not limited to Sections 11, 13 and Sections 14, which ***strictly limit the kinds of securities*** the Fed had the authority to purchase and otherwise transact with the banks and other parties. It also required the Federal Reserve Board of Governors to force write offs at the Federal Reserve Banks.

THE ACT DOES NOT SAY THE FEDERAL RESERVE BANKS CAN TAKE IN WORTHLESS SECURITIES AND EXCHANGE THEM FOR U.S. TAXPAYER CASH, ELECTRONIC FED CREDITS OR CASH-EQUIVALENTS.

The Act ***does say*** the Federal Reserve must use ***sound risk management practices***, which is an utter and sheer impossibility with the intake of nearly $30 Trillion in toxic securities from the banks and elite.

Additionally, the Fed allowed banks and non-banks who were FAILING, to be bailed out---strictly prohibited by the Federal Reserve Act in both its original form and in its amended form.

FINALLY, THE FED SPENT DURING 2½ YEARS, AT LEAST $26 TRILLION DOLLARS IN UNAUTHORIZED, SECRET BAILOUTS.

The sheer magnitude of the heist seems like it is not only treasonous, but also, treacherous (as Merriam-Webster defines these words) and anyone else who might ever engage in these kinds of heinous, vile, nefarious and secret activities would be put in jail.

The reader and Congress must decide if the Federal Reserve System, its member banks and co-conspiring wealthy elite declared economic war on America.

If they did declare war on America,
then they are also GUILTY OF TREASON,
as it is defined in the U.S. Constitution.

The destruction from this economic warfare against America is worse and will become much worse, than any other war in the history of our country. The author urges you to consider:

- IF the results are showing up in the destruction of our cities; and
- IF the results are showing up in consistently high unemployment amongst the people; and
- IF the results are showing up with increased costs of living; and
- IF the results are showing up in the apparently illegal and/or corrupt seizing of millions of homeowner properties; and
- IF the results are showing up in what appears to be the fraudulent conveyance of TRILLIONS OF DOLLARS in U.S. assets to domestic and international parties---accomplished via the transmission and use of wire facilities and/or U.S. mail; and
- IF the results are showing up in what was the transfer of TRILLIONS OF DOLLARS of U.S. assets overseas to foreign entities and foreign people who freely and secretly conspired with the Federal Reserve, the banks and the elite to secretly heist from the U.S. taxpayer over $10 Trillion in taxpayer-backed cash, equaling approximately 2/3s of the U.S. GDP—making such foreigners enemies of America; THEN

IF TWO witnesses can stand in front of Congress and if Congress holds this to be true,

THEN TREASON HAS BEEN COMMITTED.

Likewise, the courts and the U.S. Justice Department have a chance to determine if mail and wire fraud were committed, as well as if there were other serious violations and fraud committed against the American people, as this book has outlined and questioned.

Lack of action will likely not bode well for anyone party to the cover up and fraud when D'Apocalypse™ strikes, as often times in history, when the people are crying out in anguish, they will punish those responsible for their plight, as well as those who protected the evil doers and were corrupted by their money, power and influence---taking no action to help the masses before, during or after the crisis.

As is evidenced by the GAO audit, the foreign banks formed an integral part of the apparent deception to defraud, becoming partners with the Federal Reserve, member banks and elite, which quite frankly, appears to be a declaration of war on America's economy and people.

If Congress agrees, the Federal Reserve and any parties associated with the transactions are guilty of treason (according to the U.S. Constitution), by reason of declaring economic war on America and aiding and abetting the enemy---who in a co-conspiracy with the Fed, the member banks and elite, on a pre-meditated basis, determined to steal the wealth of America and destroy its economy.

Definition of TREASON
1: the betrayal of a trust **:** TREACHERY

2: the offense of attempting by overt acts to overthrow the government of the state to which the offender owes allegiance or to kill or personally injure the sovereign or the sovereign's family.

Definition of TREACHERY
1: violation of allegiance or of faith and confidence **:** TREASON
(Source: Merriam-Webster dictionary, as retrieved from http://www.merriam-webster.com/dictionary/treason and http://www.merriam-webster.com/dictionary/treachery).

U.S. Constitution Definition of TREASON
U.S. Constitution, Article III, Section 3, Clause I: "Treason against the United States, shall consist only in levying War against them, or in adhering to their Enemies, giving them Aid and Comfort. No person shall be convicted of Treason unless on the Testimony of two Witnesses to the same overt Act, or on Confession in open Court.

The Congress shall have Power to declare the Punishment of Treason, but no Attainder of Treason shall work Corruption of Blood, or Forfeiture except during the Life of the Person attainted."

Section 3-"Treason is the only crime specifically defined in the Constitution. According to Article III, Section 3, a person is guilty of treason if he or she goes to war against the United States or gives "aid or comfort" to an enemy. He or she does not have to physically pick up a weapon and fight in combat against U.S. troops. Actively helping the enemy…can lead to charges of treason. Congress may set the punishment, but it must be directed only at the guilty person and not at his or her friends or family if they were not involved in the crime." (Source: Annenberg Classroom, http://www.annenbergclassroom.org/page/article-iii-section-3).

Destruction of Jobs, Economies, Cities & States

The Federal Reserve, the member banks and the wealthy elite utterly ensured the destruction of jobs, cities and entire state economies, including but not limited to Detroit, Cleveland, Philadelphia, Phoenix, Miami, California, Michigan and many, many others.

War Declared---Young People Without Jobs & Middle-Aged Laid Off

All you have to do is ask young people if there are jobs, or not, or ask the middle-aged, laid-off people if they have any prospect of being re-employed again, at anywhere close to their old salaries---and then ask ***yourself*** whether, or not, food costs and rents have gone sky high!

When you do, you will have the answer as to whether, or not, these people declared war on the majority of people in America. The subtle drip, drip, drip of inflation, Assflation™, layoffs, downsizing, outsourcing to foreign countries, reductions in pay, cheating long-time workers out of pension retirements by firing them early, tax hikes, fee hikes, health insurance cost escalation, etc. are all signs of something truly evil descending on the American economy. The only people doing well are those in the upper class and the uber wealthy---and the companies they own and control. The banks and the Federal Reserve made sure of this because they need the most powerful part of the population to support them and not question their heist of nearly $30 Trillion.

The first step in the process is to connect the dots and recognize these events are all related---and collectively, amount to war on the regular American citizen and every small business owner in the land.

Old People's Fixed Income Squeezed

Additionally, perhaps the weakest group in physical strength, but not the weakest in terms of vote count, is retirees. They have seen their fixed incomes get ***squeezed*** as the effect of Assflation™ kicks in (see The $30 Trillion Heist---Follow The Money!, Volume II, Chapter 6, subsection "Assflation™ and VaR—it's Déjà vu, All Over Again!") and the price of everything from groceries, to gasoline and nearly all other staples increase in cost. Yes, even commodities are controlled by the banks (see Chapter 5, "Say Goodbye to Your Money," subsection, "Record Rents.").

Should Congress Investigate Sedition, or Other High Crimes Against the U.S.?

Congress has prosecuted for sedition and other high crimes before in its history and it is high time they reviewed some of the questions this book raises and take up a debate on this matter. Did the Federal Reserve rebel against the law by taking completely unreasonable actions, given the clear limitations of authority it had in the Act? Did Reserve Banks, the rich, the wealthy elite families and member banks collude to recover their bad debts and soak the American taxpayer with the bill?

Any kind of investigation probably won't happen until D'Apocalypse™ erupts and financial doomsday appears on our doorstep. Congress has a duty and an obligation, in accordance with the oaths of office they took when they were elected, as do our military and President. Both Congress and the military have a duty to protect us from enemies both foreign and domestic and all three have a duty to uphold our laws and Constitution.

The actual oaths of office for our elected officials in the federal government and our armed forces are as follows. These men and women, as history has taught us, have come to the aid of the righteous when our backs have been against the wall. Remind them, as often as you can, of their oath—and then ask them why they haven't gone after those who appear to have stolen the national treasury.

Every Senator and Congressman's Oath of Office

> *"I do solemnly swear (or affirm) that I will support and defend the Constitution of the United States* **against all enemies, foreign and domestic;** *that I will bear true faith and allegiance to the same; that I take this obligation freely, without any mental reservation or purpose of evasion; and that I will well and faithfully discharge the duties of the office on which I am about to enter: So help me God."*

History of the Oath

At the start of each new Congress, in January of every odd-numbered year, the entire House of Representatives and one-third of the Senate performs a solemn and festive constitutional rite that is as old as the Republic. While the oath-taking dates back to the First Congress in 1789, the current oath is a product of the 1860s, drafted by Civil War-era members of Congress intent on ensnaring traitors.

The Constitution contains an oath of office only for the President. For other officials, including members of Congress, the Constitution specifies only they "shall be bound by Oath or Affirmation to support this constitution." In 1789, the First Congress reworked this requirement into a simple fourteen-word oath: "I do solemnly swear (or affirm) that I will support the Constitution of the United States."

The Armed Forces Oath

> *"I, (NAME), do solemnly swear (or affirm) that I will support and defend the Constitution of the United States* ***against all enemies, foreign and domestic****; that I will bear true faith and allegiance to the same; and that I will obey the orders of the President of the United States and the orders of the officers appointed over me, according to regulations and the Uniform Code of Military Justice. So help me God."*

The President's Oath of Office

The oath of office of the President of the United States is an oath or affirmation required by the United States Constitution, as specified in Article Two, Section One, Clause Eight, before the President begins the execution of the office:

> "Before he enter on the Execution of his Office, he shall take the following Oath or Affirmation:— '*I do solemnly swear (or affirm) that I will faithfully execute the Office of President of the United States, and will* ***to the best of my Ability, preserve, protect and defend the Constitution of the United States.*'"**

The Den of Thieves Purposely Avoid Congressional Scrutiny

The den of thieves and their eager handlers simply figured out, via a poorly veiled deception, how to avoid Congressional scrutiny and authorization to secretly bail out the banks and the elite.

They empowered themselves to SECRETLY UNLOAD their worthless securities onto an unsuspecting United States public in exchange for taxpayer-backed Federal Reserve credits, U.S. cash, U.S. Treasury Securities and/or other cash-equivalents. Every one of these transactions was backed and guaranteed by the U.S. Taxpayer. In one fell swoop every elite and every bank had their credit crisis losses disappear onto the backs of the U.S. taxpayer—to the tune of nearly $30 Trillion.

Ben Bernanke, Tim Geithner, Henry Paulson and every single member of management in the Federal Reserve System, its member banks, Wall Street Executives and ever trader and salesman participating in the scam, allowed the United States' future to be placed in jeopardy.

The Fed, Wall Street and the banks---as controlled by the wealthiest families on earth, used the Federal Reserve System and deceived Congress and the American public.

They created the crisis in the first place by lowering rates to nearly zero and lent money to virtually ANYONE who came through the door for a loan.

Then, when everyone was "in" and loaded to the gills with loans, mortgages and credit lines, the banks suddenly refused to lend money, directly causing the housing and stock market crash of 2007-2010 and the ongoing economic depression for the masses through 2013.

This allowed the banks to absorb an entire mortgage industry and pick off several jewels of the banking and investment banking industry, allowing them to accomplish their immediate objectives.

Once the bankers realized their greed was too great and they reached too far, with the entire system crashing down on top of their heads, these vultures cried to the government for help—and it came in the form of hundreds of billions of dollars in TARP bailouts.

When it was clear to the bankers, the elite, Wall Street and the Fed no more bailouts were forthcoming and TARP wasn't enough to make up for their losses, they disguised, hid and otherwise veiled MASSIVE SECRET bailouts to themselves in the form of self-dealing and self-enriching purchases, swaps and loans by tendering worthless securities to the Federal Reserve.

With the consent of Bernanke, Geithner, Paulson, et al., they exchanged their dead money---their worthless Monopoly money---for pure gold in the form of American taxpayer-backed cash and cash-equivalents, U.S. Treasury Securities and taxpayer-backed Federal Reserve electronic credits worth.

The heist they conducted totaled twice the size of the United States annual Gross Domestic Product, totaling nearly $30 Trillion Dollars---ergo, the title of this work, "The $30 Trillion Heist."

Epilogue

Author's Personal Note & Invitation to Make a Commitment

Please note: if you have read either Volume II of The $30 Trillion Heist---Follow The Money! or D'Apocalypse™ Now!—The Doomsday Cycle, this Epilogue is repeated as the author's personal note and invitation to the reader.

The Federal Reserve Trilogy tells three very important interrelated stories. The author incorporated a few important sections of The $30 Trillion Heist into D'Apocalypse™ Now!---The Doomsday Cycle to provide continuity and perspective for new readers of the author's work---just in case a person hadn't read either Volume I or Volume II of The $30 Trillion Heist. Each book of the trilogy has a unique message and is distinct. Together, they may be vital to any person seeking to discover the truth and become prepared for the dangers heading our way.

Without a proper understanding of the Federal Reserve, readers may find it difficult to understand why America has changed dramatically---in seemingly dastardly ways, at all points of the compass. Understanding the fact the Federal Reserve is ***the problem*** is critical to the reader's ability to educate Congressmen, Senators, neighbors and friends. It is only through this process of education can real reform be accomplished.

It is hoped these works will help all Americans in their quest for justice against the elite, the banks and the Federal Reserve System in the aftermath of the great D'Apocalypse™. They have heisted trillions from future generations of Americans---and we need to recover these assets if our children and our children's children have any chance for recovery.

Attempting such a work against such powerful people and organizations is a daunting task. When you read these words, thoughts and theories from The Federal Reserve Trilogy, please remember these words were written by a mere man applying his worldly knowledge to facts he uncovered and events he foresees from a Christian's and businessman's perspective.

If I am wrong with respect to any outcome prognosticated or reported in these works, don't blame God.

Just blame it on a mortal man who was doing the best job he could to interpret events and evidence the best *way* he could, while turning to God in prayer. Personally, I hope I am wrong with events I expect to unfold and a miracle does happen, because the D'Apocalypse™ expected is extremely severe and extremely traumatic; hundreds of millions of people will suffer unbelievably as a result.

Real, global war will VERY LIKELY begin in and around D'Apocalypse™, but with near certainty by 2019, as there has never been a collapse of this nature before in history---and nearly all historic collapses which create massive economic hardship have led to great wars, as one economic tribe battles another to maintain control, feed its people and attempt to spark economic recovery.

When Life Isn't Easy

As you might have guessed by now, despite the ability to look ahead of the curve, nothing in my life has ever come easy. I did not grow up with a silver spoon in my mouth and it seems God has always been testing me and my faith. The funny part of it is each and every time I thought there was just too much pressure—the Holy Spirit somehow provided relief and a solution for me to follow; and I can promise you, the Holy Spirit has sustained me throughout significant trials in my life.

If you have found yourself in a similar position, where you may have been challenged, are under duress, are having a tough time, or otherwise find yourself at wits end, just read the book of Job (or even sections of it) from The Bible and you will see how truly blessed we all are.

When the roof feels like it is caving in and financially you feel like a train wreck, just look on the Internet, or on TV (CNN International, or the BBC, for example) and witness the absolute poverty which abounds outside of the confines of the United States and Western Europe. You will see it, but will not probably fully appreciate it, as you cannot smell rotting stench through television, or through the computer screen. Nevertheless, reminding ourselves of how fortunate we are, compared to many billions of other people, will lend some perspective and help you stop worrying, while keeping you strong in your faith and convictions. This will allow you to focus on the positives, which is what you need to do to survive what is lying dead ahead during the firestorm of D'Apocalypse™.

If the words written in this book touch you, or make sense and you are convinced of the evidence presented within these pages, then immediately take to heart some of the advice and get prepared for a complete meltdown in the financial markets and economic structure of society---it is coming and soon.

Then, if you don't know Jesus Christ and you are led by the Holy Spirit, pray to Jesus for your salvation and watch the miracle of a changed life begin to take place. You will no longer fear for the future, but will find you are now in the army of God and one of His confident foot soldiers who KNOWS they will be victorious in the end.

At any time when you read this book, depending on who you are, I leave three, and only three, decision boxes to help you open your heart to the Lord our God, Jesus Christ His son and the Holy Spirit.

God Bless You in your new walk with the Lord! He is mighty, indeed!!

1) FOREVER CHANGE YOUR LIFE!

"Dear God, the sole God for all eternity, I pray in your son's name, Jesus Christ, to please forgive my sins and hear my prayer. I accept Jesus Christ as my Lord and personal savior and believe you sent Him from heaven to earth, where He was born of the Virgin Mary. I believe in His life, His teachings, His horrible death and the sacrifice He made for my sins---and all mankind's sins. I KNOW AND BELIEVE HIS RESURRECTION IS TRUE AND I KNOW AND BELIEVE HE ASCENDED INTO HEAVEN AND SITS AT THE RIGHT HAND OF THE FATHER. I accept your gift and promise of eternal life through faith in Jesus Christ, for you have promised us by your grace, the grace of the one and only eternal God, I can be saved through the gift of faith. I also know my earthly works will not get me into your heavenly kingdom, as you don't want any man to boast, but I know we are created in Jesus to do good works out of the love and gratefulness we have for your mercy, power and gift of eternal life through the sacrifice made for us by Jesus Christ, your son and savior. AMEN"

"For it is by grace you have been saved, through faith—and this is not from yourselves, it is the gift of God—not by works, so that no one can boast. For we are God's handiwork, created in Christ Jesus to do good works, which God prepared in advance for us to do."
(Source: The Bible, Ephesians 2:8-10, New International Version).

"For God so loved the world that He gave His only begotten son, that whosever believeth in Him should not perish, but have eternal life." (Source: The Bible, John 3:16, King James Version)

If you pray this prayer, or a form of prayer accepting Jesus Christ as your Lord and Savior, I urge you to find brothers and sisters in Christ to nurture your walk with God. The Holy Spirit will guide you and you will notice a difference in the way you walk and talk through life.....you will see differences in your attitudes and actions. Embrace these, read and study His Holy Word, The Bible, and REPENT of your sins. Your heart will naturally want to do good works, because you realize what an amazing ***free*** gift has been given to you---ETERNAL LIFE!

In today's hurry-up world, it is becoming even more important to immediately embrace Jesus Christ as your savior, as God gave us Jesus to allow us to enter heaven. The Quickening is upon us all…he who has ears, let him hear….he or she who has heart, let them give it to the Lord our God—the one God of eternity. In the name of the Father, the Son and the Holy Spirit, AMEN!

Finally, after all the reading, studying, successes, failures, sacrifices and opportunities in life---there is only one thing which matters.

Jesus.

For those of you who are trapped in the sleek corporate confines of our banks and the thousands of companies thirsting for profits, worldwide, this book is especially for you. It is written to those living in comfort in the most American and Western-European sense of the word, with children and young adults honey-stuck to their smart phones and video games, while Mom and Dad are living, eating and drinking like kings and queens, with everyone engrossed in the TV set. Unfortunately for one all, they are completely ignoring the dark, ominous clouds on the horizon foreshadowing their very own deaths. Without Jesus you are doomed.

To any and all backsliders who are out there—I urge you to read the Holy Scripture and take heed and warning…! Take up the courage of conviction and KNOW The Bible is TRUE!! The evidence is overwhelming…pray for the strength to overcome evil with good….AND DO SO!!

2) THE BACKSLIDER'S MAKE OR BREAK TIME!

> **"What good is it, my brothers and sisters, if someone claims to have faith but has no deeds? Can such faith save them? Suppose a brother or a sister is without clothes and daily food. If one of you says to them, "Go in peace; keep warm and well fed," but does nothing about their physical needs, what good is it? In the same way, faith by itself, if it is not accompanied by action, is dead.**
>
> **But someone will say, "You have faith; I have deeds."**
>
> **Show me your faith without deeds, and I will show you my faith by my deeds. You believe that there is one God. Good! Even the demons believe that—and shudder.**
>
> **You foolish person, do you want evidence that faith without deeds is useless? Was not our father Abraham considered righteous for what he did when he offered his son Isaac on the altar? You see that his faith and his actions were working together, and his faith was made complete by what he did. And the scripture was fulfilled that says, "Abraham believed God, and it was credited to him as righteousness," and he was called God's friend. You see that a person is considered righteous by what they do and not by faith alone.**
>
> **In the same way, was not even Rahab the prostitute considered righteous for what she did when she gave lodging to the spies and sent them off in a different direction? As the body without the spirit is dead, so faith without deeds is dead."**
>
> (Source: The Bible, James 2:14-24, New International Version).

Sadly, there are millions of souls who believe in Jesus, but go back to their old ways of sin after they have received Jesus as their savior and don't do any good works. The Holy Scripture is very clear on this topic….FAITH WITHOUT WORKS IS DEAD.

As even the History Channel recounts the story of Abraham being obedient to God---The Bible—in both the Old and New Testaments---informed us of God's principle of obedience long before it streamed into our living rooms courtesy of your cable provider. If you truly have given your heart and life to Jesus Christ, your natural desire---and your own predetermined destiny, is to do good deeds!

Backsliders, one and all, you must believe in the imminence of His arrival and I implore you to make a different, real change in your life.

Remember... ***"Even the demons believe...and they shudder."***

It is not enough to just "believe." Make a difference in the life around you---just as Jesus and the disciples did, and "do" for other people. Help them, pray for them, feed them, cloth them, return to a simpler life (e.g., Jesus and His disciples didn't have any worldly possessions). Do not go down the slippery slope of, "Well, the Lord blessed me with this, so it is all OK...."

We probably all know numbers of wealthy Christians who have been blessed with much---but have done very little for other people in relation to what was given to them. To these people, I implore you to remember what Jesus said:

> **"It is easier for a camel to go through the eye of a needle, than for a rich man to enter into the kingdom of God."**
> (Source: The Bible, Matthew 19:23-24, King James Version).

Of course, the wealthy will go on to the next words of Jesus when the disciples asked Him who can be saved and Jesus replied all things are possible for God.

The admonition is clear, however, the wealthy shall be scrutinized very carefully by our heavenly and just God.

The disciples themselves gave up EVERYTHING THEY HAD TO FOLLOW JESUS. They all changed. They were all afraid at His death and went into hiding (fearful the Romans and the Jews would crucify them, just as they had Jesus), but they became ferocious and vociferous zealots for Christ---brandishing the helmet of salvation, the shield of faith, while swinging with all of their might, the sword of the Holy Spirit---and they died martyrs' deaths, with one spared to write the Book of Revelation---the Book of the Apocalypse, who of course was the Apostle John.

It was quite a change for a small group of men---all once terrified and in hiding and all unafraid to die for Christ. I don't know of a single case in history where any person, let alone an entire group of people (except John, spared to write the Book of Revelation, the Book of the Apocalypse) would die for a lie when they could have just walked away if they had just chosen to denounce Jesus Christ as their Lord and Savior!

These men are as relevant to us today more than ever before in history.

If you have ears to hear, then listen; if you have eyes to see, then read:

3) THE MOST DANGEROUS ROUTE TO HELL IS BEING TOO COMFORTABLE!

"Then Peter said to Him, 'Behold, we have left everything and followed You; what then will there be for us?' And Jesus said to them, 'Truly I say to you, that you who have followed Me, in the regeneration when the Son of Man will sit on His glorious throne, you also shall sit upon twelve thrones, judging the twelve tribes of Israel. And everyone who has left houses or brothers or sisters or father or mother or children or farms for My name's sake, will receive many times as much, and will inherit eternal life. But many who are first will be last; and the last, first.'"
(Source: The Bible, Matthew 19:27-30, New American Standard Version).

The author, Robert Lyman Peter Kelly (as a boy, I chose "Peter" as my confirmation name), just like you, the reader, and just like the Apostle Peter, is a sinner and the words I write are only possible because I have been forgiven by the grace of God through the faith I have in the sacrifice and resurrection of the son of God, Jesus Christ. I know He shed His blood for me and for all mankind. He was born of the Virgin Mary and Jesus truly lived, taught, breathed, witnessed, suffered, died, buried, was resurrected AND ascended into heaven in front of many, many witnesses--all in fulfillment of the scriptures. He performed (and performs today) many miracles for the living while He walked among the disciples—and continues to perform those miracles after His earthly death.

The biggest miracle Jesus gives us ALL is the miraculous change He brings to those who truly give themselves to Him. This is the miracle of a changed life. If you are not saved through the blood of Christ and your absolute faith in His resurrection and teachings, pray to God as you have been led by the Holy Spirit in one of the DECISION BOXES of this book, above, or otherwise. Ask for His forgiveness in His son's name, Jesus Christ, and commit your life to Him. SEEK other like-minded individuals who can help you learn more about your new walk and birth in Jesus. This is what Jesus meant when He said you cannot enter the Kingdom of Heaven---UNLESS YOU ARE BORN AGAIN!!

> Finally, for all you backsliders out there, whether RICH or POOR, **Jesus did not put a limit on how many times you can ask for, AND RECEIVE, complete forgiveness and thus eternal life in Heaven.**

With your new life, you have a new beginning. Make the most of it for His glory and not your own. When the disaster of D'Apocalypse™ strikes, remain calm and KNOW the Lord is our God and has complete control of EVERYTHING. This is part of the battle which must be fought before Jesus returns to earth.

I hope and pray you choose the side of might for right.

To this, the people said, in Jesus name,

Amen!

Christian Cross in the Roman Coliseum

Made in United States
Troutdale, OR
11/03/2026

56852531R00149